THE DAYS ARE JUST PACKED

Other Books by Bill Watterson

Calvin and Hobbes
Something Under the Bed Is Drooling
Yukon Ho!
Weirdos from Another Planet
The Revenge of the Baby-Sat
Scientific Progress Goes "Boink"
Attack of the Deranged Mutant Killer Monster Snow Goons
Homicidal Psycho Jungle Cat
The Calvin and Hobbes Tenth Anniversary Book
There's Treasure Everywhere
It's a Magical World
Calvin and Hobbes Sunday Pages 1985-1995
The Complete Calvin and Hobbes

Treasury Collections

The Essential Calvin and Hobbes
The Calvin and Hobbes Lazy Sunday Book
The Authoritative Calvin and Hobbes
The Indispensable Calvin and Hobbes
The Calvin and Hobbes 10th Anniversary Book

THE DAYS ARE JUST *PACKED*

A Calvin and Hobbes Collection by Bill Watterson

IS THE COAST CLEAR? GIVE ME A BOOST!
WHAT'S THE PLAN?
WE WAIT FOR SUSIE TO WALK UNDERNEATH THIS TREE AND THEN WE DROP THE WATER BALLOON ON HER!
WHAT IF SHE DOESN'T WALK BY?
THEN WE JUST SIT IN THE TREE ALL DAY.
I LOVE SUMMER.
THE DAYS ARE JUST **PACKED**.
WATTERSON

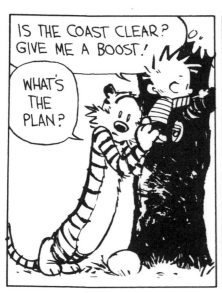

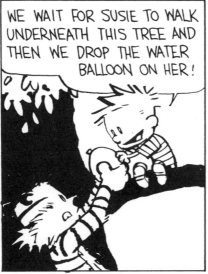

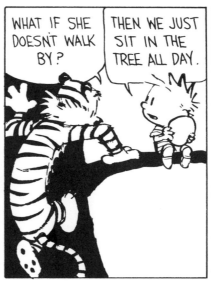

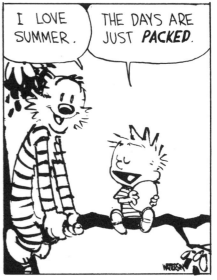

Andrews McMeel Publishing, LLC
Kansas City

Calvin and Hobbes is distributed internationally by Universal Press Syndicate.

The Days Are Just Packed copyright © 1993 by Bill Watterson. All rights reserved.
Printed in China. No part of this book may be used or reproduced in any manner whatsoever without
written permission except in the case of reprints in the context of reviews. For information write Andrews
McMeel Publishing, LLC, an Andrews McMeel Universal Company, 1130 Walnut Street, Kansas City, Missouri 64106

ISBN-13: 978-0-8362-1735-3 paperback
ISBN-10: 0-8362-1735-7 paperback
ISBN-10: 0-8362-1809-4 hardback

Library of Congress Control Number 93-71863

09 10 SDB 21 20 19

www.andrewsmcmeel.com

─────────── ATTENTION: SCHOOLS AND BUSINESSES ───────────

Andrews McMeel books are available at quantity discounts with bulk purchase for educational, business, or sales
promotional use. For information write to: Special Sales Department, Andrews McMeel Publishing, LLC, 1130
Walnut Street, Kansas City, Missouri 64106

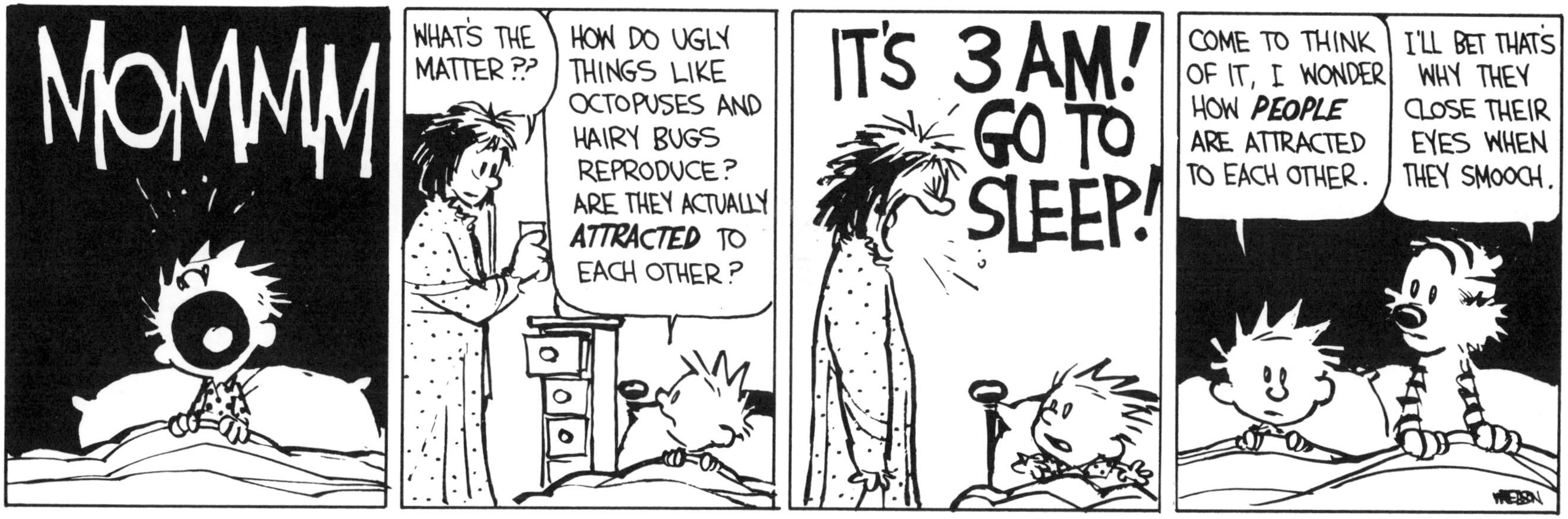
MOMMM
WHAT'S THE MATTER ??
HOW DO UGLY THINGS LIKE OCTOPUSES AND HAIRY BUGS REPRODUCE? ARE THEY ACTUALLY ATTRACTED TO EACH OTHER?
IT'S 3 AM! GO TO SLEEP!
COME TO THINK OF IT, I WONDER HOW PEOPLE ARE ATTRACTED TO EACH OTHER.
I'LL BET THAT'S WHY THEY CLOSE THEIR EYES WHEN THEY SMOOCH.

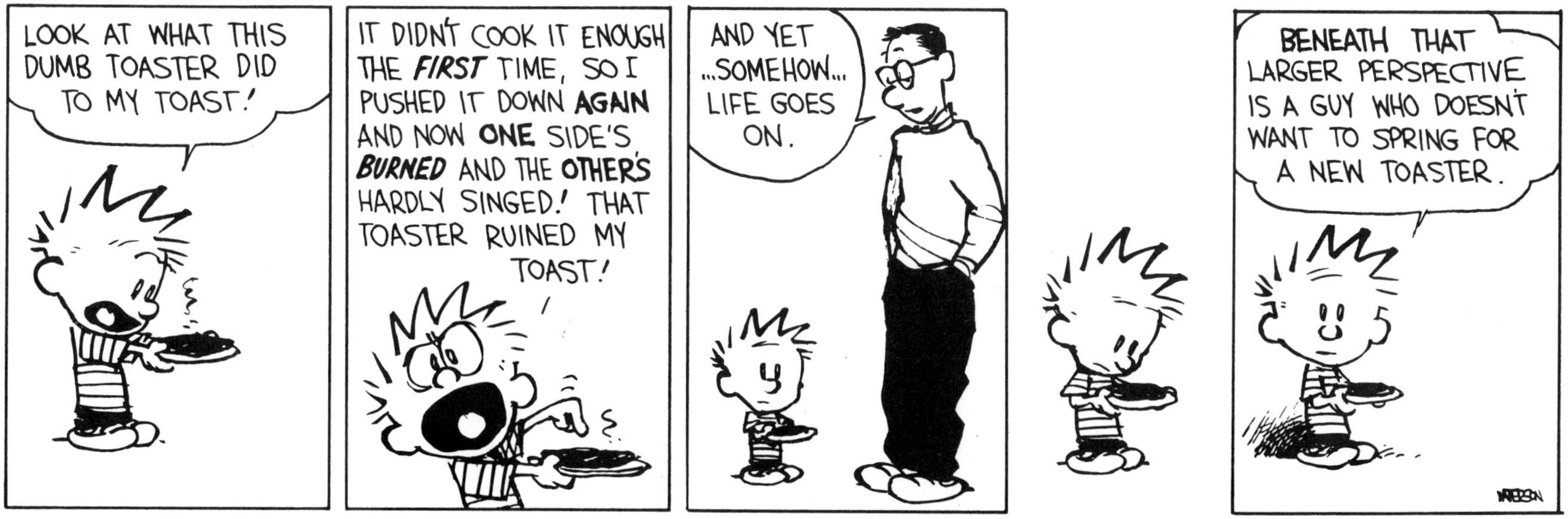
LOOK AT WHAT THIS DUMB TOASTER DID TO MY TOAST!
IT DIDN'T COOK IT ENOUGH THE FIRST TIME, SO I PUSHED IT DOWN AGAIN AND NOW ONE SIDE'S BURNED AND THE OTHER'S HARDLY SINGED! THAT TOASTER RUINED MY TOAST!
AND YET ...SOMEHOW... LIFE GOES ON.
BENEATH THAT LARGER PERSPECTIVE IS A GUY WHO DOESN'T WANT TO SPRING FOR A NEW TOASTER.

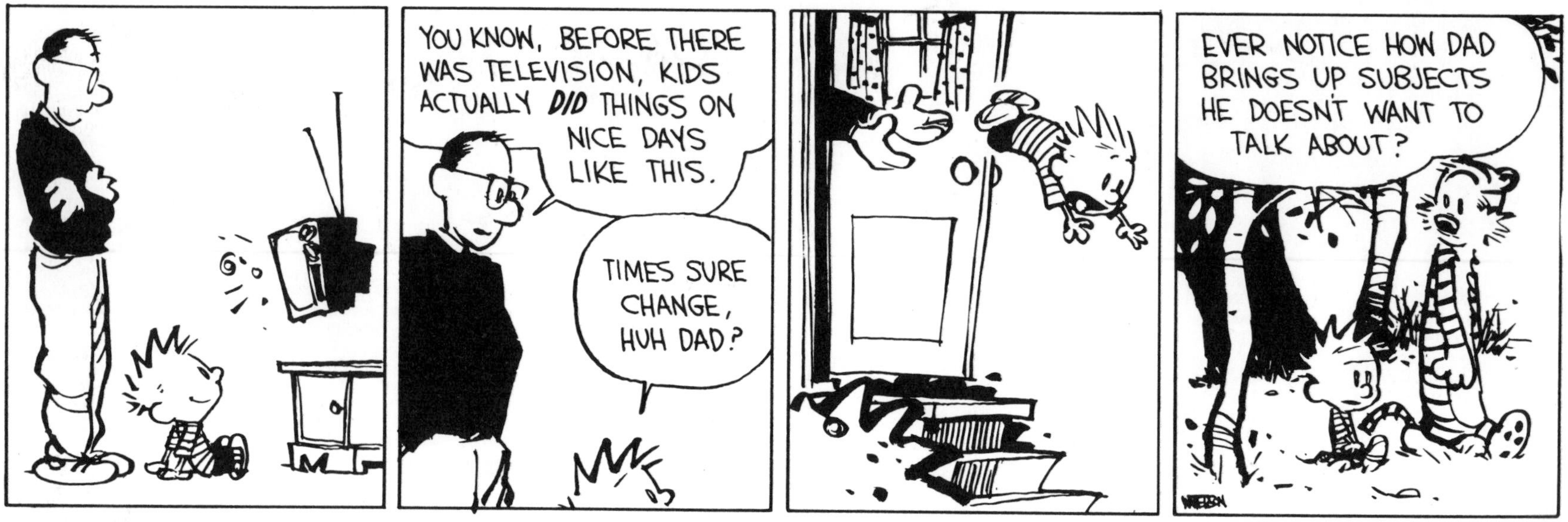
YOU KNOW, BEFORE THERE WAS TELEVISION, KIDS ACTUALLY DID THINGS ON NICE DAYS LIKE THIS.
TIMES SURE CHANGE, HUH DAD?
EVER NOTICE HOW DAD BRINGS UP SUBJECTS HE DOESN'T WANT TO TALK ABOUT?

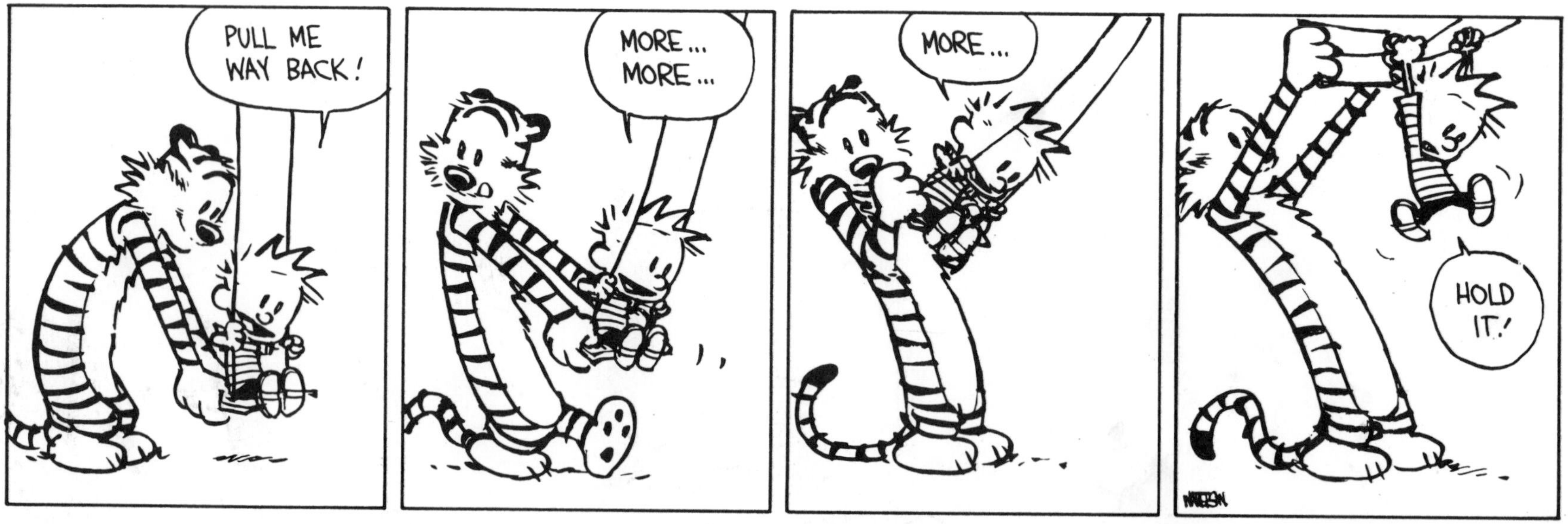
PULL ME WAY BACK!
MORE... MORE...
MORE...
HOLD IT!

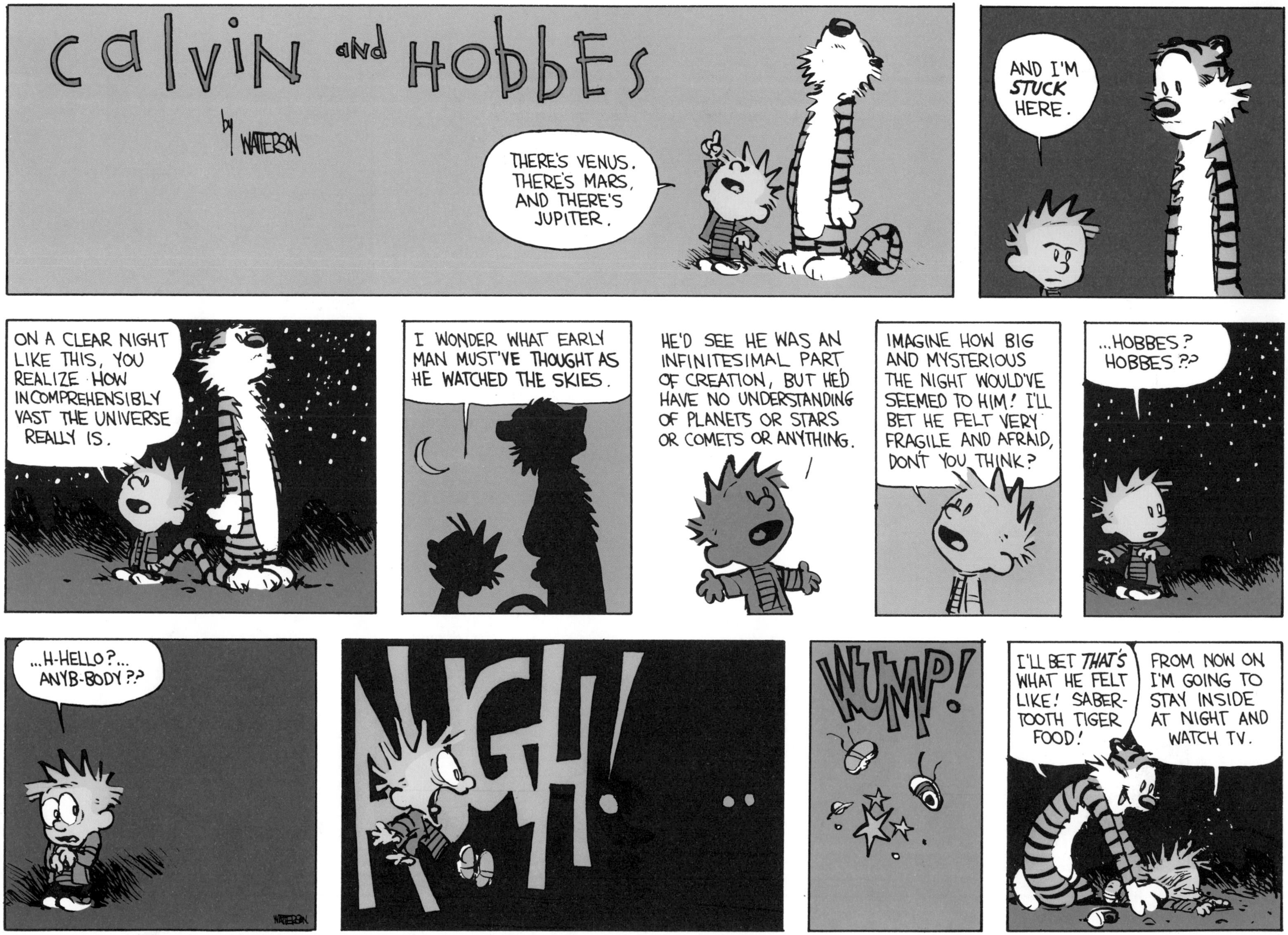
Calvin and HOBBES
by WATTERSON
THERE'S VENUS. THERE'S MARS, AND THERE'S JUPITER.
AND I'M STUCK HERE.
ON A CLEAR NIGHT LIKE THIS, YOU REALIZE HOW INCOMPREHENSIBLY VAST THE UNIVERSE REALLY IS.
I WONDER WHAT EARLY MAN MUST'VE THOUGHT AS HE WATCHED THE SKIES.
HE'D SEE HE WAS AN INFINITESIMAL PART OF CREATION, BUT HE'D HAVE NO UNDERSTANDING OF PLANETS OR STARS OR COMETS OR ANYTHING.
IMAGINE HOW BIG AND MYSTERIOUS THE NIGHT WOULD'VE SEEMED TO HIM! I'LL BET HE FELT VERY FRAGILE AND AFRAID, DON'T YOU THINK?
...HOBBES? HOBBES??
...H-HELLO?... ANYB-BODY??
WATTERSON
NNGH!
WUMP!
I'LL BET THAT'S WHAT HE FELT LIKE! SABER-TOOTH TIGER FOOD!
FROM NOW ON I'M GOING TO STAY INSIDE AT NIGHT AND WATCH TV.

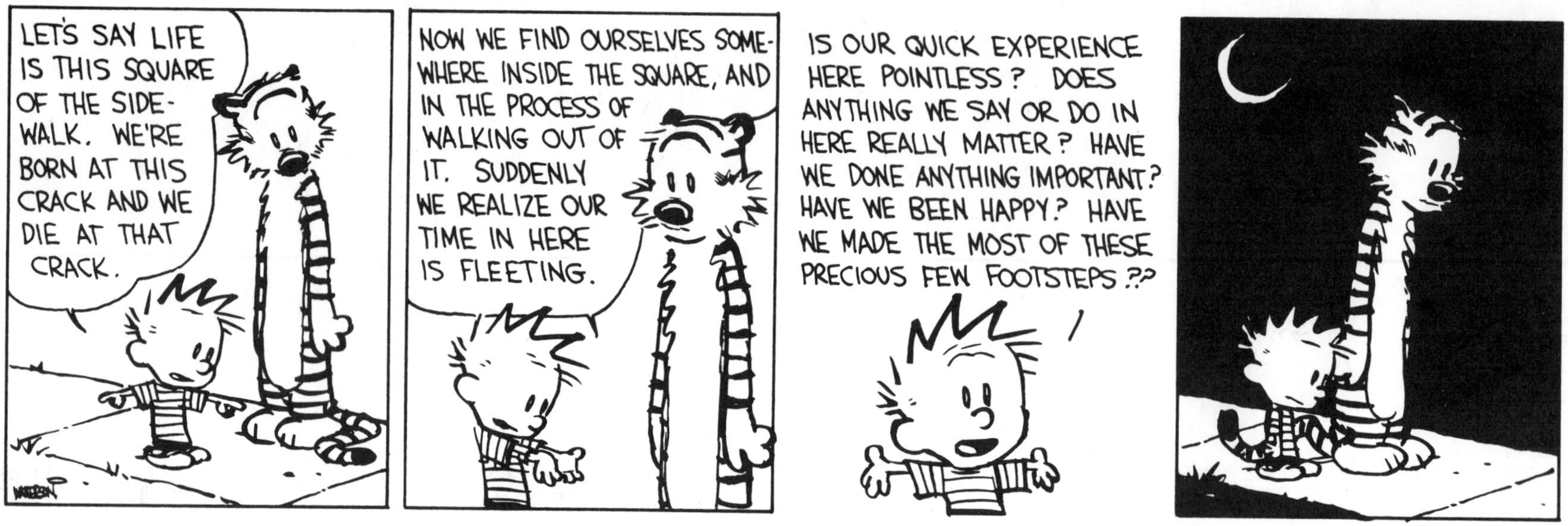
LET'S SAY LIFE IS THIS SQUARE OF THE SIDE-WALK. WE'RE BORN AT THIS CRACK AND WE DIE AT THAT CRACK.
NOW WE FIND OURSELVES SOME-WHERE INSIDE THE SQUARE, AND IN THE PROCESS OF WALKING OUT OF IT. SUDDENLY WE REALIZE OUR TIME IN HERE IS FLEETING.
IS OUR QUICK EXPERIENCE HERE POINTLESS? DOES ANYTHING WE SAY OR DO IN HERE REALLY MATTER? HAVE WE DONE ANYTHING IMPORTANT? HAVE WE BEEN HAPPY? HAVE WE MADE THE MOST OF THESE PRECIOUS FEW FOOTSTEPS?!?

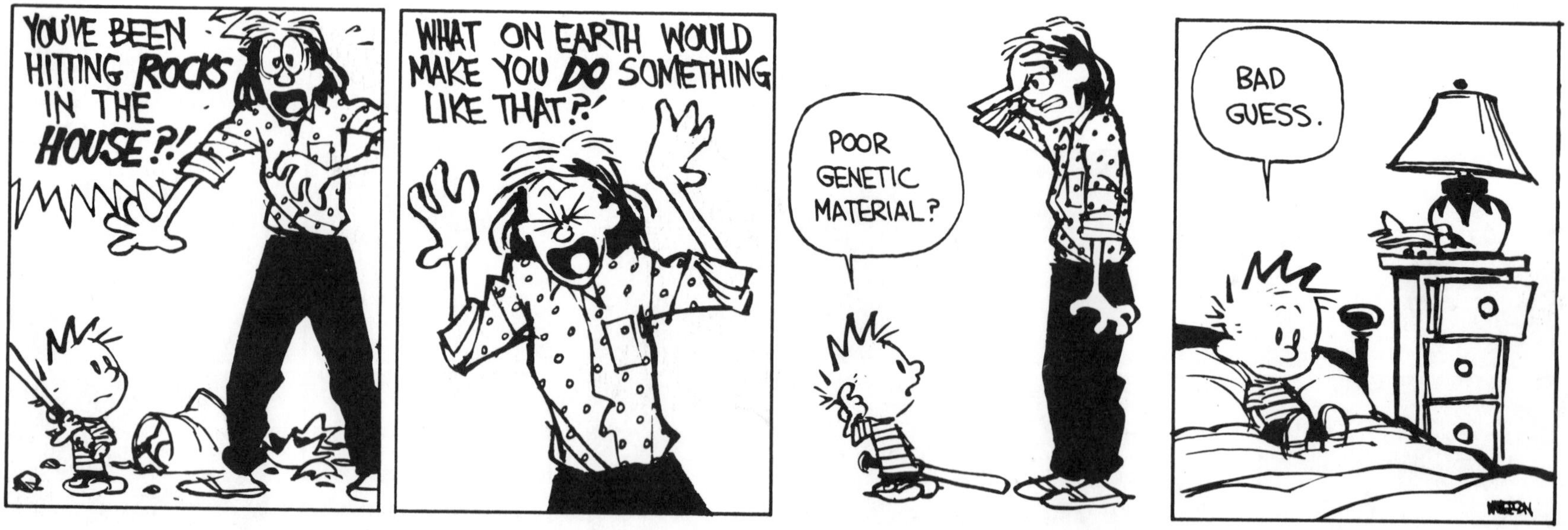
YOU'VE BEEN HITTING ROCKS IN THE HOUSE?!
WHAT ON EARTH WOULD MAKE YOU DO SOMETHING LIKE THAT?!
POOR GENETIC MATERIAL?
BAD GUESS.

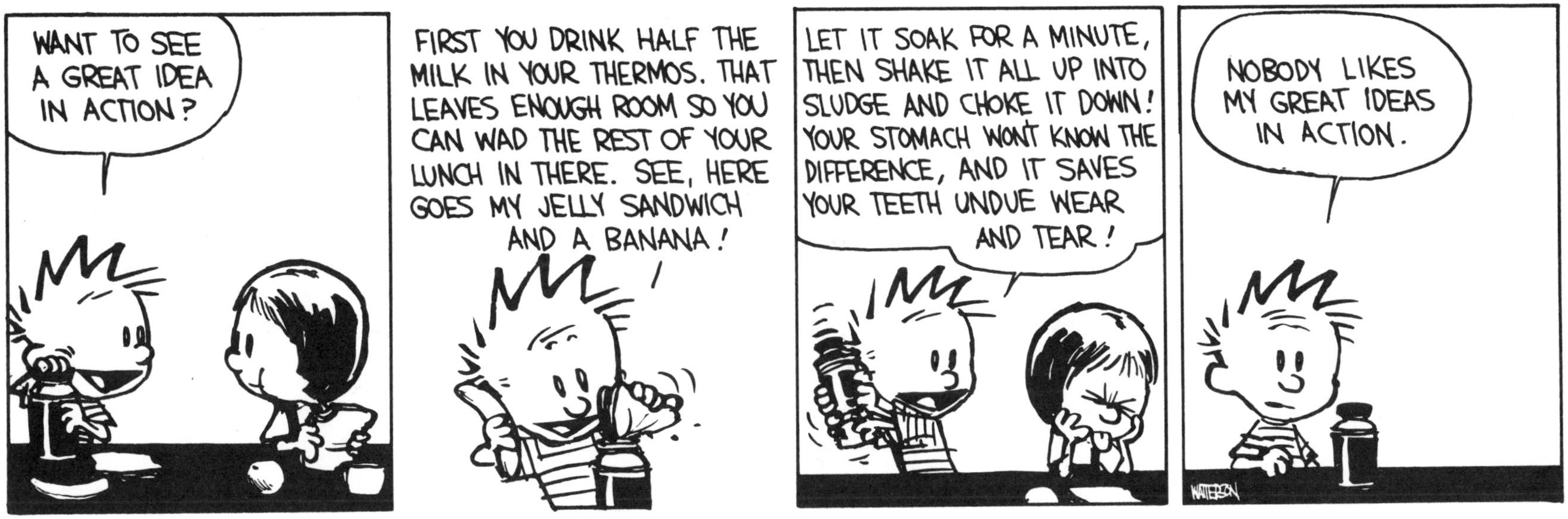
WANT TO SEE A GREAT IDEA IN ACTION?
FIRST YOU DRINK HALF THE MILK IN YOUR THERMOS. THAT LEAVES ENOUGH ROOM SO YOU CAN WAD THE REST OF YOUR LUNCH IN THERE. SEE, HERE GOES MY JELLY SANDWICH AND A BANANA!
LET IT SOAK FOR A MINUTE, THEN SHAKE IT ALL UP INTO SLUDGE AND CHOKE IT DOWN! YOUR STOMACH WON'T KNOW THE DIFFERENCE, AND IT SAVES YOUR TEETH UNDUE WEAR AND TEAR!
NOBODY LIKES MY GREAT IDEAS IN ACTION.

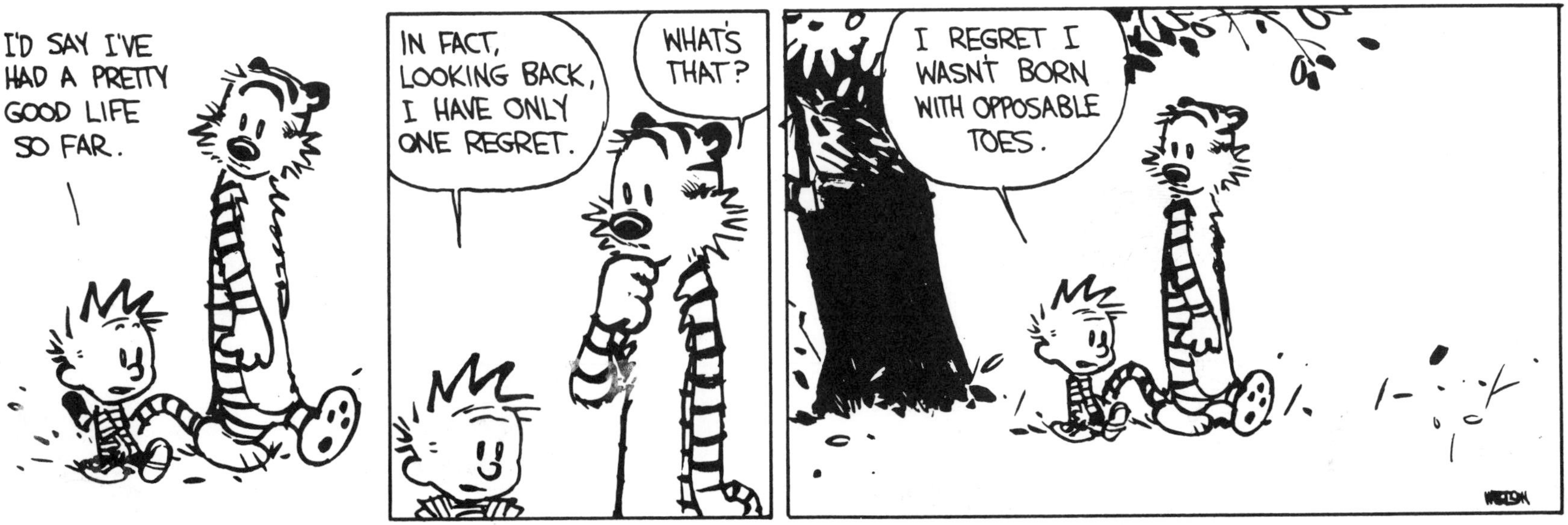
I'D SAY I'VE HAD A PRETTY GOOD LIFE SO FAR.
IN FACT, LOOKING BACK, I HAVE ONLY ONE REGRET.
WHAT'S THAT?
I REGRET I WASN'T BORN WITH OPPOSABLE TOES.

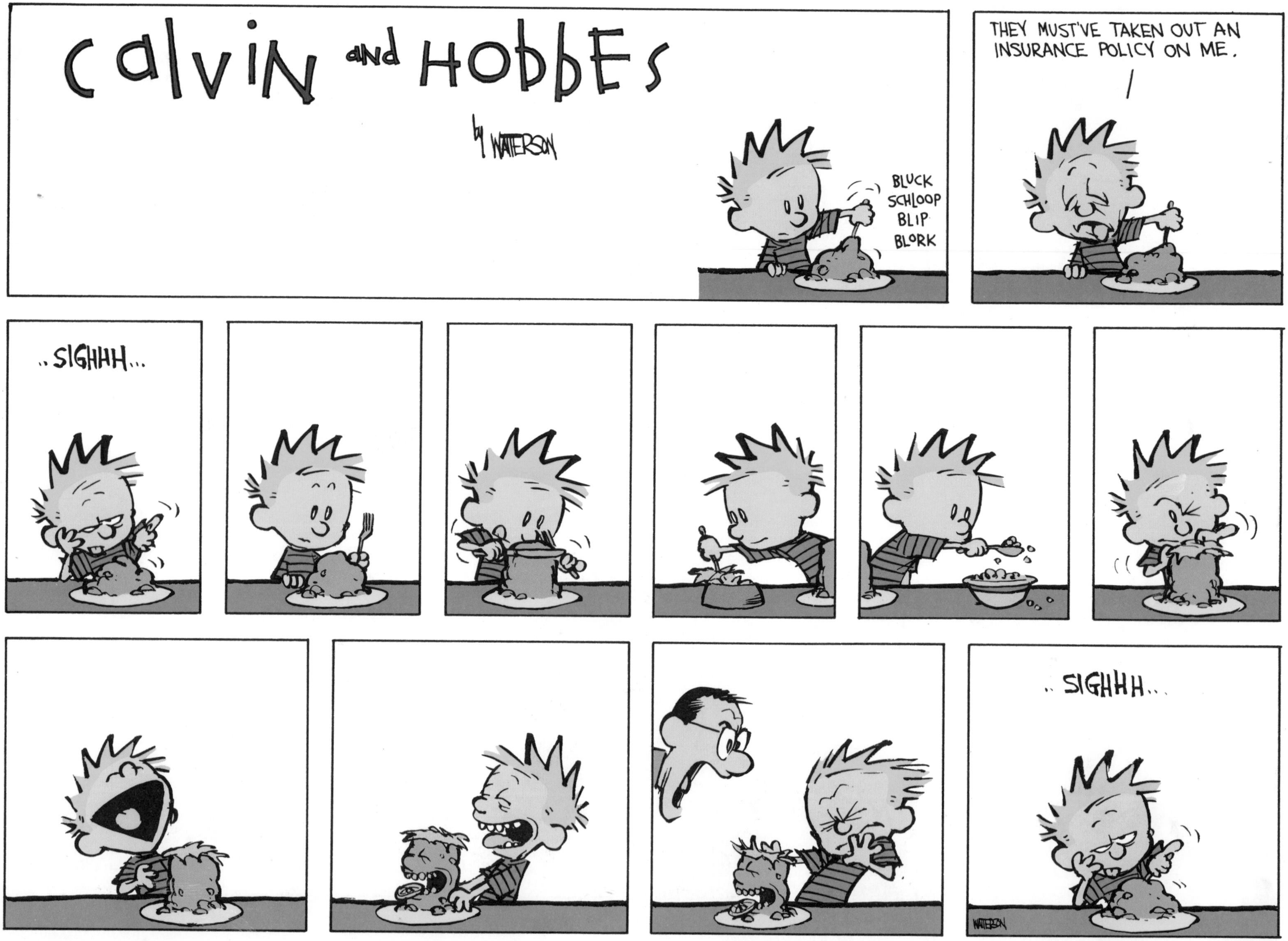
Calvin and HOBBES
by WATTERSON
BLUCK
SCHLOOP
BLIP
BLORK
THEY MUST'VE TAKEN OUT AN INSURANCE POLICY ON ME.
.. SIGHHH...
.. SIGHHH...
WATTERSON

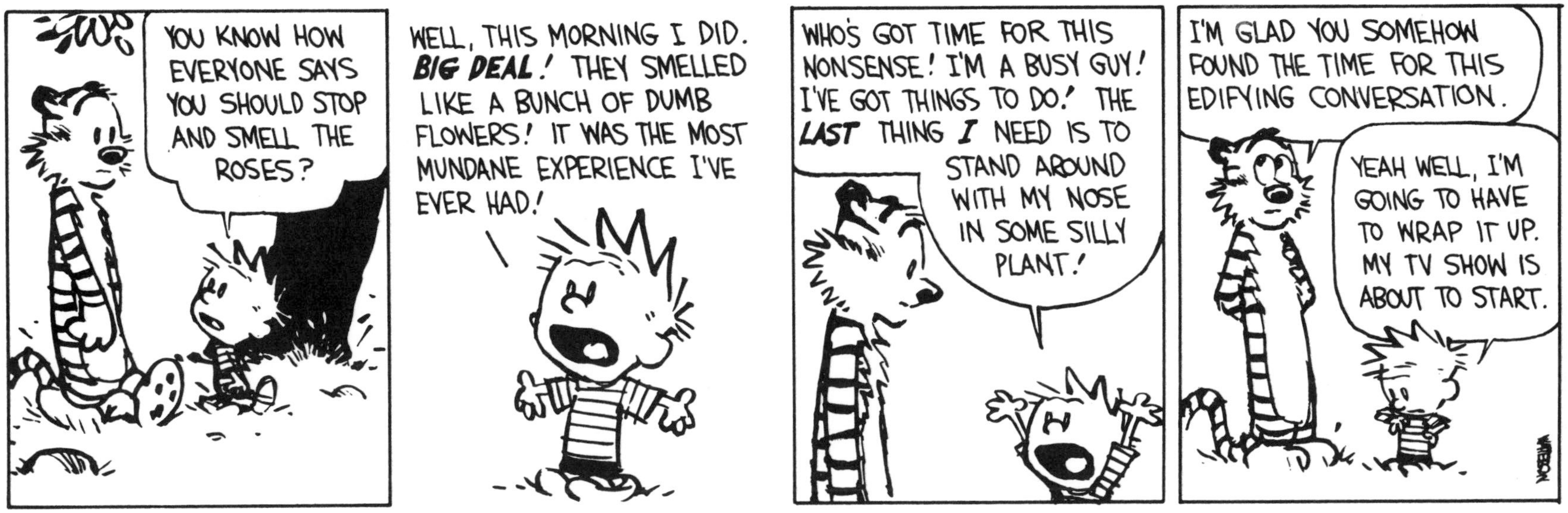
YOU KNOW HOW EVERYONE SAYS YOU SHOULD STOP AND SMELL THE ROSES?
WELL, THIS MORNING I DID. **BIG DEAL!** THEY SMELLED LIKE A BUNCH OF DUMB FLOWERS! IT WAS THE MOST MUNDANE EXPERIENCE I'VE EVER HAD!
WHO'S GOT TIME FOR THIS NONSENSE! I'M A BUSY GUY! I'VE GOT THINGS TO DO! THE **LAST** THING **I** NEED IS TO STAND AROUND WITH MY NOSE IN SOME SILLY PLANT!
I'M GLAD YOU SOMEHOW FOUND THE TIME FOR THIS EDIFYING CONVERSATION.
YEAH WELL, I'M GOING TO HAVE TO WRAP IT UP. MY TV SHOW IS ABOUT TO START.

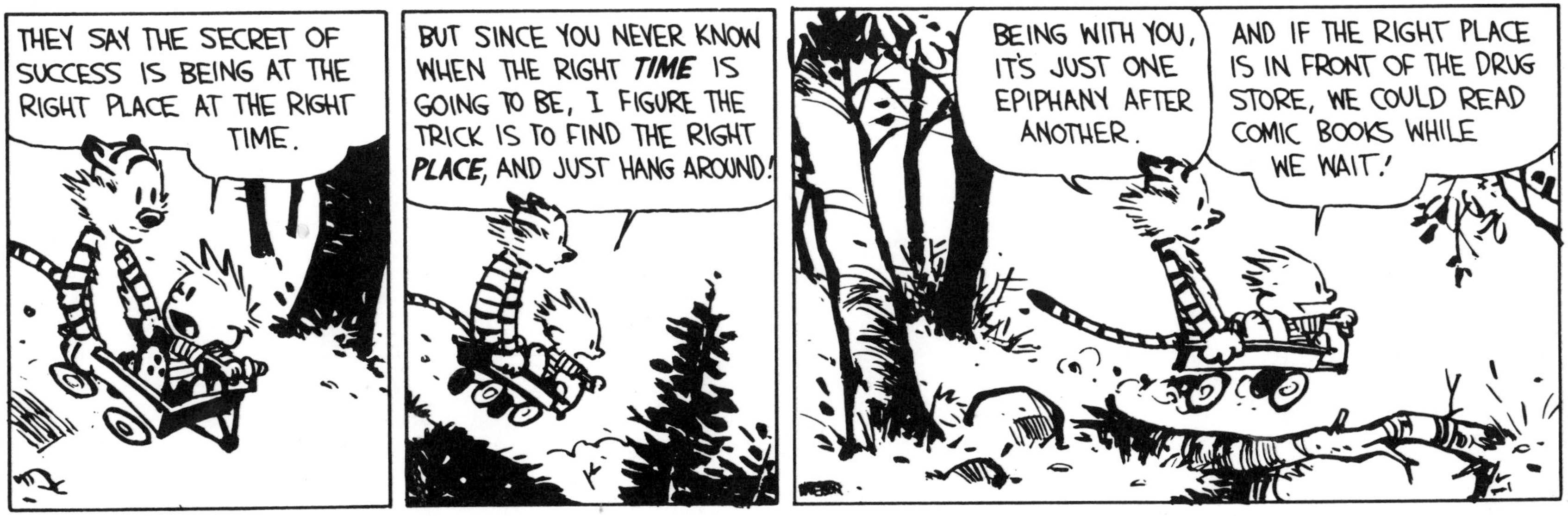
THEY SAY THE SECRET OF SUCCESS IS BEING AT THE RIGHT PLACE AT THE RIGHT TIME.
BUT SINCE YOU NEVER KNOW WHEN THE RIGHT **TIME** IS GOING TO BE, I FIGURE THE TRICK IS TO FIND THE RIGHT **PLACE**, AND JUST HANG AROUND!
BEING WITH YOU, IT'S JUST ONE EPIPHANY AFTER ANOTHER.
AND IF THE RIGHT PLACE IS IN FRONT OF THE DRUG STORE, WE COULD READ COMIC BOOKS WHILE WE WAIT!

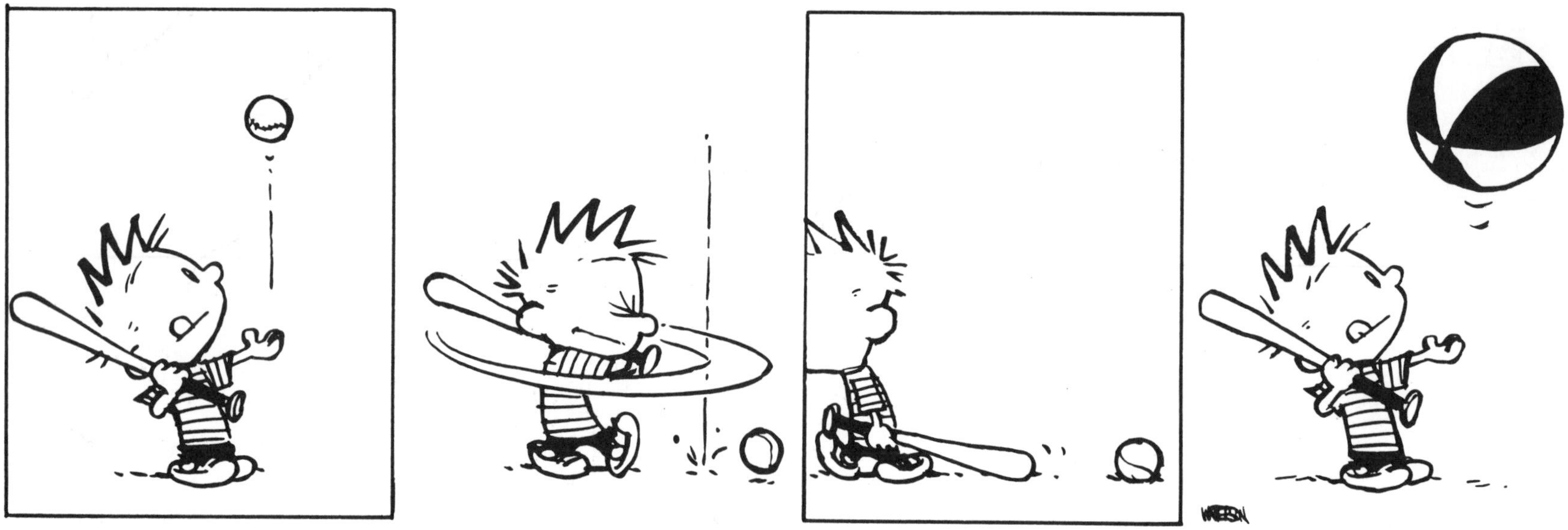

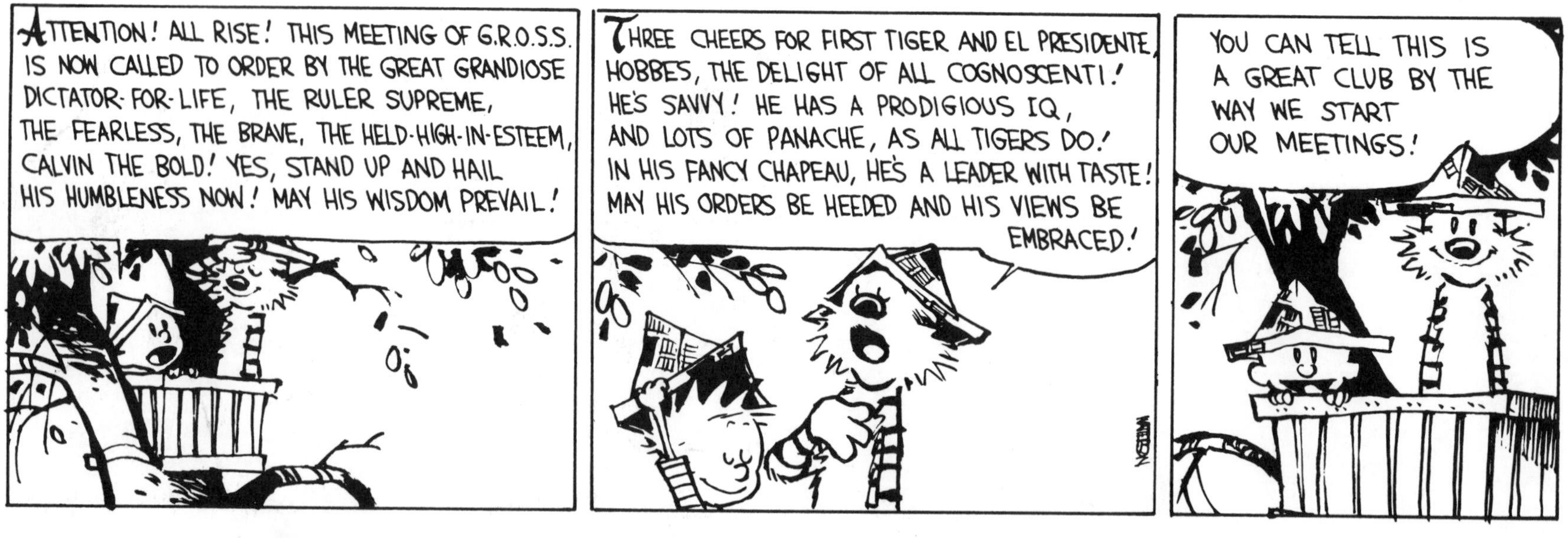
ATTENTION! ALL RISE! THIS MEETING OF G.R.O.S.S. IS NOW CALLED TO ORDER BY THE GREAT GRANDIOSE DICTATOR-FOR-LIFE, THE RULER SUPREME, THE FEARLESS, THE BRAVE, THE HELD-HIGH-IN-ESTEEM, CALVIN THE BOLD! YES, STAND UP AND HAIL HIS HUMBLENESS NOW! MAY HIS WISDOM PREVAIL!
THREE CHEERS FOR FIRST TIGER AND EL PRESIDENTE, HOBBES, THE DELIGHT OF ALL COGNOSCENTI! HE'S SAVVY! HE HAS A PRODIGIOUS IQ, AND LOTS OF PANACHE, AS ALL TIGERS DO! IN HIS FANCY CHAPEAU, HE'S A LEADER WITH TASTE! MAY HIS ORDERS BE HEEDED AND HIS VIEWS BE EMBRACED!
YOU CAN TELL THIS IS A GREAT CLUB BY THE WAY WE START OUR MEETINGS!

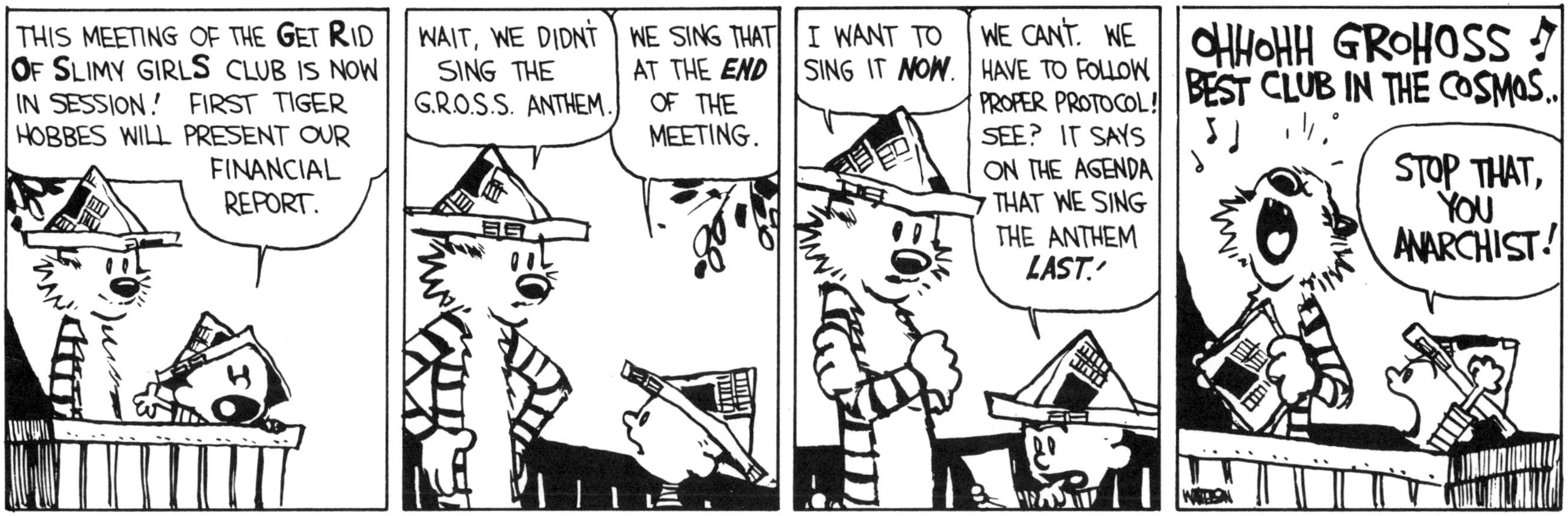
THIS MEETING OF THE GET RID OF SLIMY GIRLS CLUB IS NOW IN SESSION! FIRST TIGER HOBBES WILL PRESENT OUR FINANCIAL REPORT.
WAIT, WE DIDN'T SING THE G.R.O.S.S. ANTHEM.
WE SING THAT AT THE END OF THE MEETING.
I WANT TO SING IT NOW.
WE CAN'T. WE HAVE TO FOLLOW PROPER PROTOCOL! SEE? IT SAYS ON THE AGENDA THAT WE SING THE ANTHEM LAST!
OHHOHH GROHOSS BEST CLUB IN THE COSMOS..
STOP THAT, YOU ANARCHIST!

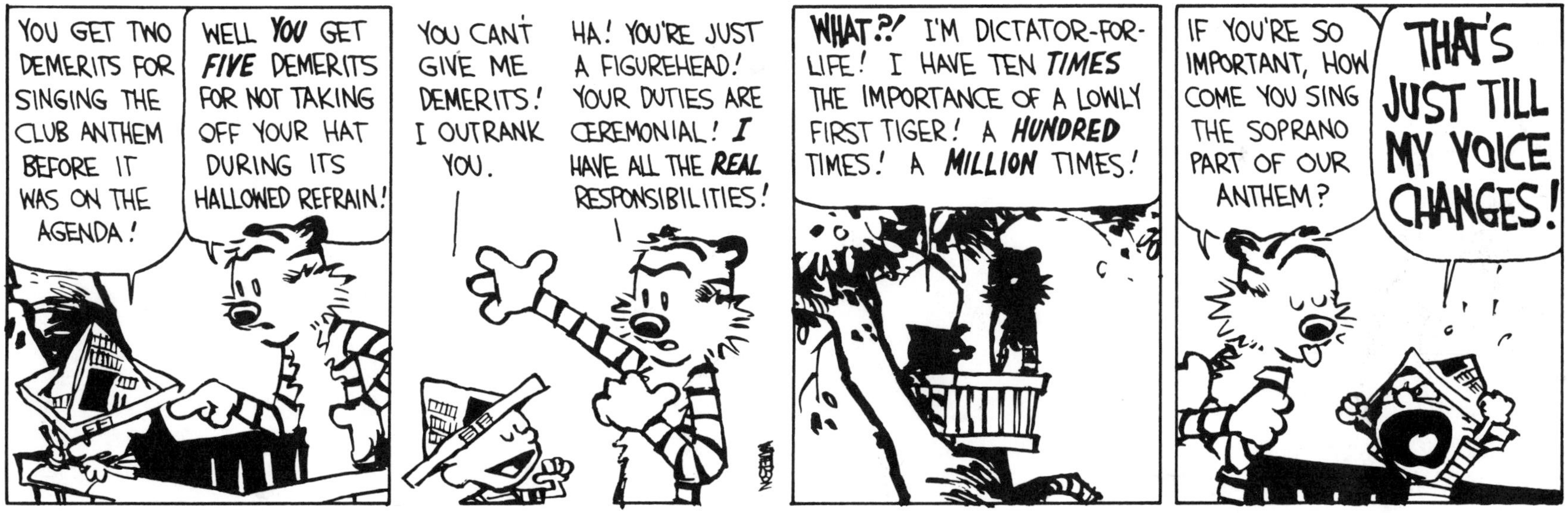
YOU GET TWO DEMERITS FOR SINGING THE CLUB ANTHEM BEFORE IT WAS ON THE AGENDA!
WELL YOU GET FIVE DEMERITS FOR NOT TAKING OFF YOUR HAT DURING ITS HALLOWED REFRAIN!
YOU CAN'T GIVE ME DEMERITS! I OUTRANK YOU.
HA! YOU'RE JUST A FIGUREHEAD! YOUR DUTIES ARE CEREMONIAL! I HAVE ALL THE REAL RESPONSIBILITIES!
WHAT?! I'M DICTATOR-FOR-LIFE! I HAVE TEN TIMES THE IMPORTANCE OF A LOWLY FIRST TIGER! A HUNDRED TIMES! A MILLION TIMES!
IF YOU'RE SO IMPORTANT, HOW COME YOU SING THE SOPRANO PART OF OUR ANTHEM?
THAT'S JUST TILL MY VOICE CHANGES!

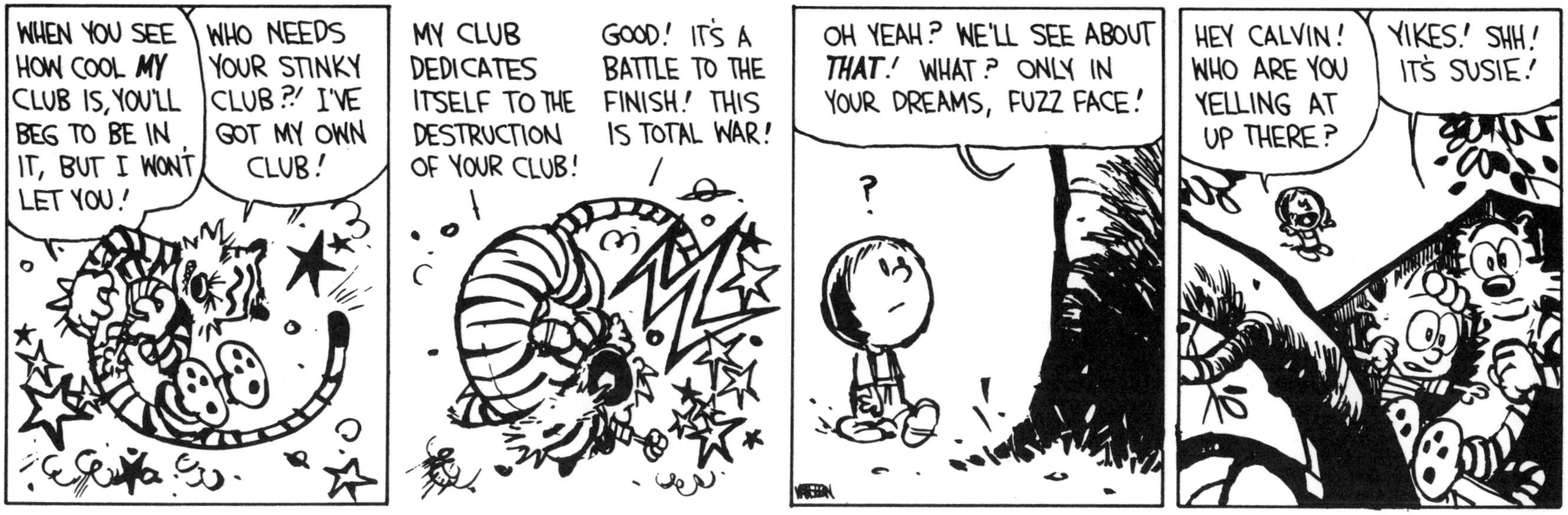
WHEN YOU SEE HOW COOL MY CLUB IS, YOU'LL BEG TO BE IN IT, BUT I WON'T LET YOU!
WHO NEEDS YOUR STINKY CLUB?! I'VE GOT MY OWN CLUB!
MY CLUB DEDICATES ITSELF TO THE DESTRUCTION OF YOUR CLUB!
GOOD! IT'S A BATTLE TO THE FINISH! THIS IS TOTAL WAR!
OH YEAH? WE'LL SEE ABOUT THAT! WHAT? ONLY IN YOUR DREAMS, FUZZ FACE!
?
HEY CALVIN! WHO ARE YOU YELLING AT UP THERE?
YIKES! SHH! IT'S SUSIE!

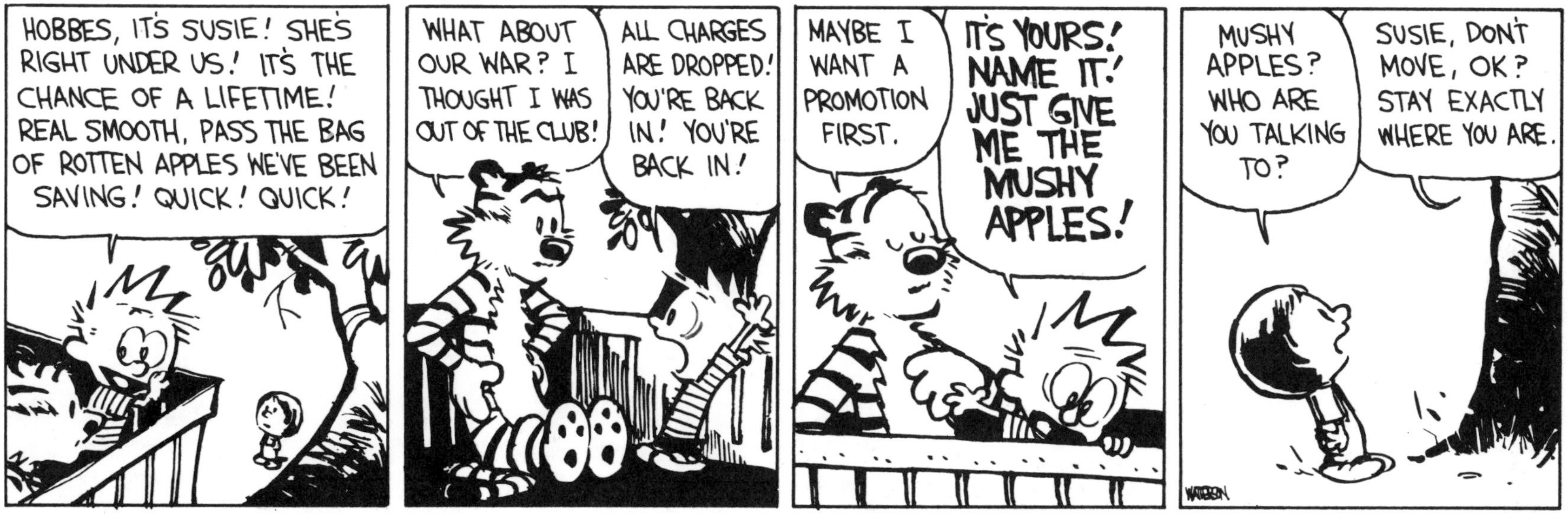
HOBBES, IT'S SUSIE! SHE'S RIGHT UNDER US! IT'S THE CHANCE OF A LIFETIME! REAL SMOOTH, PASS THE BAG OF ROTTEN APPLES WE'VE BEEN SAVING! QUICK! QUICK!
WHAT ABOUT OUR WAR? I THOUGHT I WAS OUT OF THE CLUB!
ALL CHARGES ARE DROPPED! YOU'RE BACK IN! YOU'RE BACK IN!
MAYBE I WANT A PROMOTION FIRST.
IT'S YOURS! NAME IT! JUST GIVE ME THE MUSHY APPLES!
MUSHY APPLES? WHO ARE YOU TALKING TO?
SUSIE, DON'T MOVE, OK? STAY EXACTLY WHERE YOU ARE.

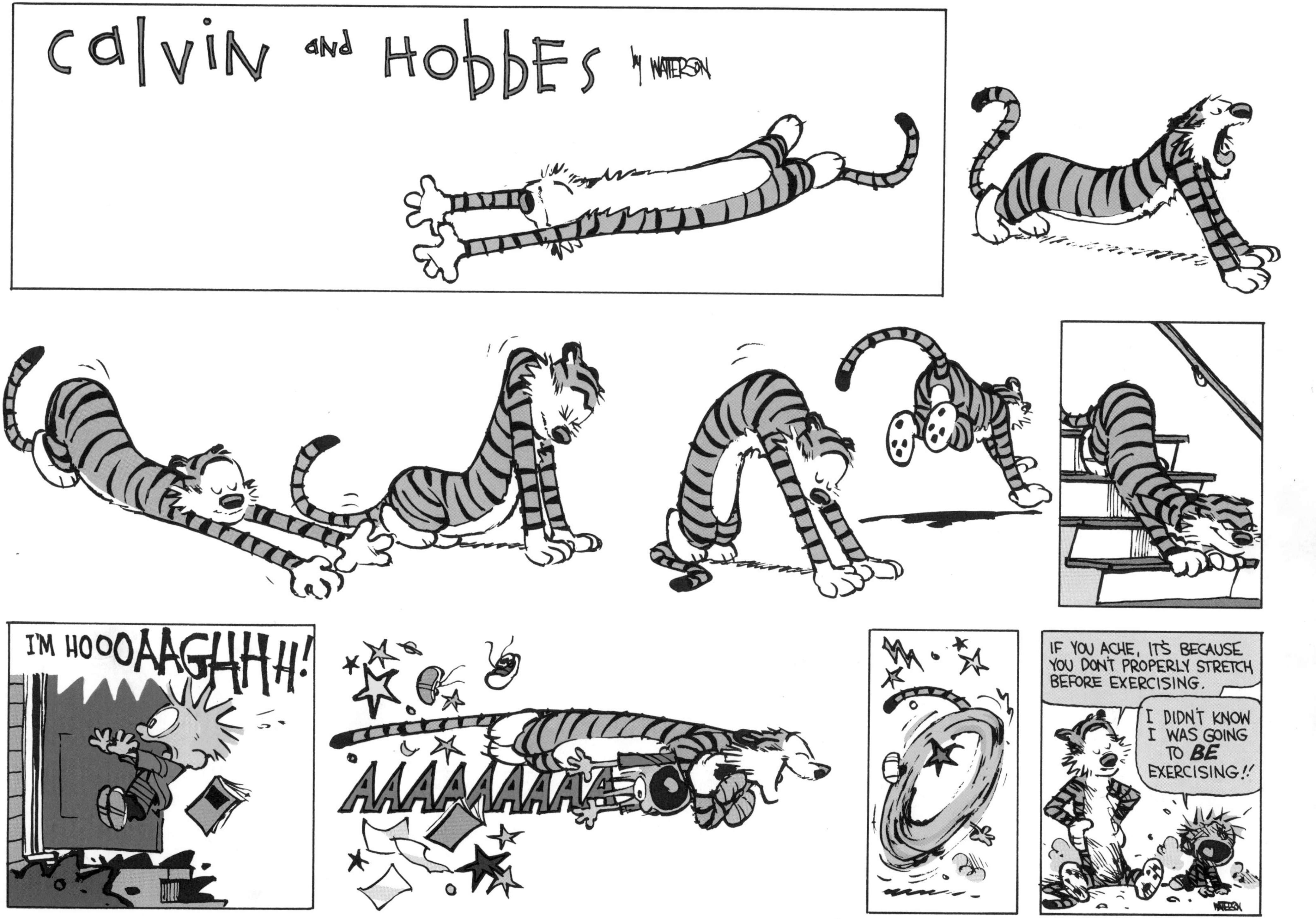
Calvin and HOBBES by WATTERSON
I'M HOOOAAGHHH!
AAAAAAAAA
IF YOU ACHE, IT'S BECAUSE YOU DON'T PROPERLY STRETCH BEFORE EXERCISING.
I DIDN'T KNOW I WAS GOING TO *BE* EXERCISING!!
WATTERSON

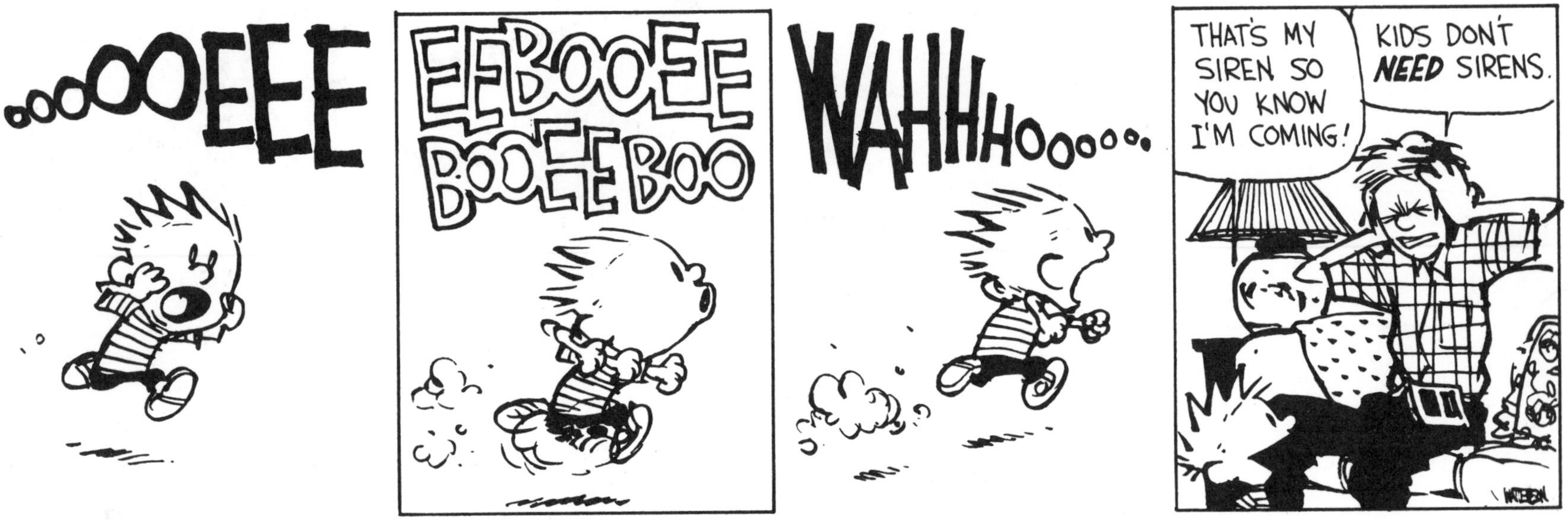
oooOOEEE
EEBOOEE BOOEEBOO
WAHHHOoooo
THAT'S MY SIREN SO YOU KNOW I'M COMING!
KIDS DON'T NEED SIRENS.

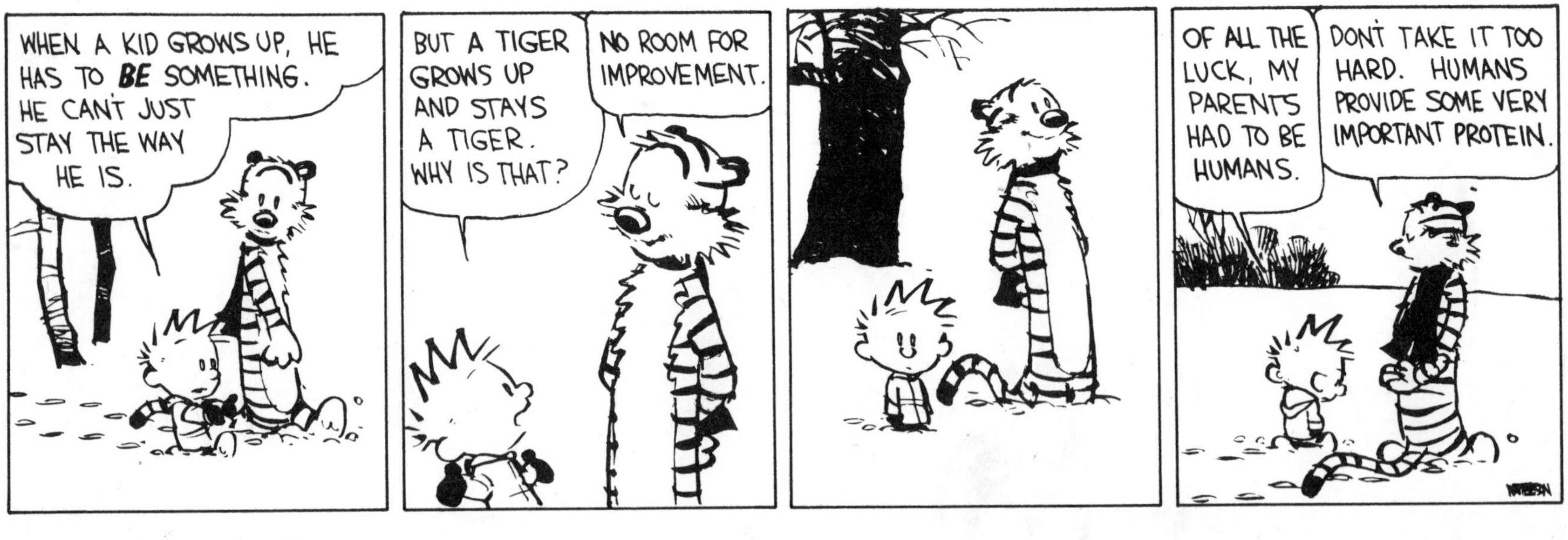
WHEN A KID GROWS UP, HE HAS TO BE SOMETHING. HE CAN'T JUST STAY THE WAY HE IS.
BUT A TIGER GROWS UP AND STAYS A TIGER. WHY IS THAT?
NO ROOM FOR IMPROVEMENT.
OF ALL THE LUCK, MY PARENTS HAD TO BE HUMANS.
DON'T TAKE IT TOO HARD. HUMANS PROVIDE SOME VERY IMPORTANT PROTEIN.

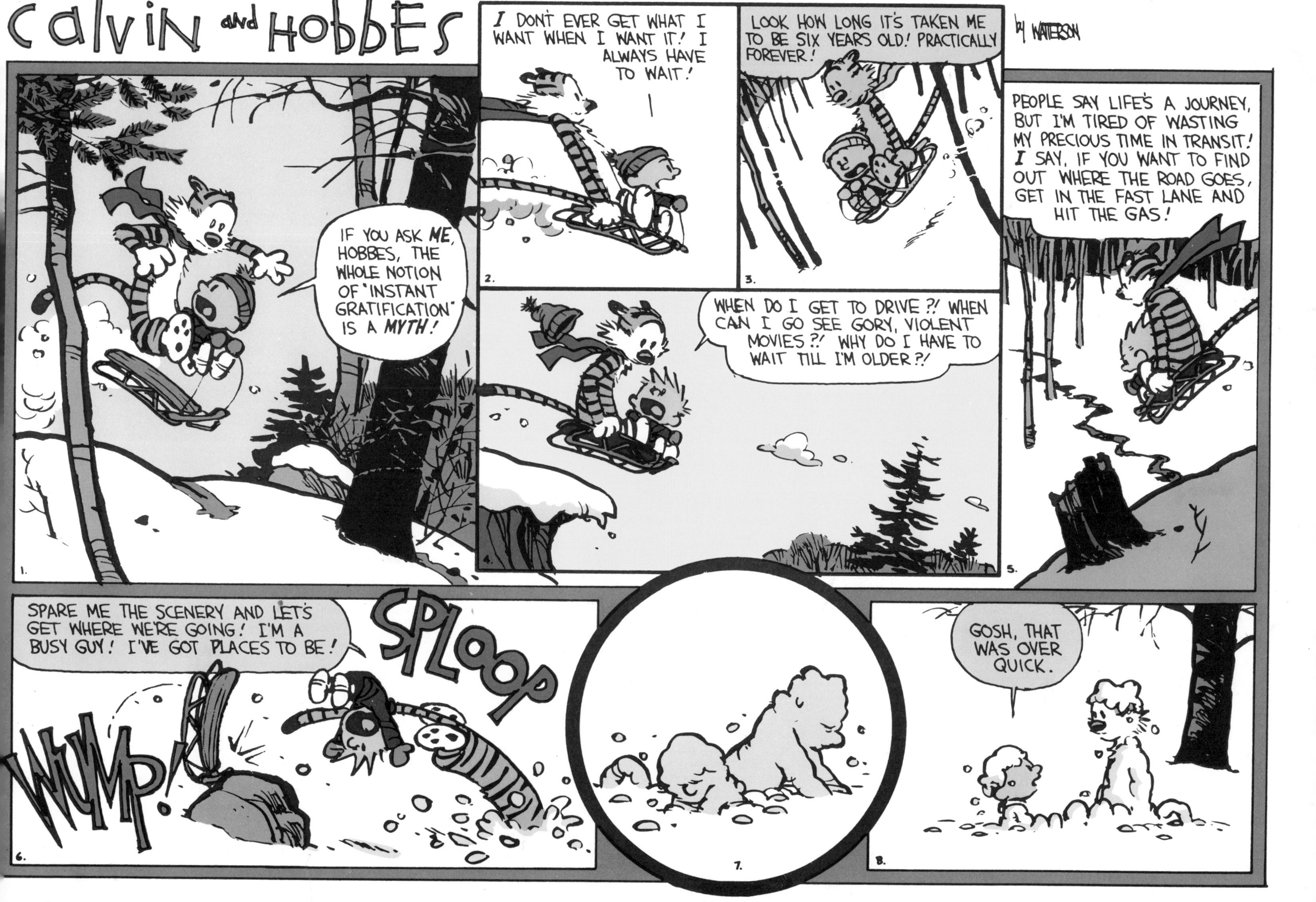
Calvin and HOBBES
by WATTERSON
IF YOU ASK ME, HOBBES, THE WHOLE NOTION OF "INSTANT GRATIFICATION" IS A MYTH!
I DON'T EVER GET WHAT I WANT WHEN I WANT IT! I ALWAYS HAVE TO WAIT!
LOOK HOW LONG IT'S TAKEN ME TO BE SIX YEARS OLD! PRACTICALLY FOREVER!
WHEN DO I GET TO DRIVE?! WHEN CAN I GO SEE GORY, VIOLENT MOVIES?! WHY DO I HAVE TO WAIT TILL I'M OLDER?!
PEOPLE SAY LIFE'S A JOURNEY, BUT I'M TIRED OF WASTING MY PRECIOUS TIME IN TRANSIT! I SAY, IF YOU WANT TO FIND OUT WHERE THE ROAD GOES, GET IN THE FAST LANE AND HIT THE GAS!
SPARE ME THE SCENERY AND LET'S GET WHERE WE'RE GOING! I'M A BUSY GUY! I'VE GOT PLACES TO BE!
WHUMP!
SPLOOP
GOSH, THAT WAS OVER QUICK.

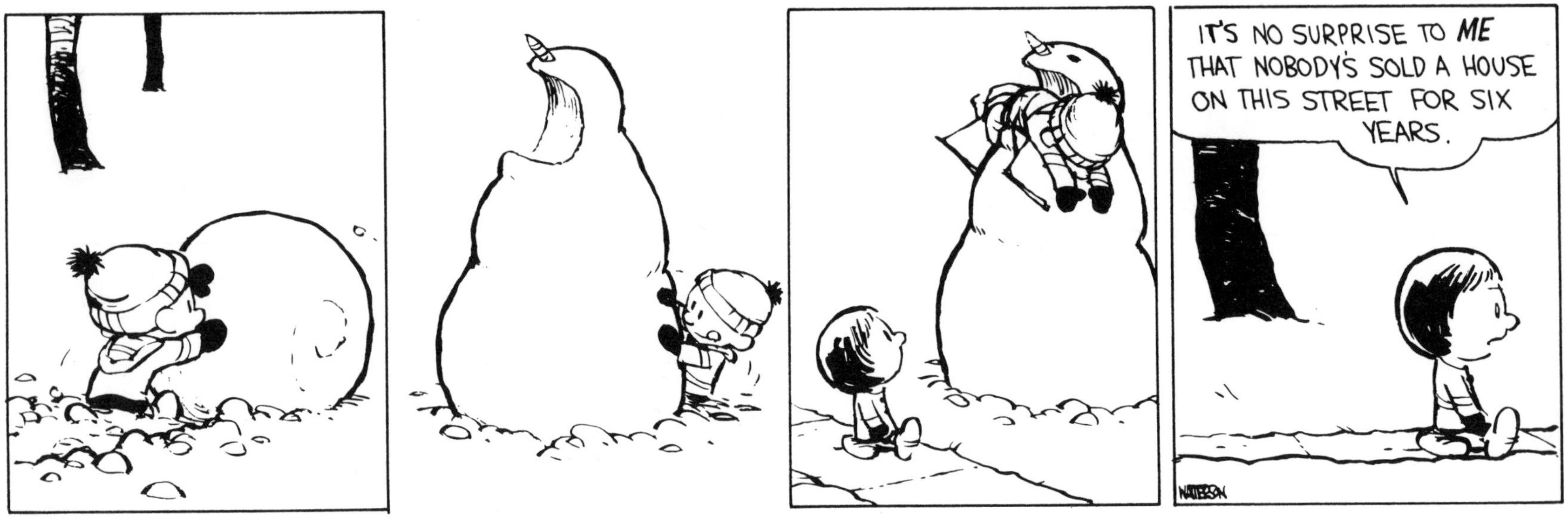
IT'S NO SURPRISE TO *ME* THAT NOBODY'S SOLD A HOUSE ON THIS STREET FOR SIX YEARS.
WATERSON

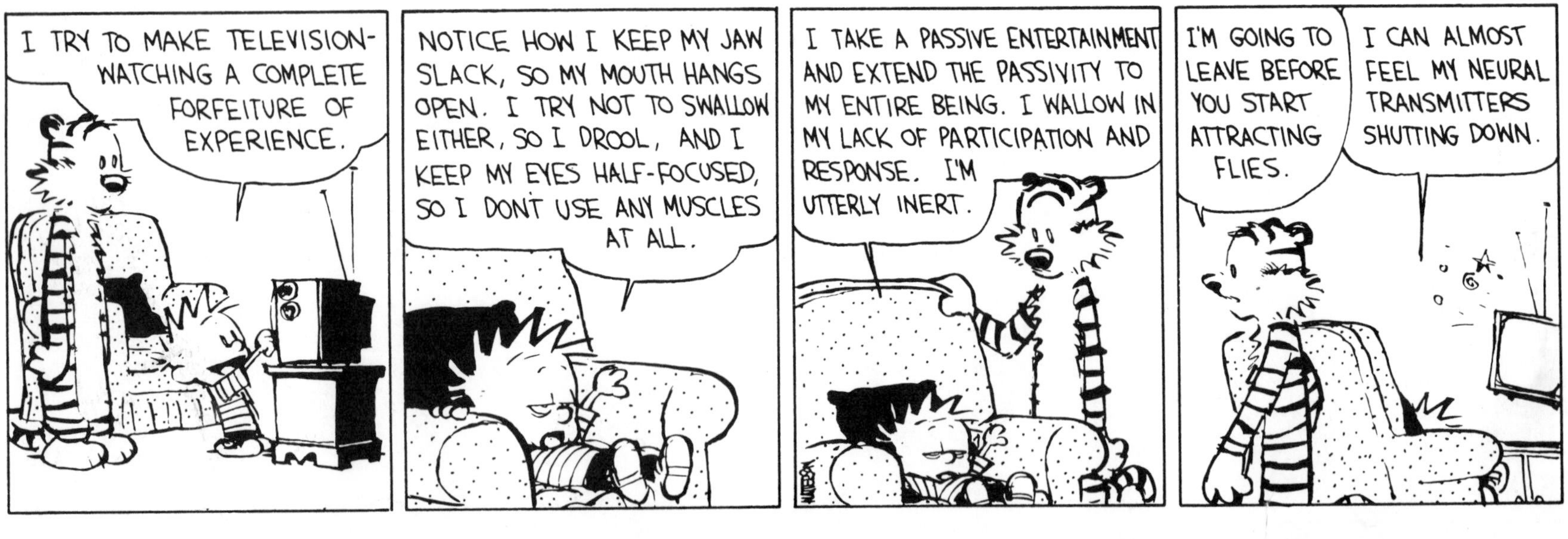
I TRY TO MAKE TELEVISION-WATCHING A COMPLETE FORFEITURE OF EXPERIENCE.
NOTICE HOW I KEEP MY JAW SLACK, SO MY MOUTH HANGS OPEN. I TRY NOT TO SWALLOW EITHER, SO I DROOL, AND I KEEP MY EYES HALF-FOCUSED, SO I DON'T USE ANY MUSCLES AT ALL.
I TAKE A PASSIVE ENTERTAINMENT AND EXTEND THE PASSIVITY TO MY ENTIRE BEING. I WALLOW IN MY LACK OF PARTICIPATION AND RESPONSE. I'M UTTERLY INERT.
WATERSON
I'M GOING TO LEAVE BEFORE YOU START ATTRACTING FLIES.
I CAN ALMOST FEEL MY NEURAL TRANSMITTERS SHUTTING DOWN.

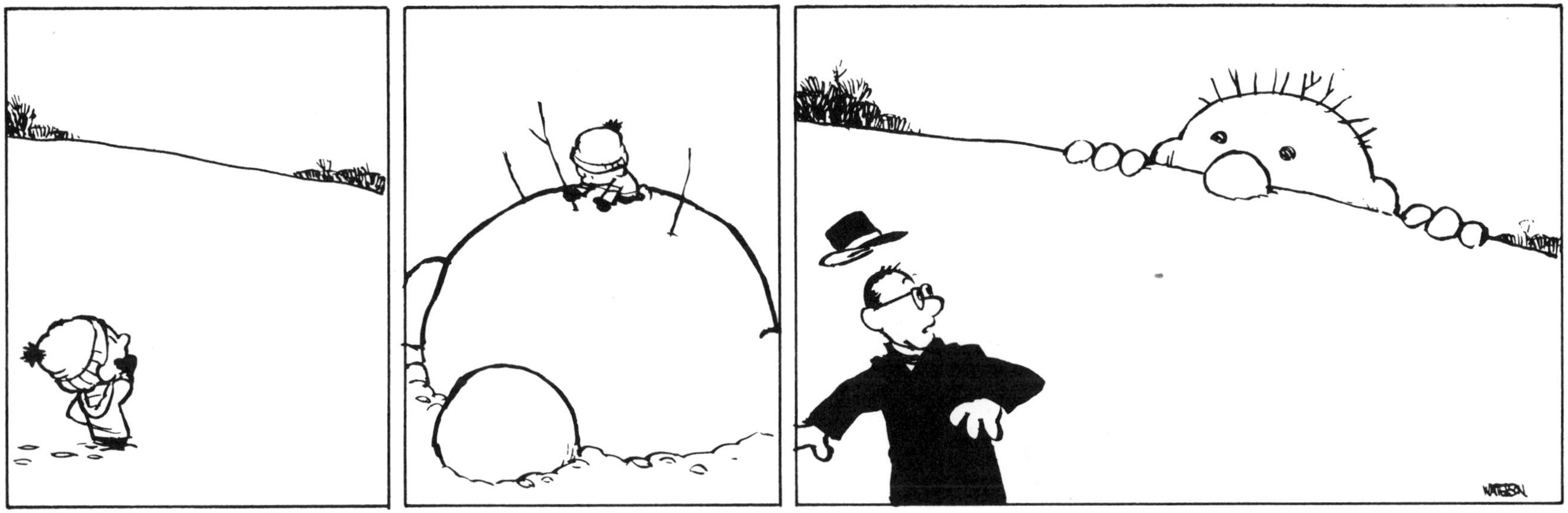

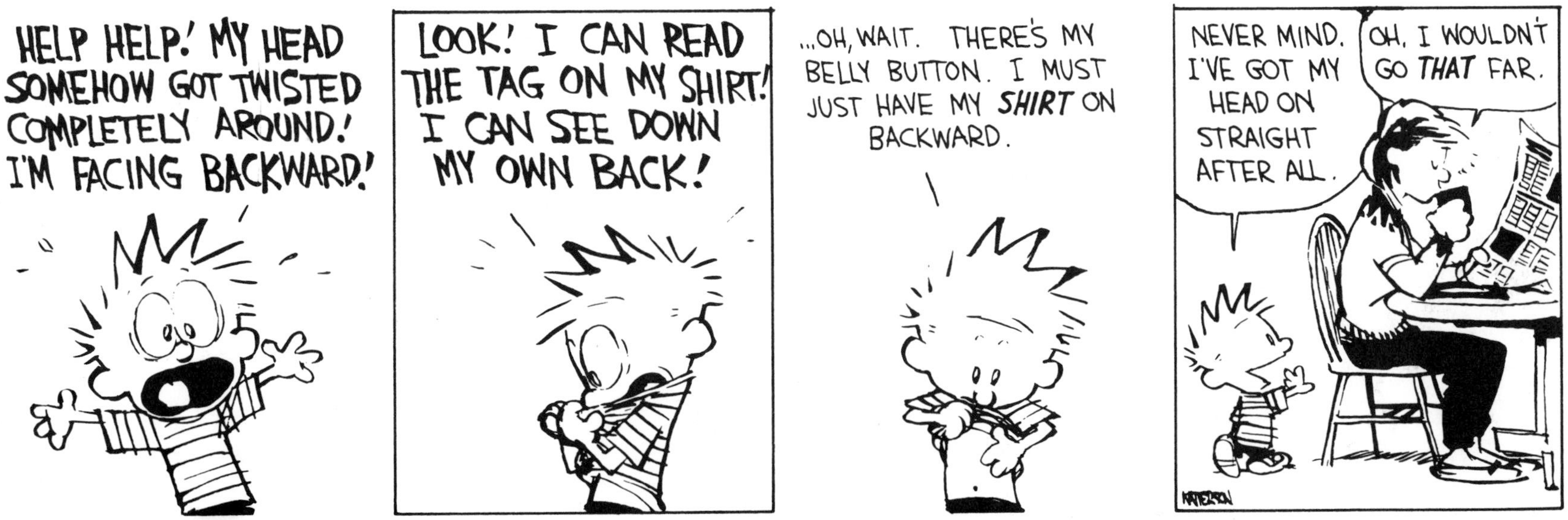
HELP HELP! MY HEAD SOMEHOW GOT TWISTED COMPLETELY AROUND! I'M FACING BACKWARD!
LOOK! I CAN READ THE TAG ON MY SHIRT! I CAN SEE DOWN MY OWN BACK!
...OH, WAIT. THERE'S MY BELLY BUTTON. I MUST JUST HAVE MY SHIRT ON BACKWARD.
NEVER MIND. I'VE GOT MY HEAD ON STRAIGHT AFTER ALL.
OH, I WOULDN'T GO THAT FAR.

PULL

PULL

PULL

OH SURE! NICE TRY!

DARN, DARN, DARN DARN, DARN!

AREN'T YOU SUPPOSED TO BE DOING HOMEWORK NOW?

I QUIT DOING HOMEWORK. HOMEWORK IS BAD FOR MY SELF-ESTEEM.

IT IS?

SURE! IT SENDS THE MESSAGE THAT I DON'T KNOW ENOUGH! ALL THAT EMPHASIS ON RIGHT ANSWERS MAKES ME FEEL BAD WHEN I GET THEM WRONG.

SO INSTEAD OF TRYING TO LEARN, I'M JUST CONCENTRATING ON LIKING MYSELF THE WAY I AM.

YOUR SELF-ESTEEM IS ENHANCED BY REMAINING AN IGNORAMUS?

PLEASE! LET'S CALL IT "INFORMATIONALLY IMPAIRED."

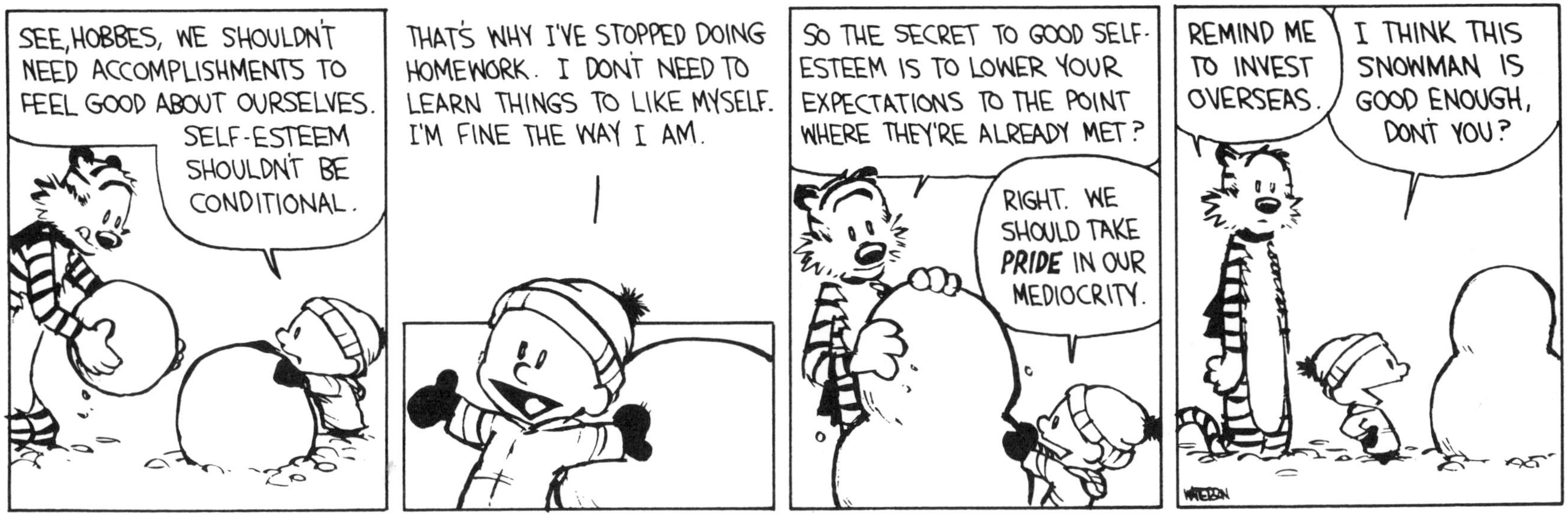
SEE, HOBBES, WE SHOULDN'T NEED ACCOMPLISHMENTS TO FEEL GOOD ABOUT OURSELVES.
SELF-ESTEEM SHOULDN'T BE CONDITIONAL.
THAT'S WHY I'VE STOPPED DOING HOMEWORK. I DON'T NEED TO LEARN THINGS TO LIKE MYSELF. I'M FINE THE WAY I AM.
SO THE SECRET TO GOOD SELF-ESTEEM IS TO LOWER YOUR EXPECTATIONS TO THE POINT WHERE THEY'RE ALREADY MET?
RIGHT. WE SHOULD TAKE PRIDE IN OUR MEDIOCRITY.
REMIND ME TO INVEST OVERSEAS.
I THINK THIS SNOWMAN IS GOOD ENOUGH, DON'T YOU?

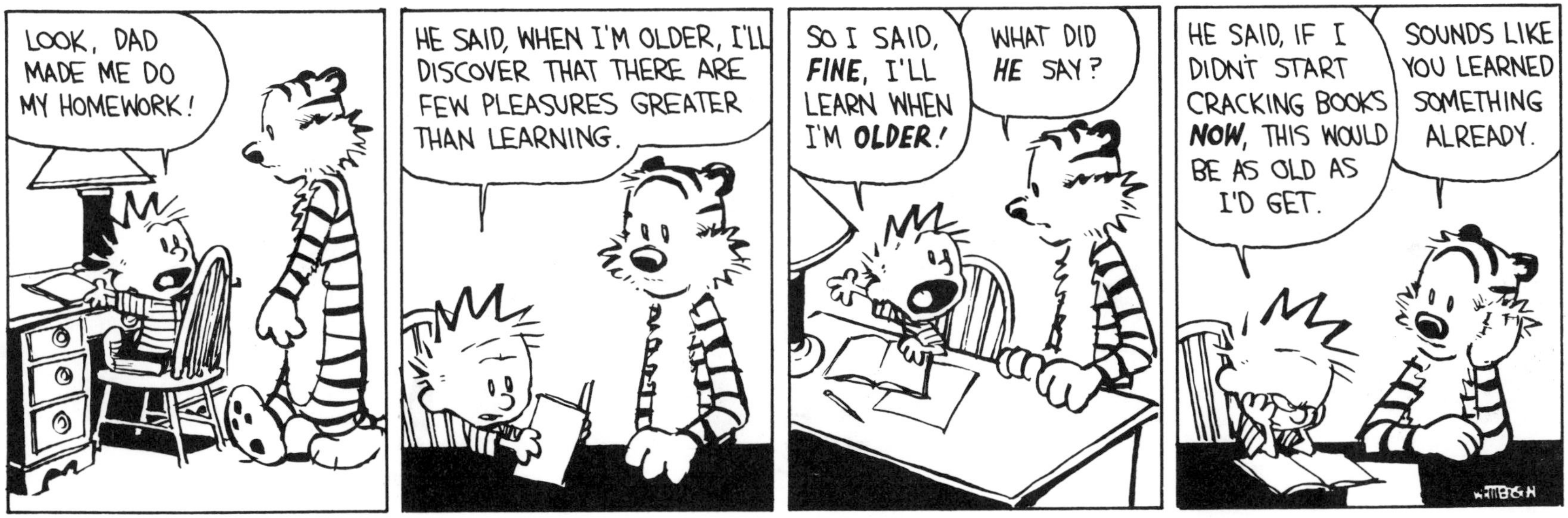
LOOK, DAD MADE ME DO MY HOMEWORK!
HE SAID, WHEN I'M OLDER, I'LL DISCOVER THAT THERE ARE FEW PLEASURES GREATER THAN LEARNING.
SO I SAID, FINE, I'LL LEARN WHEN I'M OLDER!
WHAT DID HE SAY?
HE SAID, IF I DIDN'T START CRACKING BOOKS NOW, THIS WOULD BE AS OLD AS I'D GET.
SOUNDS LIKE YOU LEARNED SOMETHING ALREADY.

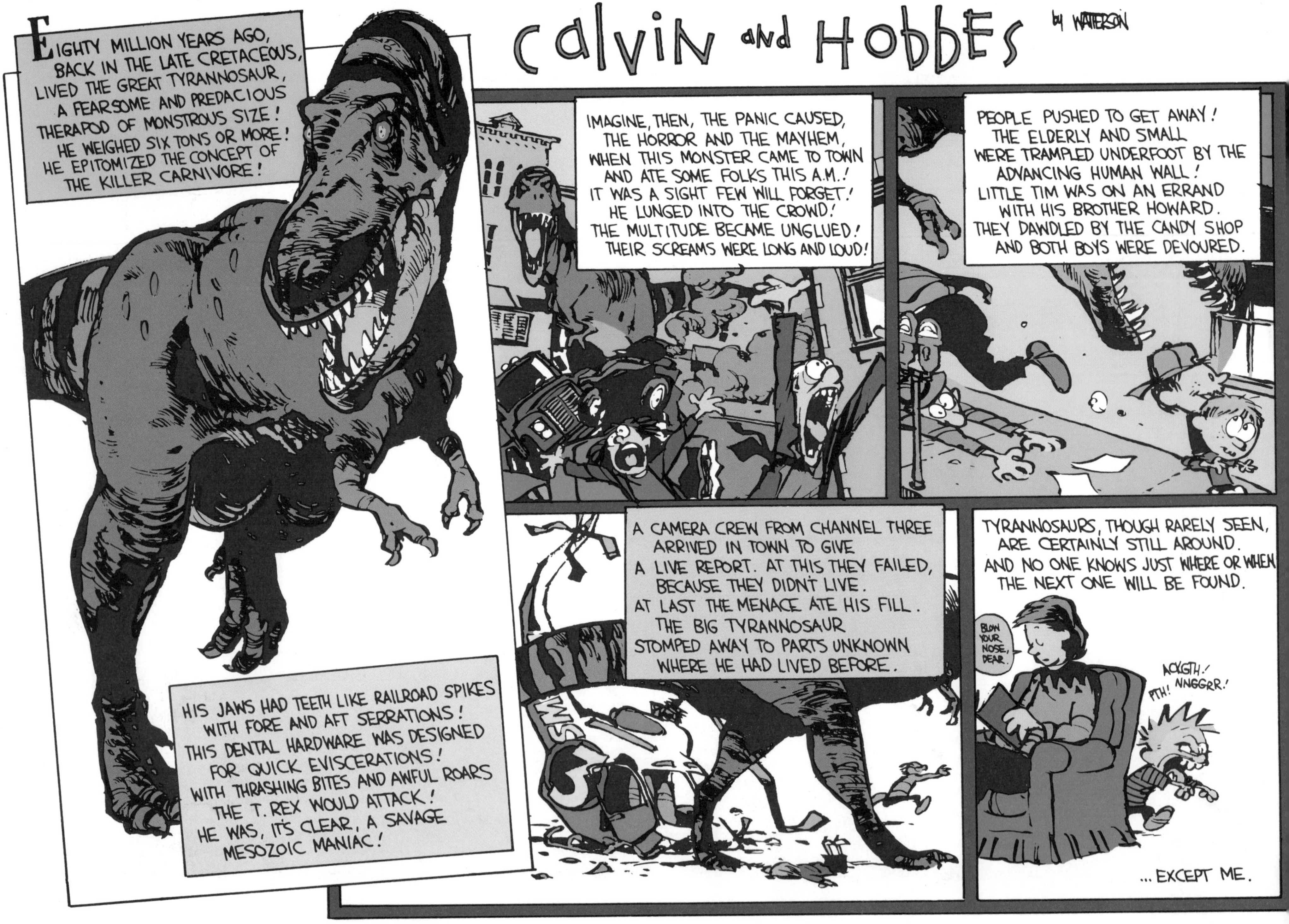
Calvin and Hobbes
by WATTERSON
EIGHTY MILLION YEARS AGO, BACK IN THE LATE CRETACEOUS, LIVED THE GREAT TYRANNOSAUR, A FEARSOME AND PREDACIOUS THERAPOD OF MONSTROUS SIZE! HE WEIGHED SIX TONS OR MORE! HE EPITOMIZED THE CONCEPT OF THE KILLER CARNIVORE!
HIS JAWS HAD TEETH LIKE RAILROAD SPIKES WITH FORE AND AFT SERRATIONS! THIS DENTAL HARDWARE WAS DESIGNED FOR QUICK EVISCERATIONS! WITH THRASHING BITES AND AWFUL ROARS THE T. REX WOULD ATTACK! HE WAS, IT'S CLEAR, A SAVAGE MESOZOIC MANIAC!
IMAGINE, THEN, THE PANIC CAUSED, THE HORROR AND THE MAYHEM, WHEN THIS MONSTER CAME TO TOWN AND ATE SOME FOLKS THIS A.M.! IT WAS A SIGHT FEW WILL FORGET! HE LUNGED INTO THE CROWD! THE MULTITUDE BECAME UNGLUED! THEIR SCREAMS WERE LONG AND LOUD!
PEOPLE PUSHED TO GET AWAY! THE ELDERLY AND SMALL WERE TRAMPLED UNDERFOOT BY THE ADVANCING HUMAN WALL! LITTLE TIM WAS ON AN ERRAND WITH HIS BROTHER HOWARD. THEY DAWDLED BY THE CANDY SHOP AND BOTH BOYS WERE DEVOURED.
A CAMERA CREW FROM CHANNEL THREE ARRIVED IN TOWN TO GIVE A LIVE REPORT. AT THIS THEY FAILED, BECAUSE THEY DIDN'T LIVE. AT LAST THE MENACE ATE HIS FILL. THE BIG TYRANNOSAUR STOMPED AWAY TO PARTS UNKNOWN WHERE HE HAD LIVED BEFORE.
TYRANNOSAURS, THOUGH RARELY SEEN, ARE CERTAINLY STILL AROUND. AND NO ONE KNOWS JUST WHERE OR WHEN THE NEXT ONE WILL BE FOUND.
BLOW YOUR NOSE, DEAR.
ACKGTH! NNGGRR! PTH!
... EXCEPT ME.

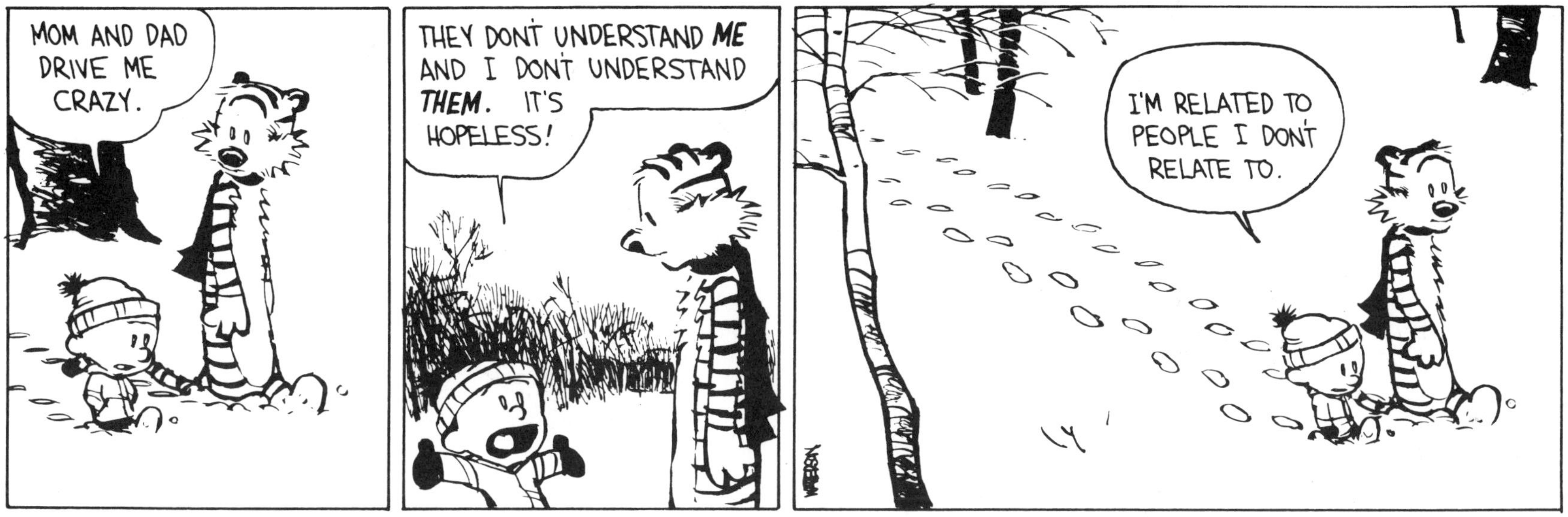
MOM AND DAD DRIVE ME CRAZY.
THEY DON'T UNDERSTAND **ME** AND I DON'T UNDERSTAND **THEM**. IT'S HOPELESS!
I'M RELATED TO PEOPLE I DON'T RELATE TO.
WATERSON

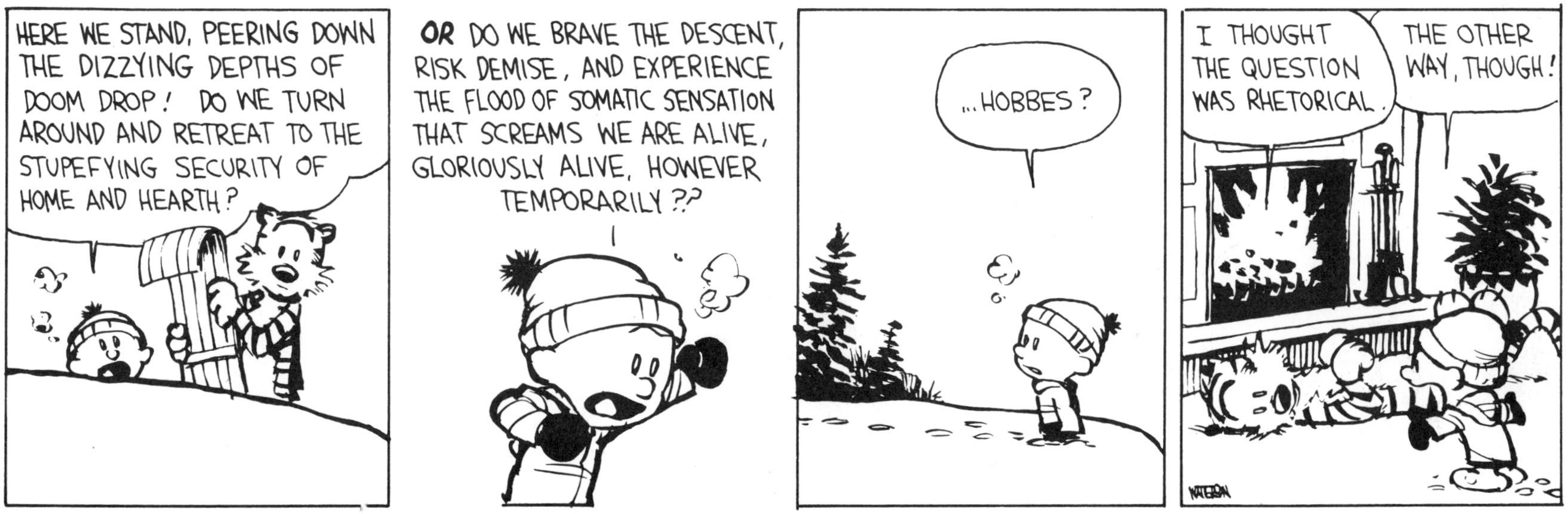
HERE WE STAND, PEERING DOWN THE DIZZYING DEPTHS OF DOOM DROP! DO WE TURN AROUND AND RETREAT TO THE STUPEFYING SECURITY OF HOME AND HEARTH?
OR DO WE BRAVE THE DESCENT, RISK DEMISE, AND EXPERIENCE THE FLOOD OF SOMATIC SENSATION THAT SCREAMS WE ARE ALIVE, GLORIOUSLY ALIVE, HOWEVER TEMPORARILY??
...HOBBES?
I THOUGHT THE QUESTION WAS RHETORICAL.
THE OTHER WAY, THOUGH!
WATERSON

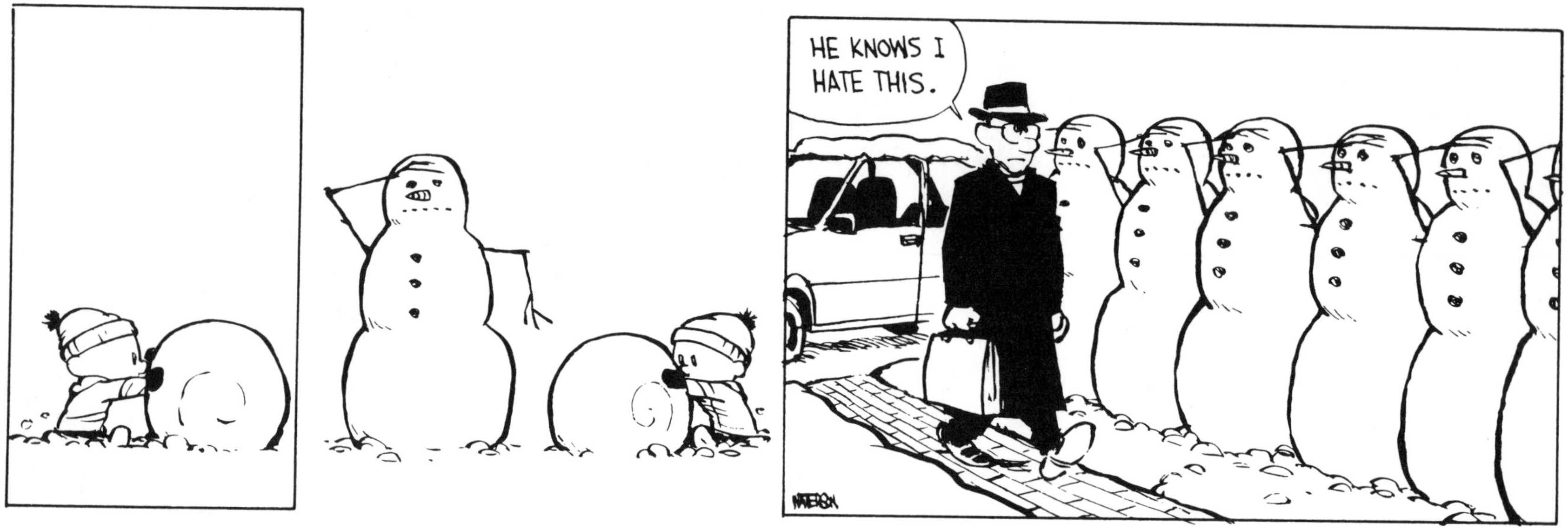
HE KNOWS I HATE THIS.

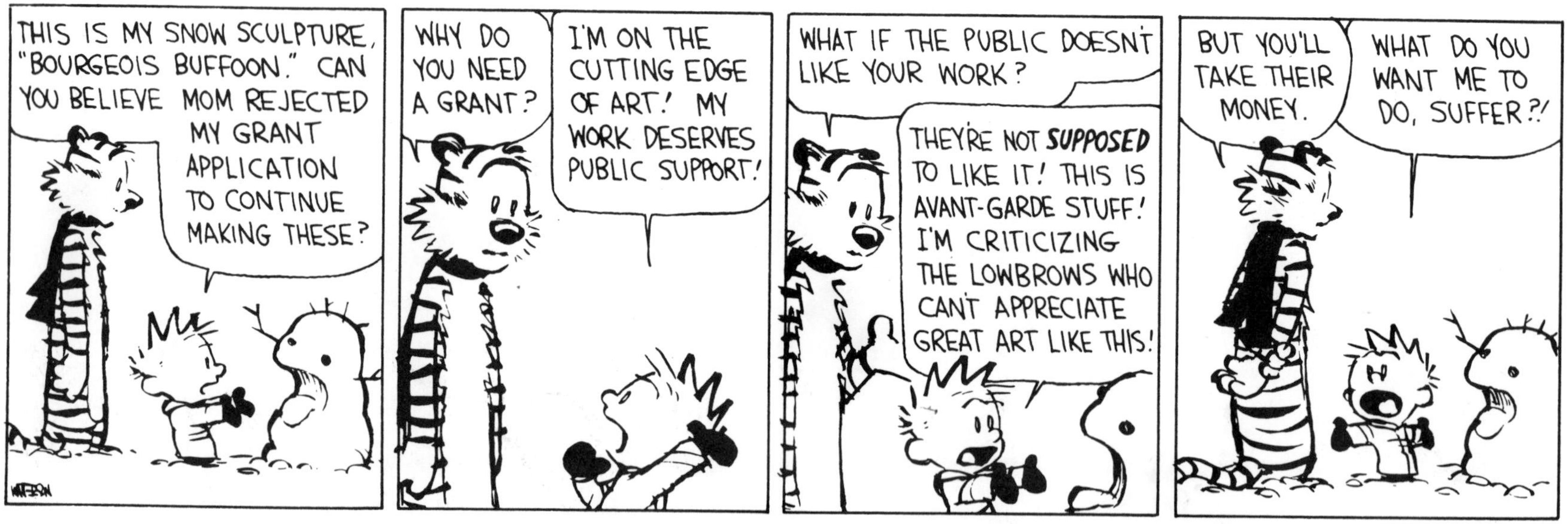
THIS IS MY SNOW SCULPTURE, "BOURGEOIS BUFFOON." CAN YOU BELIEVE MOM REJECTED MY GRANT APPLICATION TO CONTINUE MAKING THESE?
WHY DO YOU NEED A GRANT?
I'M ON THE CUTTING EDGE OF ART! MY WORK DESERVES PUBLIC SUPPORT!
WHAT IF THE PUBLIC DOESN'T LIKE YOUR WORK?
THEY'RE NOT SUPPOSED TO LIKE IT! THIS IS AVANT-GARDE STUFF! I'M CRITICIZING THE LOWBROWS WHO CAN'T APPRECIATE GREAT ART LIKE THIS!
BUT YOU'LL TAKE THEIR MONEY.
WHAT DO YOU WANT ME TO DO, SUFFER?!

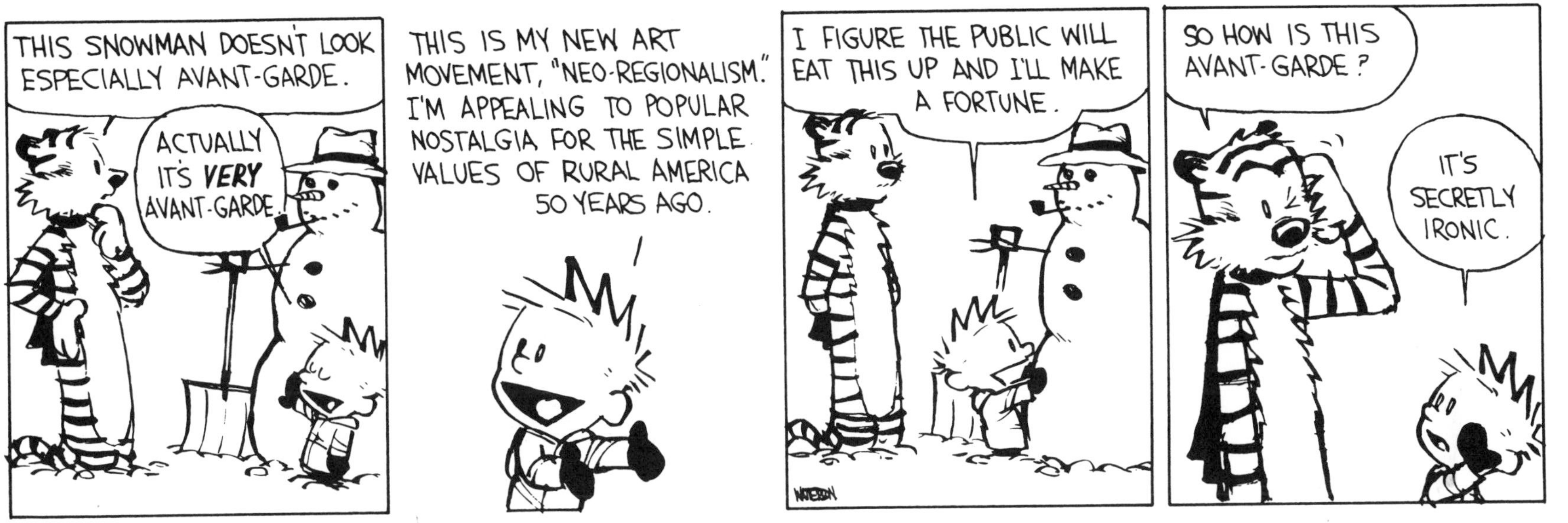
THIS SNOWMAN DOESN'T LOOK ESPECIALLY AVANT-GARDE.
ACTUALLY IT'S **VERY** AVANT-GARDE.
THIS IS MY NEW ART MOVEMENT, "NEO-REGIONALISM." I'M APPEALING TO POPULAR NOSTALGIA FOR THE SIMPLE VALUES OF RURAL AMERICA 50 YEARS AGO.
I FIGURE THE PUBLIC WILL EAT THIS UP AND I'LL MAKE A FORTUNE.
SO HOW IS THIS AVANT-GARDE?
IT'S SECRETLY IRONIC.
WATTERSON

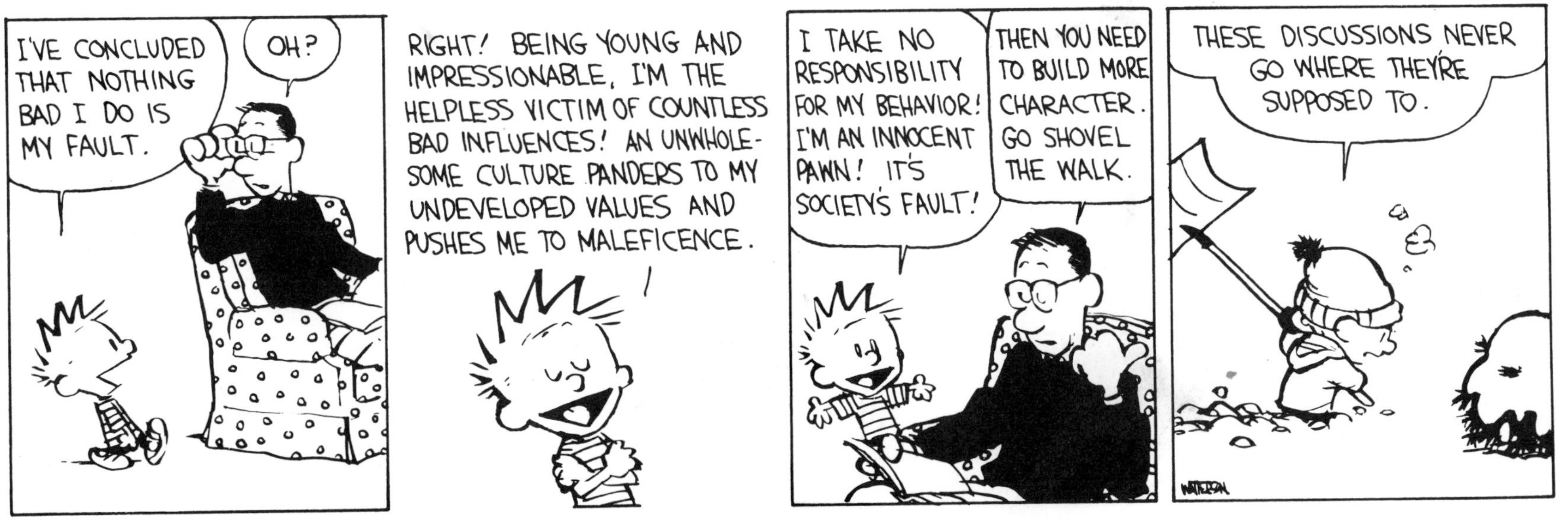
I'VE CONCLUDED THAT NOTHING BAD I DO IS MY FAULT.
OH?
RIGHT! BEING YOUNG AND IMPRESSIONABLE, I'M THE HELPLESS VICTIM OF COUNTLESS BAD INFLUENCES! AN UNWHOLESOME CULTURE PANDERS TO MY UNDEVELOPED VALUES AND PUSHES ME TO MALEFICENCE.
I TAKE NO RESPONSIBILITY FOR MY BEHAVIOR! I'M AN INNOCENT PAWN! IT'S SOCIETY'S FAULT!
THEN YOU NEED TO BUILD MORE CHARACTER. GO SHOVEL THE WALK.
THESE DISCUSSIONS NEVER GO WHERE THEY'RE SUPPOSED TO.
WATTERSON

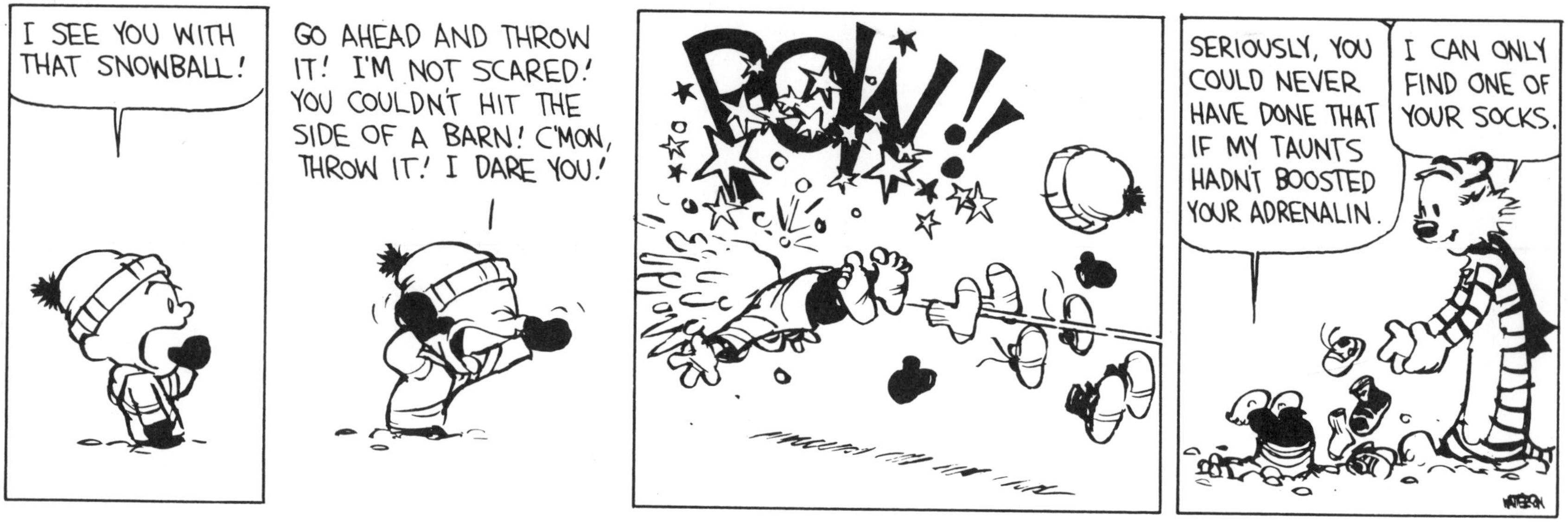
I SEE YOU WITH THAT SNOWBALL!
GO AHEAD AND THROW IT! I'M NOT SCARED! YOU COULDN'T HIT THE SIDE OF A BARN! C'MON, THROW IT! I DARE YOU!
POW!!
SERIOUSLY, YOU COULD NEVER HAVE DONE THAT IF MY TAUNTS HADN'T BOOSTED YOUR ADRENALIN.
I CAN ONLY FIND ONE OF YOUR SOCKS.

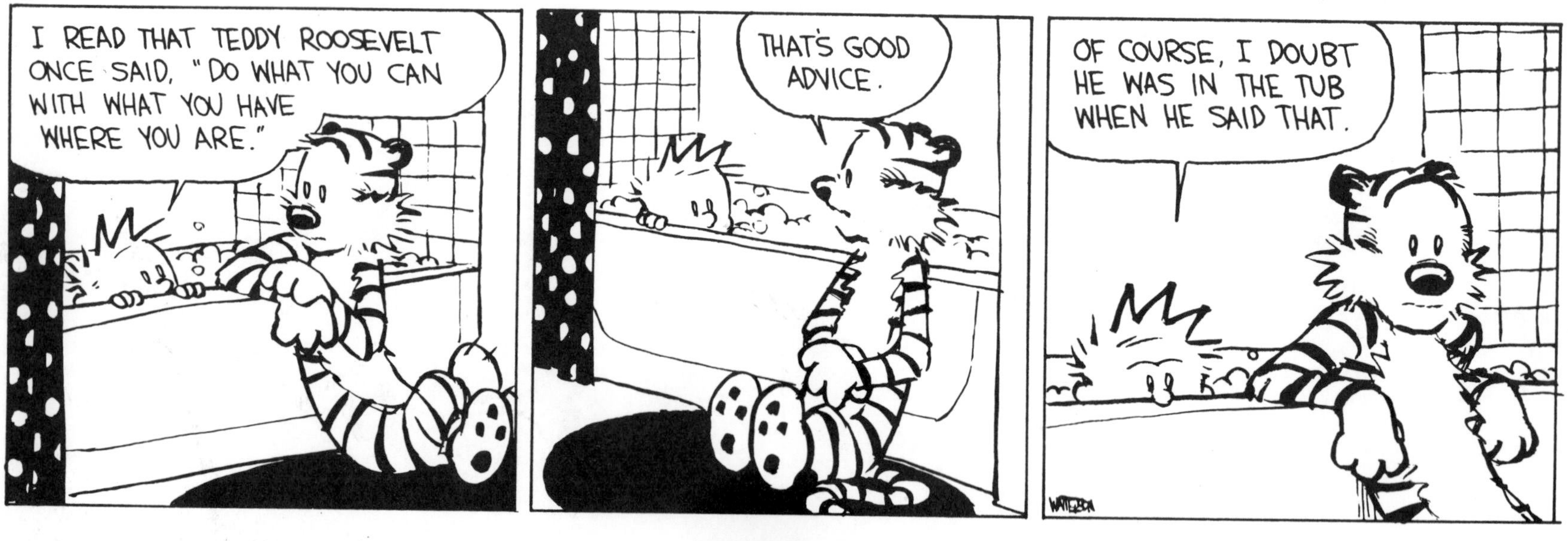
I READ THAT TEDDY ROOSEVELT ONCE SAID, "DO WHAT YOU CAN WITH WHAT YOU HAVE WHERE YOU ARE."
THAT'S GOOD ADVICE.
OF COURSE, I DOUBT HE WAS IN THE TUB WHEN HE SAID THAT.

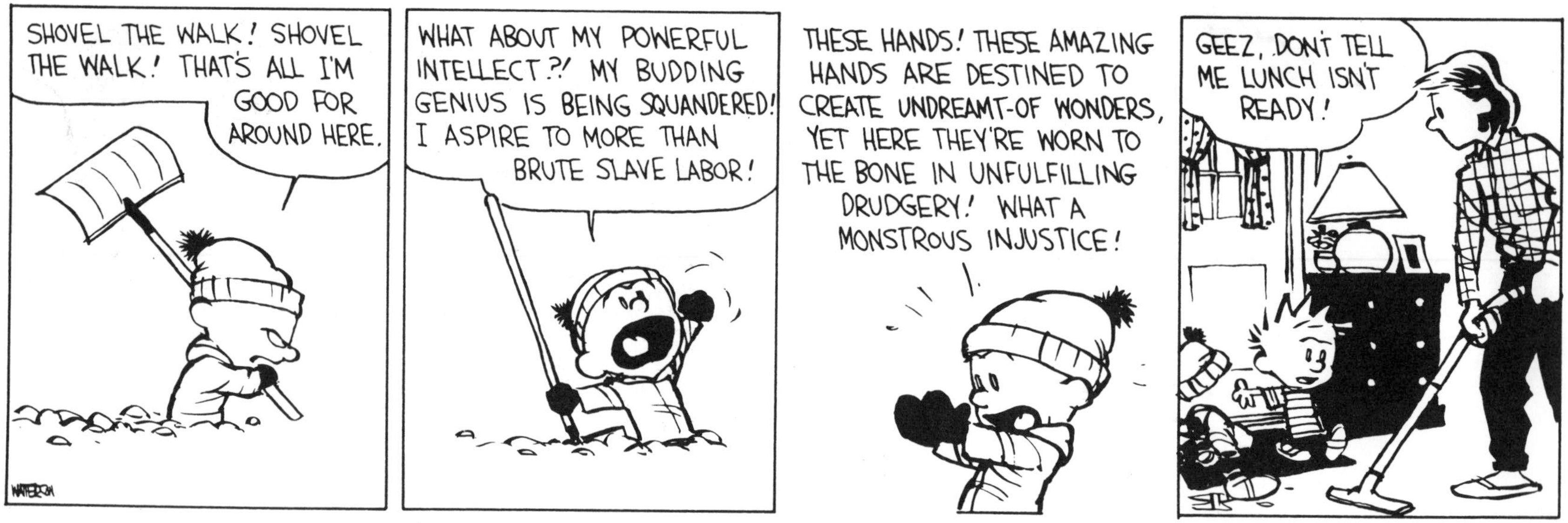
SHOVEL THE WALK! SHOVEL THE WALK! THAT'S ALL I'M GOOD FOR AROUND HERE.
WHAT ABOUT MY POWERFUL INTELLECT?! MY BUDDING GENIUS IS BEING SQUANDERED! I ASPIRE TO MORE THAN BRUTE SLAVE LABOR!
THESE HANDS! THESE AMAZING HANDS ARE DESTINED TO CREATE UNDREAMT-OF WONDERS, YET HERE THEY'RE WORN TO THE BONE IN UNFULFILLING DRUDGERY! WHAT A MONSTROUS INJUSTICE!
GEEZ, DON'T TELL ME LUNCH ISN'T READY!

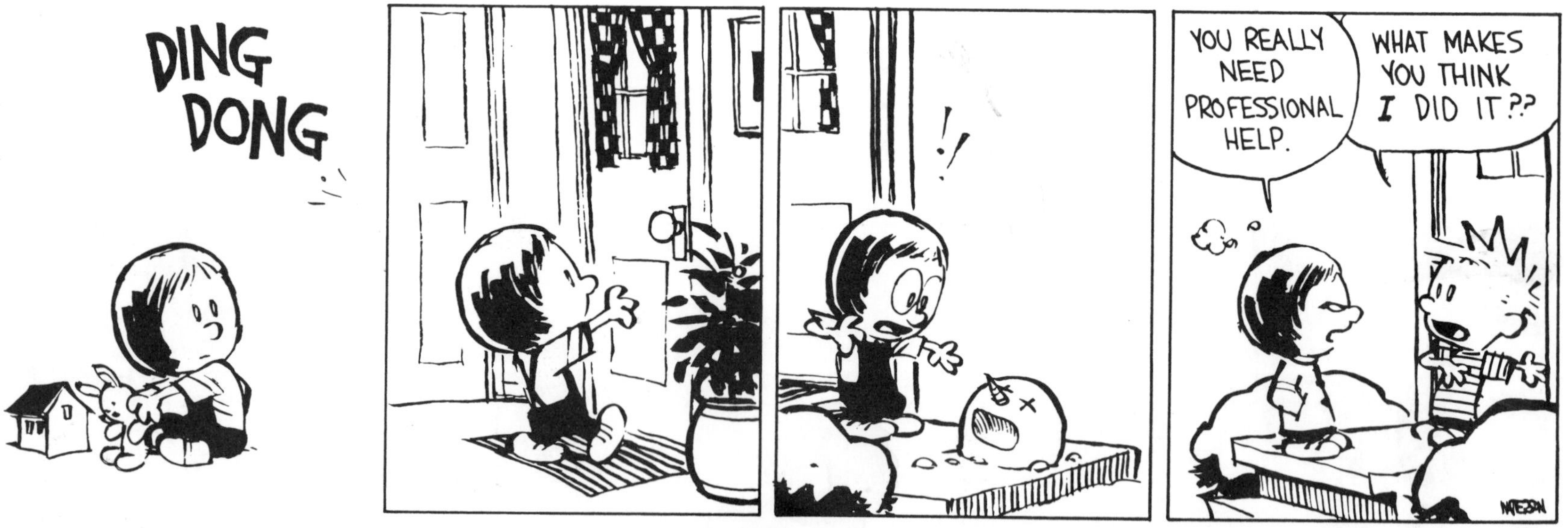
DING DONG
!!
YOU REALLY NEED PROFESSIONAL HELP.
WHAT MAKES YOU THINK I DID IT??

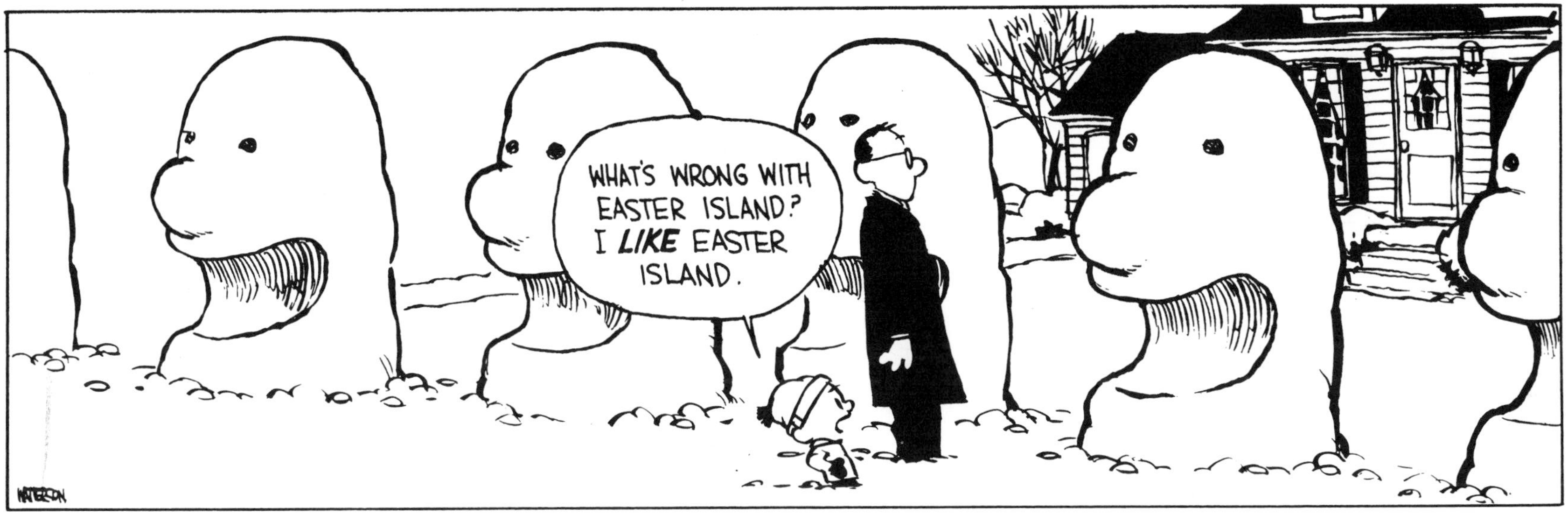
WHAT'S WRONG WITH EASTER ISLAND? I **LIKE** EASTER ISLAND.

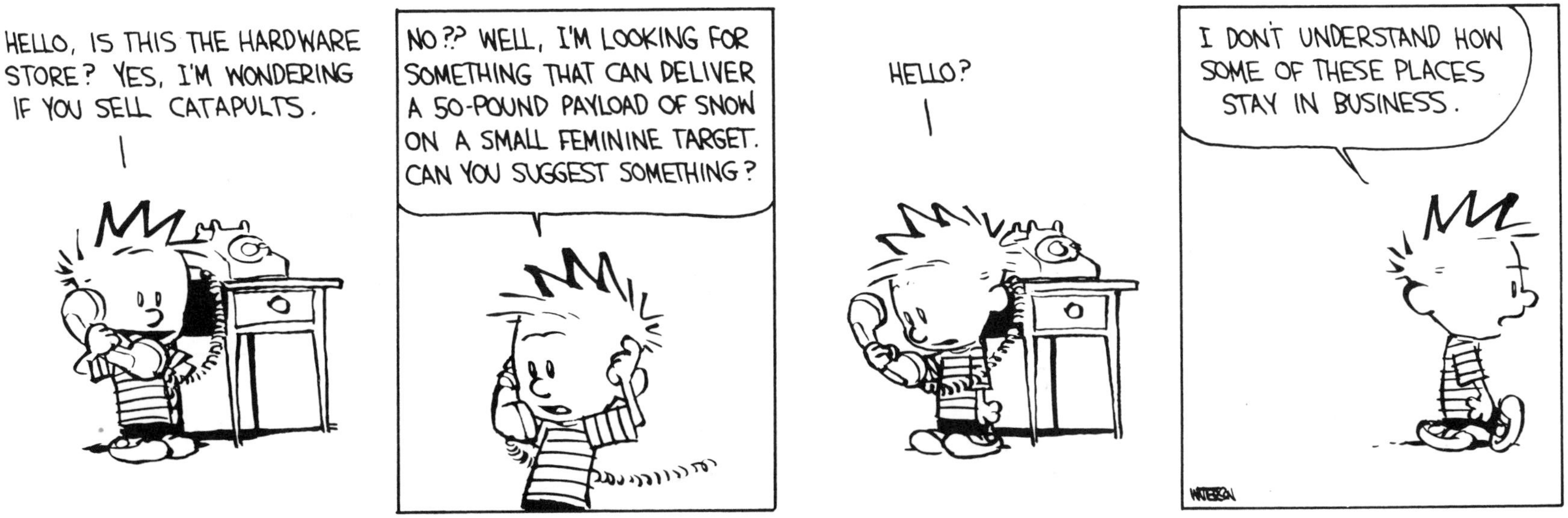
HELLO, IS THIS THE HARDWARE STORE? YES, I'M WONDERING IF YOU SELL CATAPULTS.
NO?? WELL, I'M LOOKING FOR SOMETHING THAT CAN DELIVER A 50-POUND PAYLOAD OF SNOW ON A SMALL FEMININE TARGET. CAN YOU SUGGEST SOMETHING?
HELLO?
I DON'T UNDERSTAND HOW SOME OF THESE PLACES STAY IN BUSINESS.

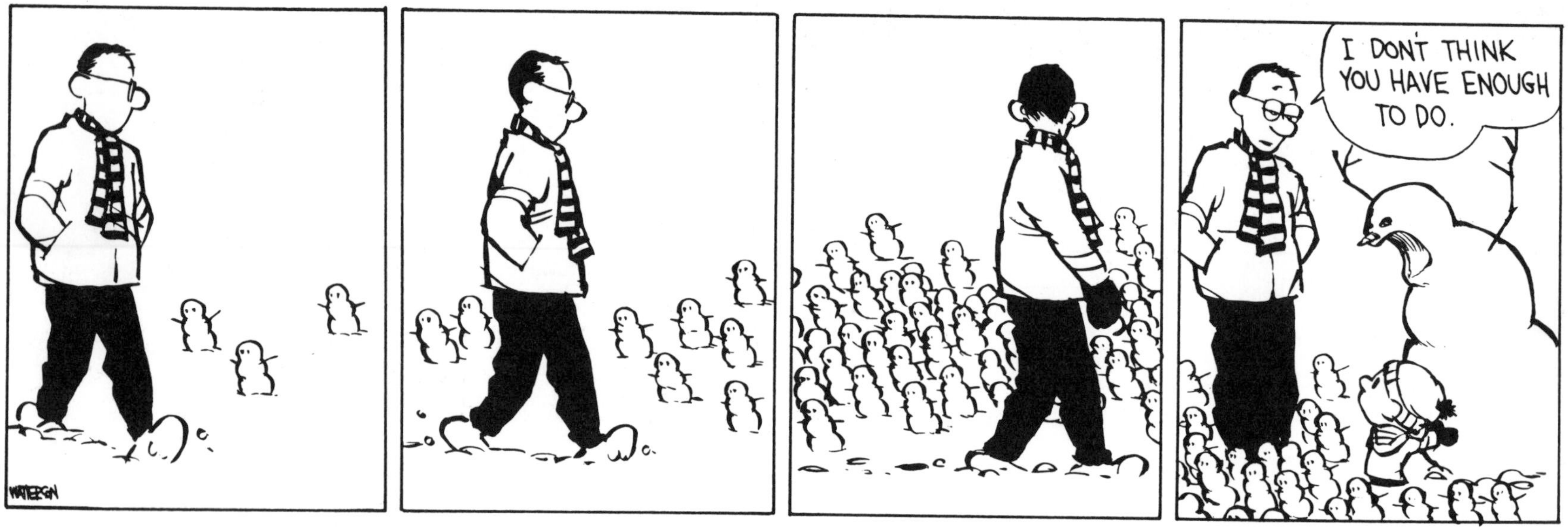
I DON'T THINK YOU HAVE ENOUGH TO DO.

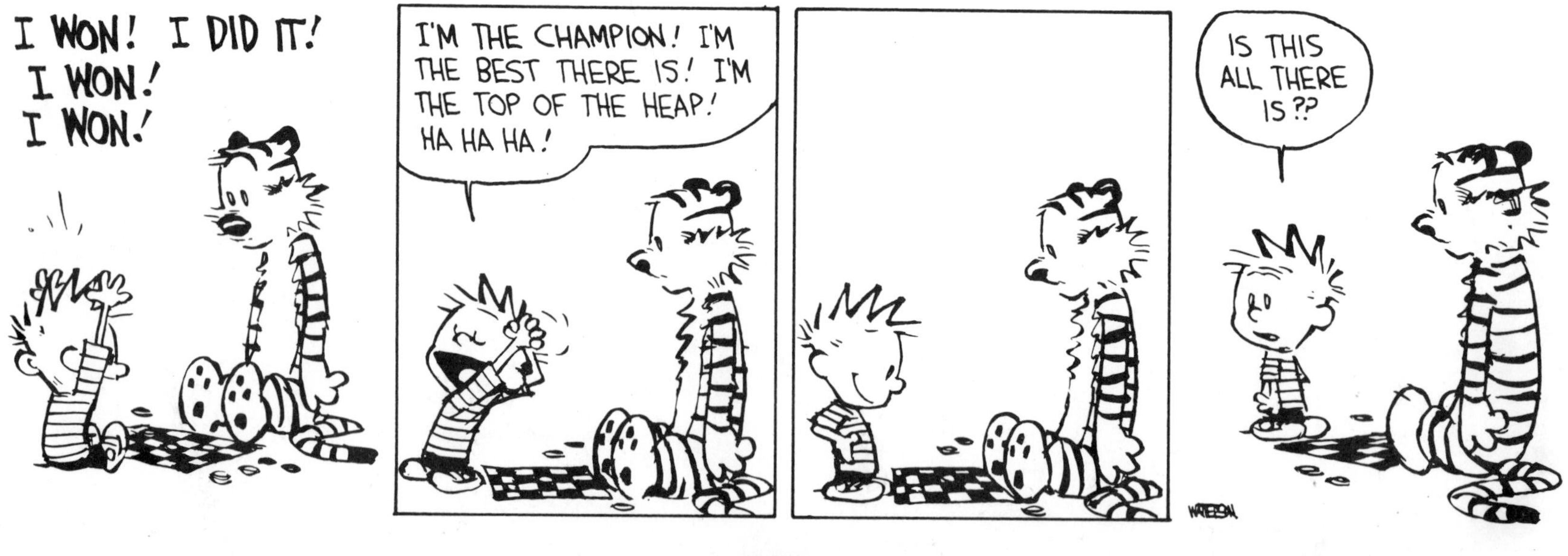
I WON! I DID IT! I WON! I WON!
I'M THE CHAMPION! I'M THE BEST THERE IS! I'M THE TOP OF THE HEAP! HA HA HA!
IS THIS ALL THERE IS??

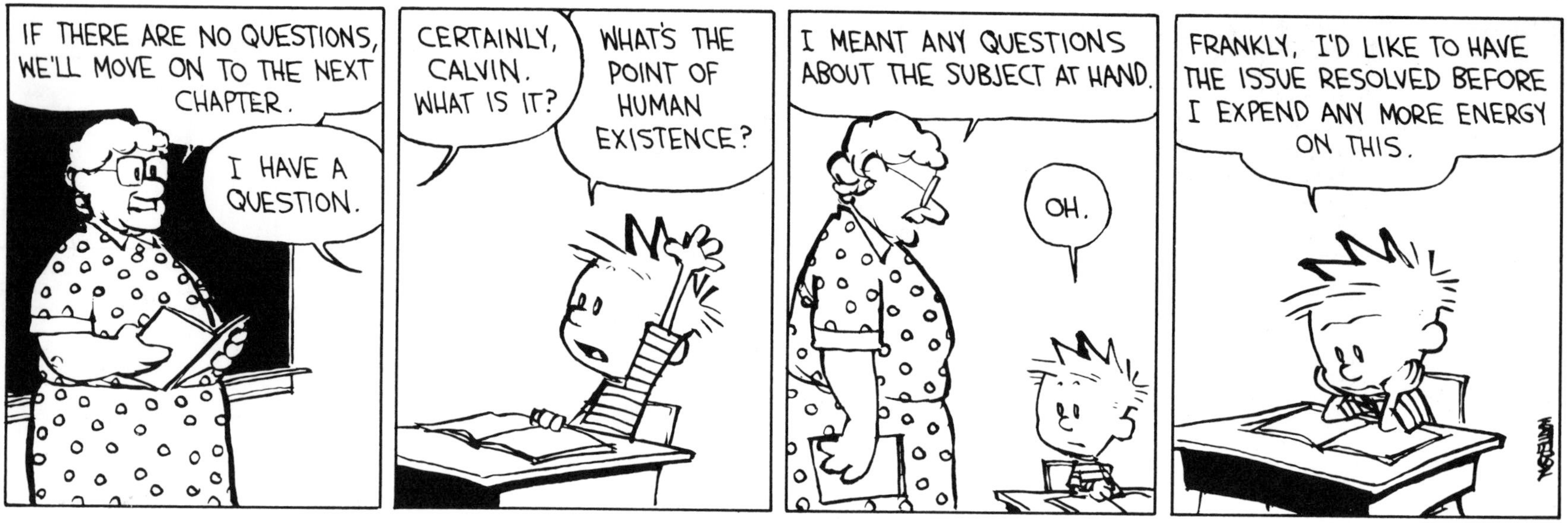
IF THERE ARE NO QUESTIONS, WE'LL MOVE ON TO THE NEXT CHAPTER.
I HAVE A QUESTION.
CERTAINLY, CALVIN. WHAT IS IT?
WHAT'S THE POINT OF HUMAN EXISTENCE?
I MEANT ANY QUESTIONS ABOUT THE SUBJECT AT HAND.
OH.
FRANKLY, I'D LIKE TO HAVE THE ISSUE RESOLVED BEFORE I EXPEND ANY MORE ENERGY ON THIS.

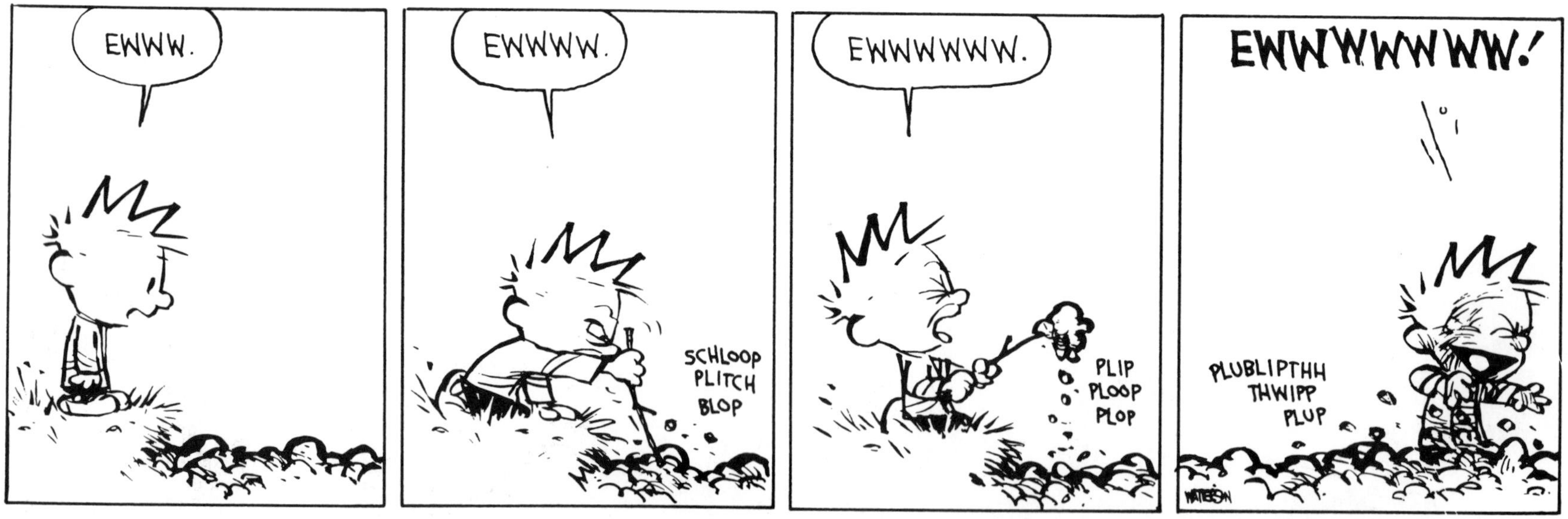
EWWW.
EWWWW.
SCHLOOP
PLITCH
BLOP
EWWWWWW.
PLIP
PLOOP
PLOP
EWWWWWWW!
PLUBLIPTHH
THWIPP
PLUP

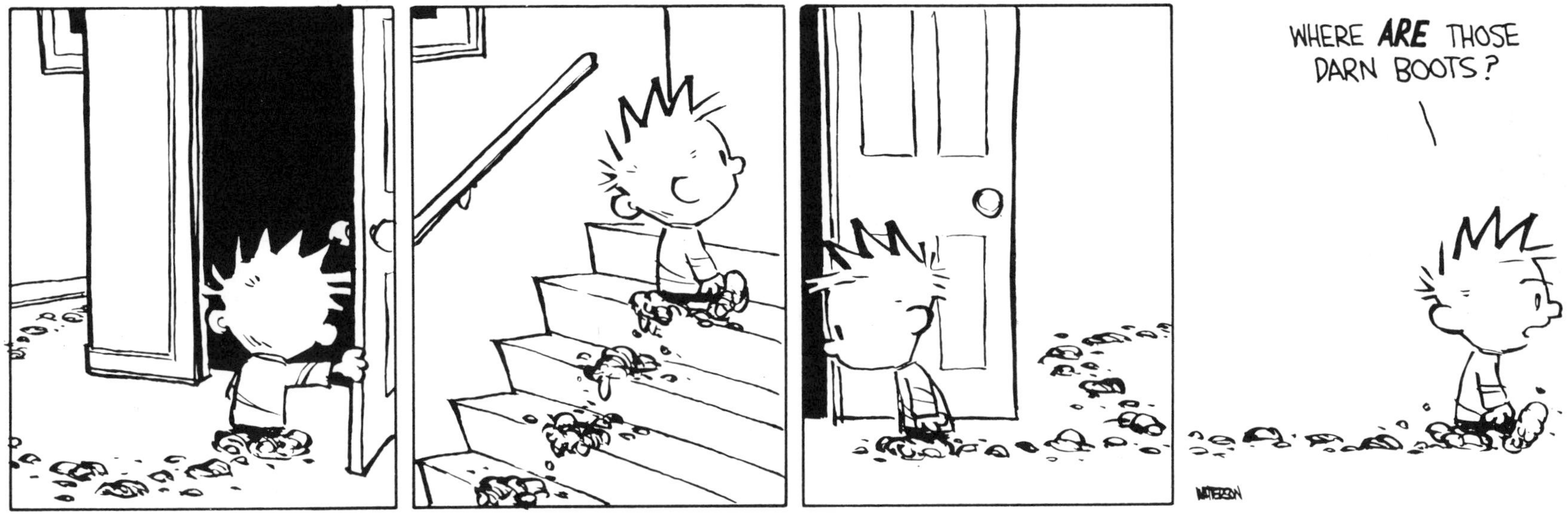
WHERE **ARE** THOSE DARN BOOTS?

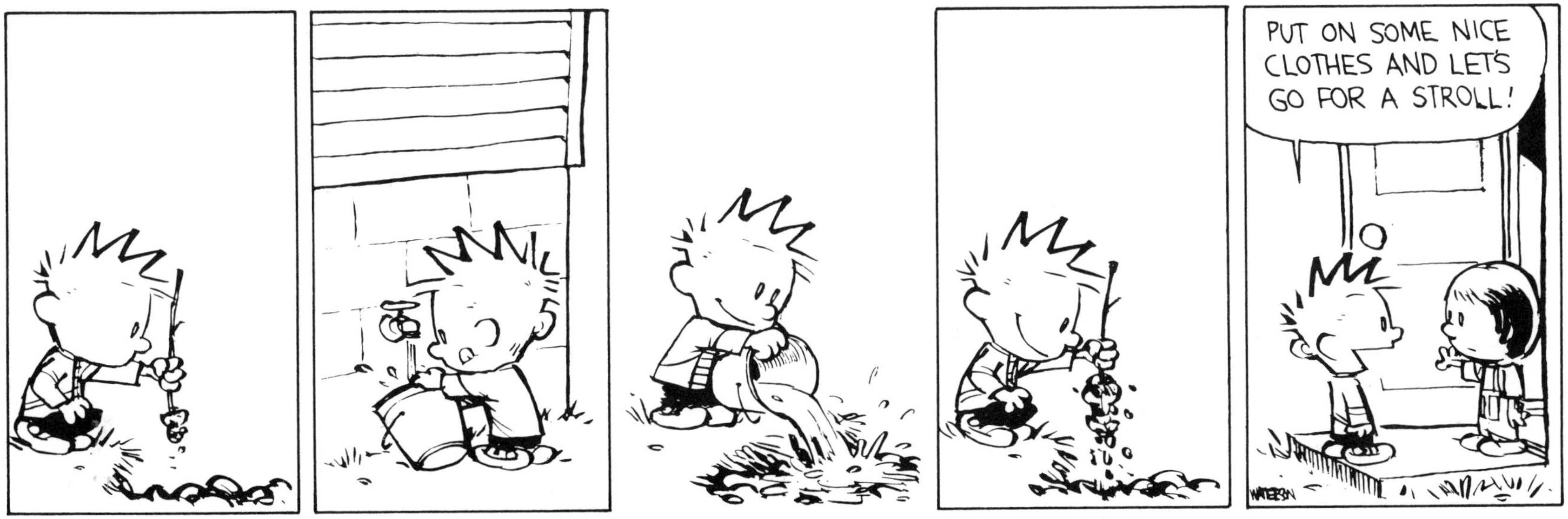
PUT ON SOME NICE CLOTHES AND LET'S GO FOR A STROLL!

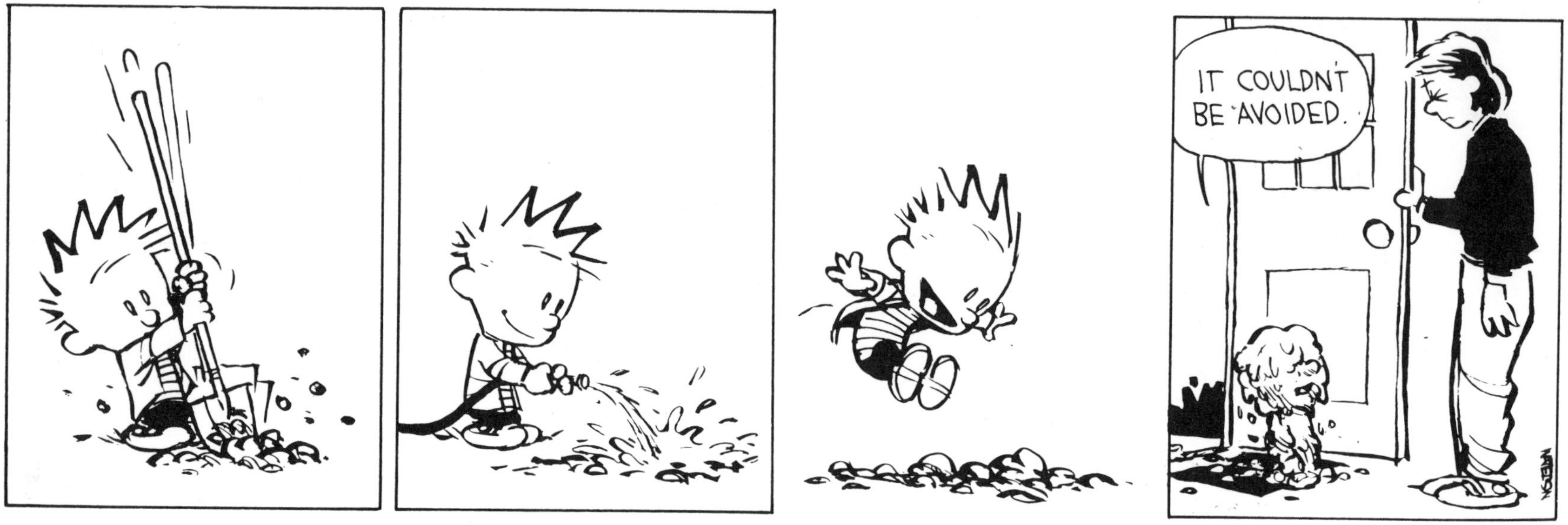
IT COULDN'T BE AVOIDED.

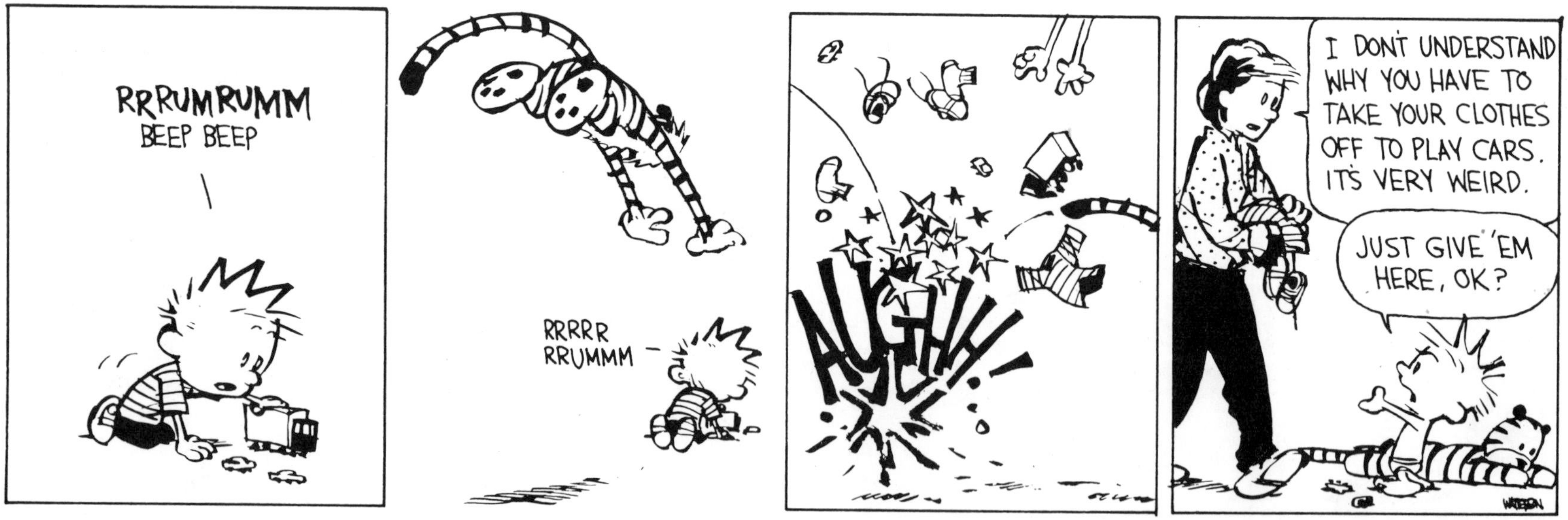
RRRUMRUMM
BEEP BEEP
RRRRR RRUMMM
AUGHH!
I DON'T UNDERSTAND WHY YOU HAVE TO TAKE YOUR CLOTHES OFF TO PLAY CARS. IT'S VERY WEIRD.
JUST GIVE 'EM HERE, OK?

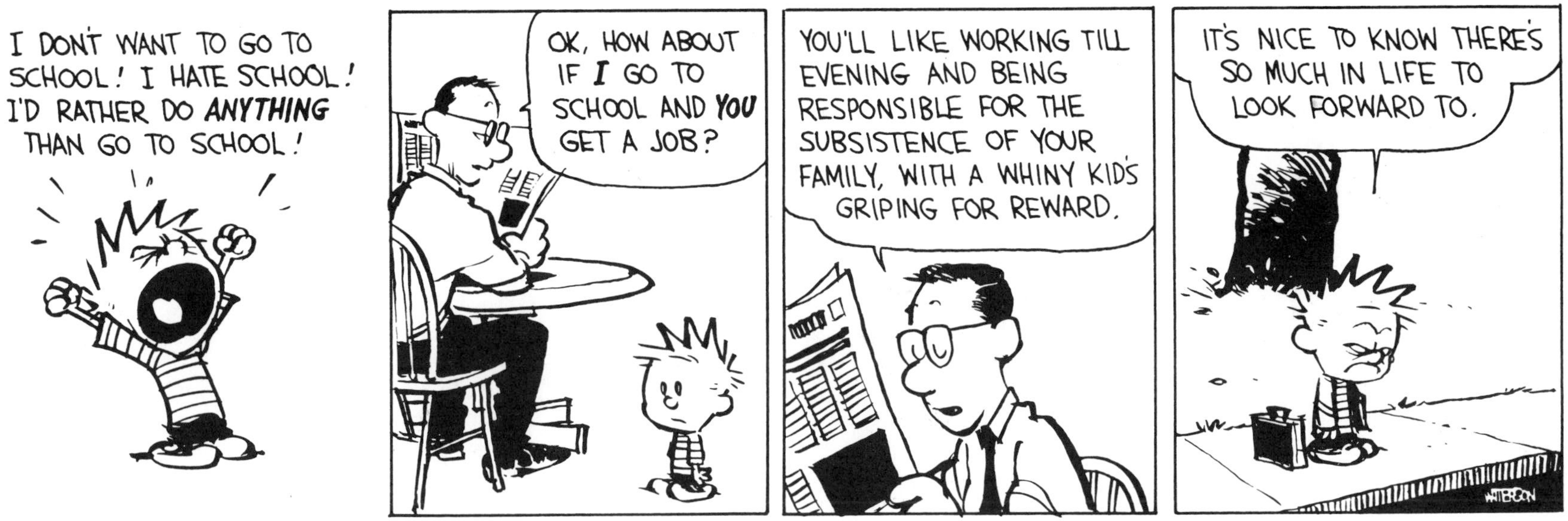
I DON'T WANT TO GO TO SCHOOL! I HATE SCHOOL! I'D RATHER DO ANYTHING THAN GO TO SCHOOL!
OK, HOW ABOUT IF I GO TO SCHOOL AND YOU GET A JOB?
YOU'LL LIKE WORKING TILL EVENING AND BEING RESPONSIBLE FOR THE SUBSISTENCE OF YOUR FAMILY, WITH A WHINY KID'S GRIPING FOR REWARD.
IT'S NICE TO KNOW THERE'S SO MUCH IN LIFE TO LOOK FORWARD TO.

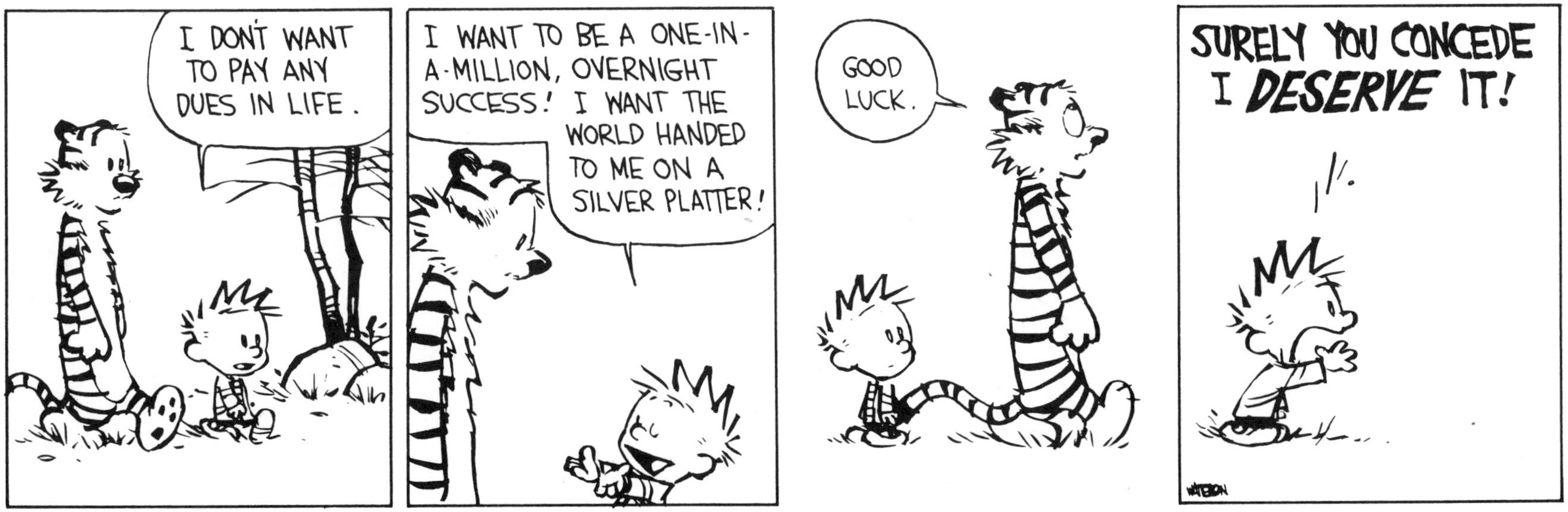
I DON'T WANT TO PAY ANY DUES IN LIFE.
I WANT TO BE A ONE-IN-A-MILLION, OVERNIGHT SUCCESS! I WANT THE WORLD HANDED TO ME ON A SILVER PLATTER!
GOOD LUCK.
SURELY YOU CONCEDE I DESERVE IT!

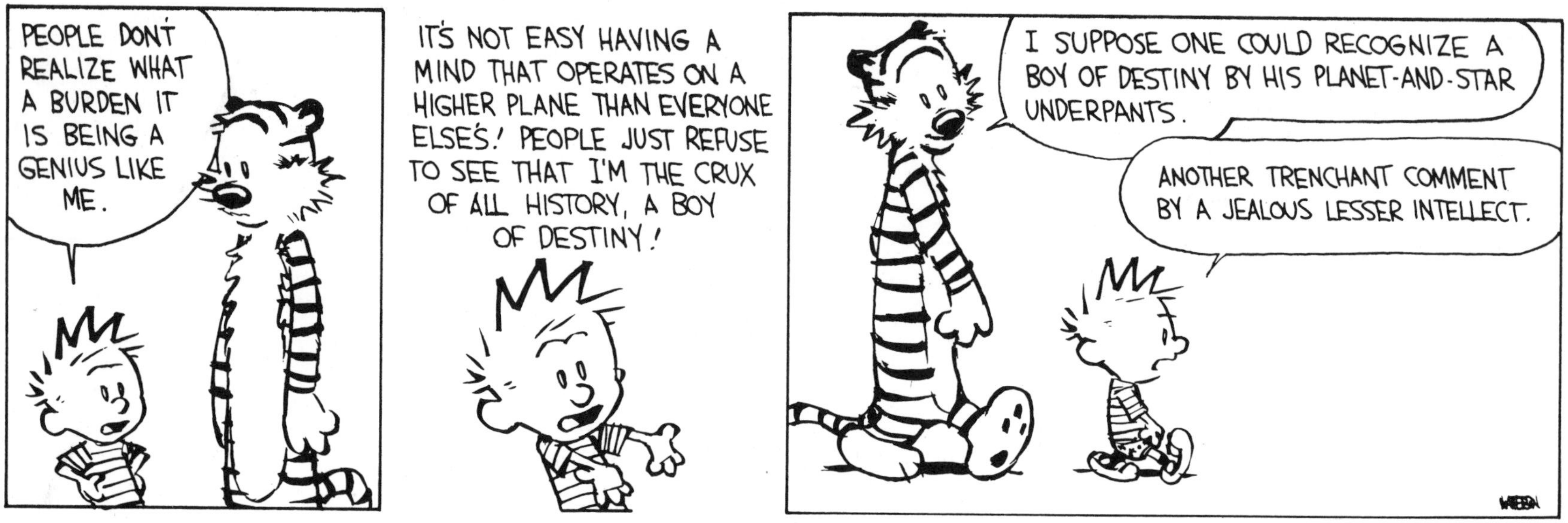
PEOPLE DON'T REALIZE WHAT A BURDEN IT IS BEING A GENIUS LIKE ME.
IT'S NOT EASY HAVING A MIND THAT OPERATES ON A HIGHER PLANE THAN EVERYONE ELSE'S! PEOPLE JUST REFUSE TO SEE THAT I'M THE CRUX OF ALL HISTORY, A BOY OF DESTINY!
I SUPPOSE ONE COULD RECOGNIZE A BOY OF DESTINY BY HIS PLANET-AND-STAR UNDERPANTS.
ANOTHER TRENCHANT COMMENT BY A JEALOUS LESSER INTELLECT.

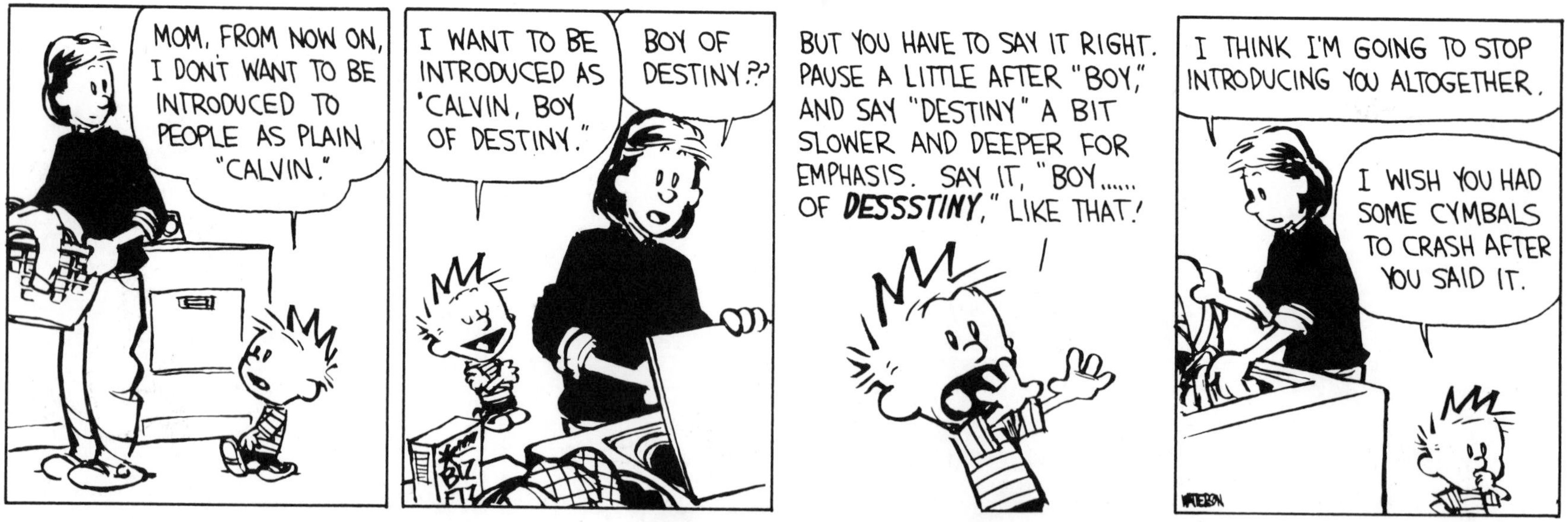
MOM, FROM NOW ON, I DON'T WANT TO BE INTRODUCED TO PEOPLE AS PLAIN "CALVIN."
I WANT TO BE INTRODUCED AS "CALVIN, BOY OF DESTINY."
BOY OF DESTINY??
BUT YOU HAVE TO SAY IT RIGHT. PAUSE A LITTLE AFTER "BOY," AND SAY "DESTINY" A BIT SLOWER AND DEEPER FOR EMPHASIS. SAY IT, "BOY...... OF DESSSTINY," LIKE THAT!
I THINK I'M GOING TO STOP INTRODUCING YOU ALTOGETHER.
I WISH YOU HAD SOME CYMBALS TO CRASH AFTER YOU SAID IT.

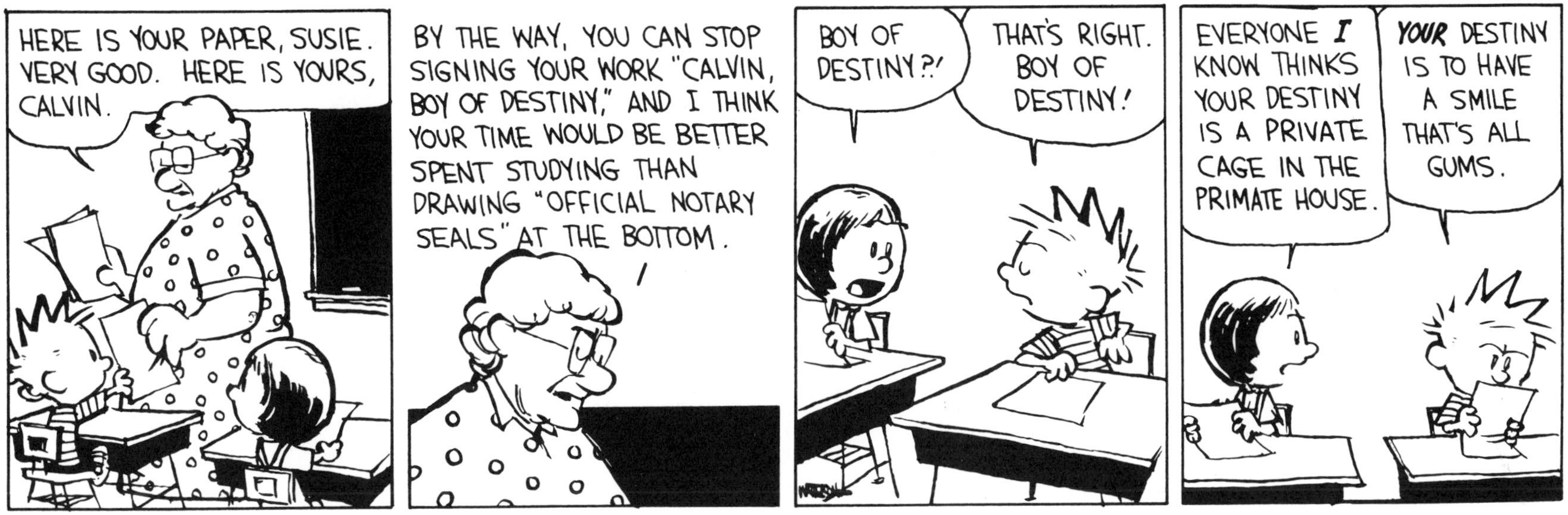
HERE IS YOUR PAPER, SUSIE. VERY GOOD. HERE IS YOURS, CALVIN.
BY THE WAY, YOU CAN STOP SIGNING YOUR WORK "CALVIN, BOY OF DESTINY," AND I THINK YOUR TIME WOULD BE BETTER SPENT STUDYING THAN DRAWING "OFFICIAL NOTARY SEALS" AT THE BOTTOM.
BOY OF DESTINY?!
THAT'S RIGHT. BOY OF DESTINY!
EVERYONE I KNOW THINKS YOUR DESTINY IS A PRIVATE CAGE IN THE PRIMATE HOUSE.
YOUR DESTINY IS TO HAVE A SMILE THAT'S ALL GUMS.

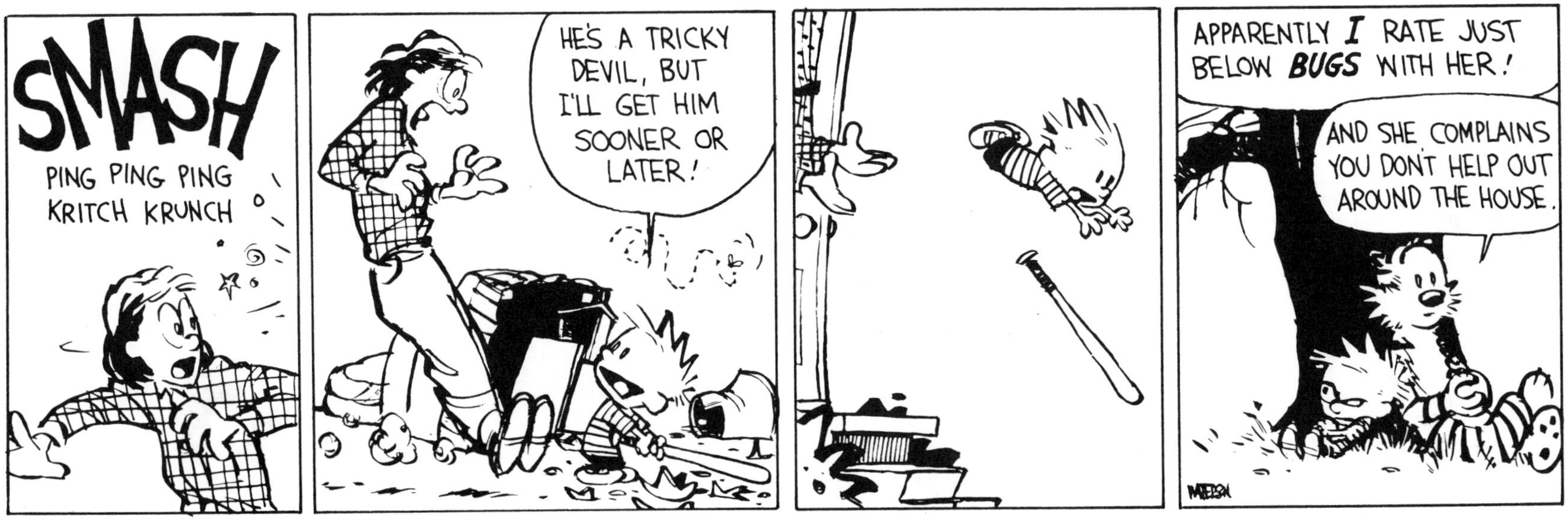
SMASH
PING PING PING
KRITCH KRUNCH
HE'S A TRICKY DEVIL, BUT I'LL GET HIM SOONER OR LATER!
APPARENTLY I RATE JUST BELOW BUGS WITH HER!
AND SHE COMPLAINS YOU DON'T HELP OUT AROUND THE HOUSE.

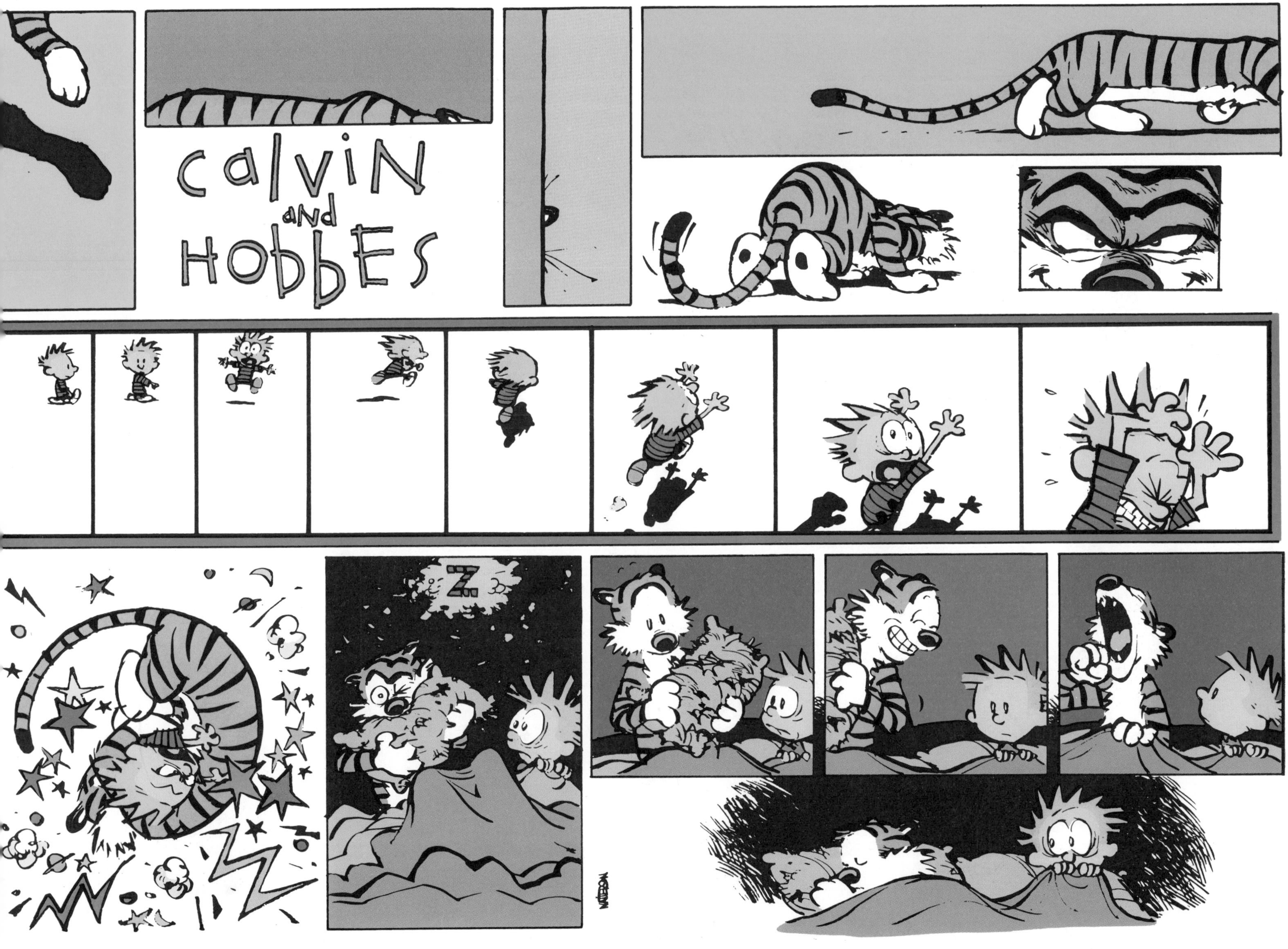
Calvin and Hobbes
Z

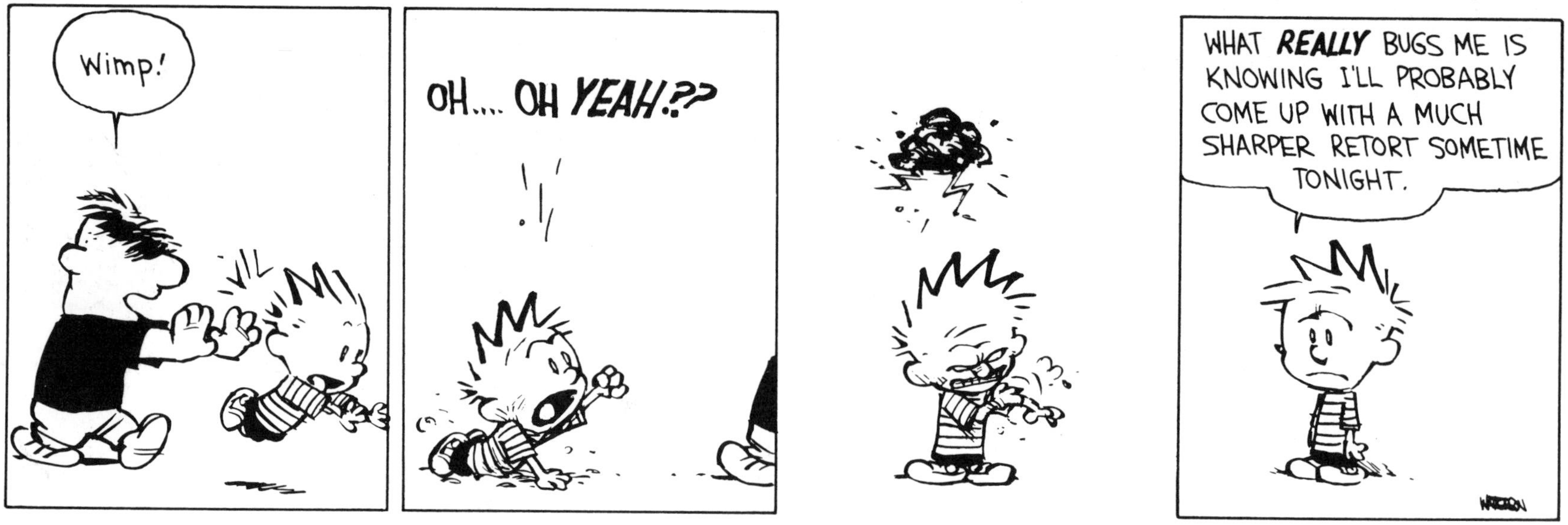
Wimp!
OH.... OH YEAH!??
WHAT REALLY BUGS ME IS KNOWING I'LL PROBABLY COME UP WITH A MUCH SHARPER RETORT SOMETIME TONIGHT.

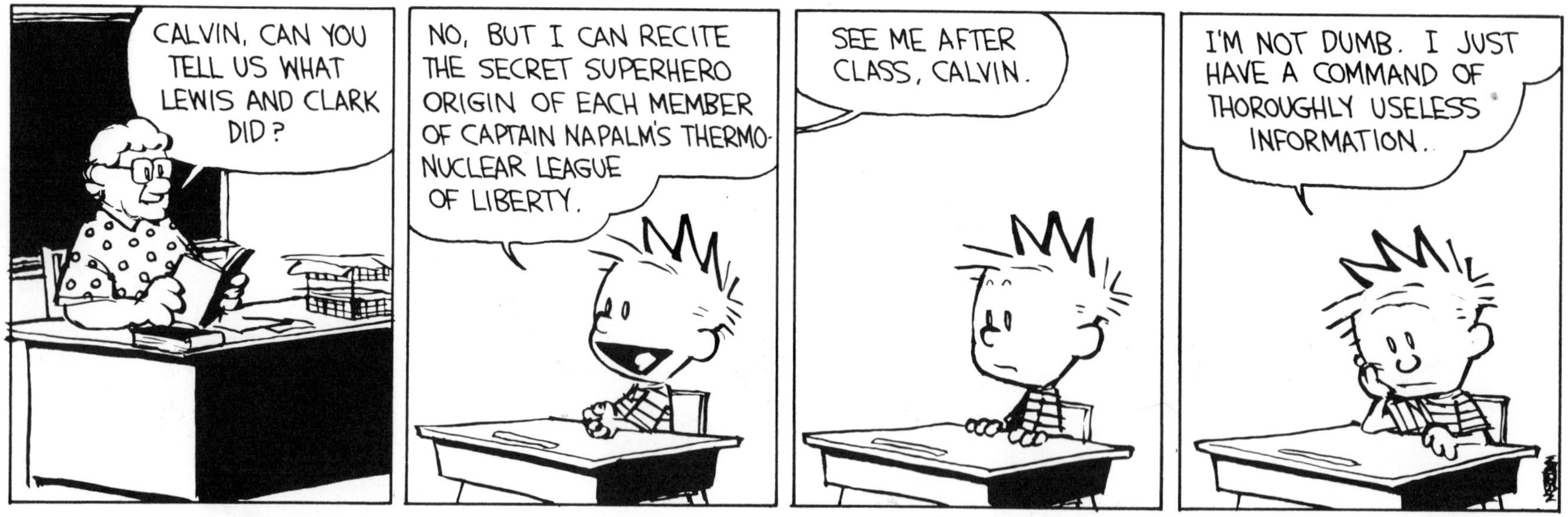
CALVIN, CAN YOU TELL US WHAT LEWIS AND CLARK DID?
NO, BUT I CAN RECITE THE SECRET SUPERHERO ORIGIN OF EACH MEMBER OF CAPTAIN NAPALM'S THERMO-NUCLEAR LEAGUE OF LIBERTY.
SEE ME AFTER CLASS, CALVIN.
I'M NOT DUMB. I JUST HAVE A COMMAND OF THOROUGHLY USELESS INFORMATION.

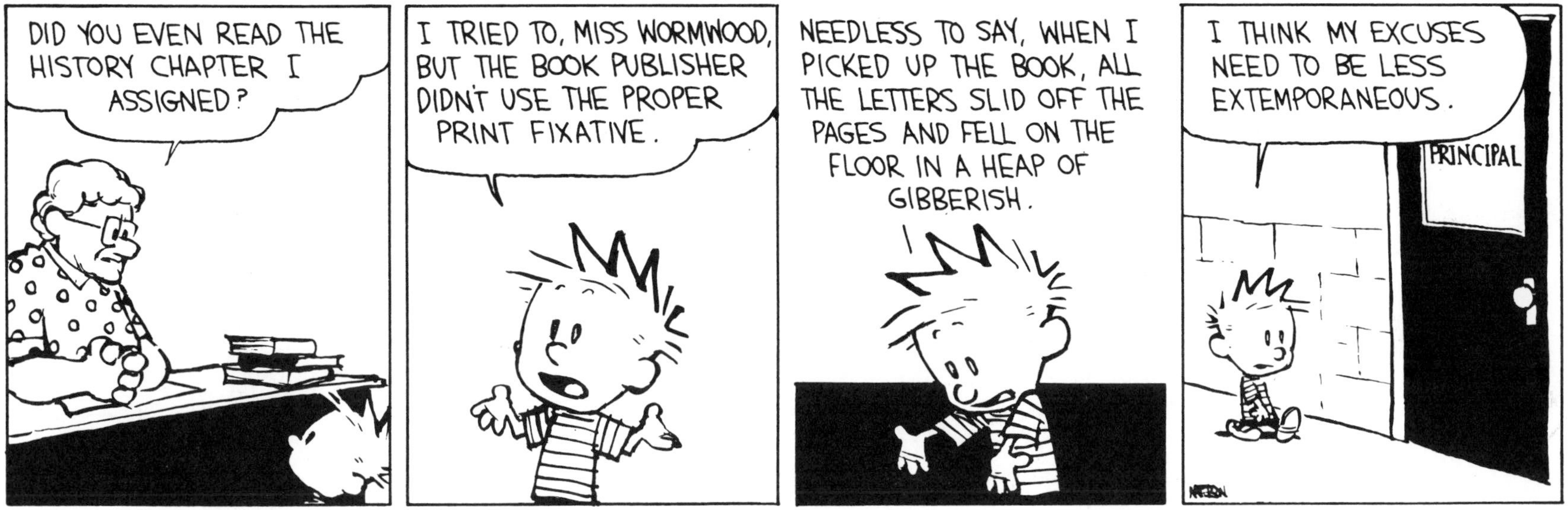
DID YOU EVEN READ THE HISTORY CHAPTER I ASSIGNED?
I TRIED TO, MISS WORMWOOD, BUT THE BOOK PUBLISHER DIDN'T USE THE PROPER PRINT FIXATIVE.
NEEDLESS TO SAY, WHEN I PICKED UP THE BOOK, ALL THE LETTERS SLID OFF THE PAGES AND FELL ON THE FLOOR IN A HEAP OF GIBBERISH.
I THINK MY EXCUSES NEED TO BE LESS EXTEMPORANEOUS.
PRINCIPAL

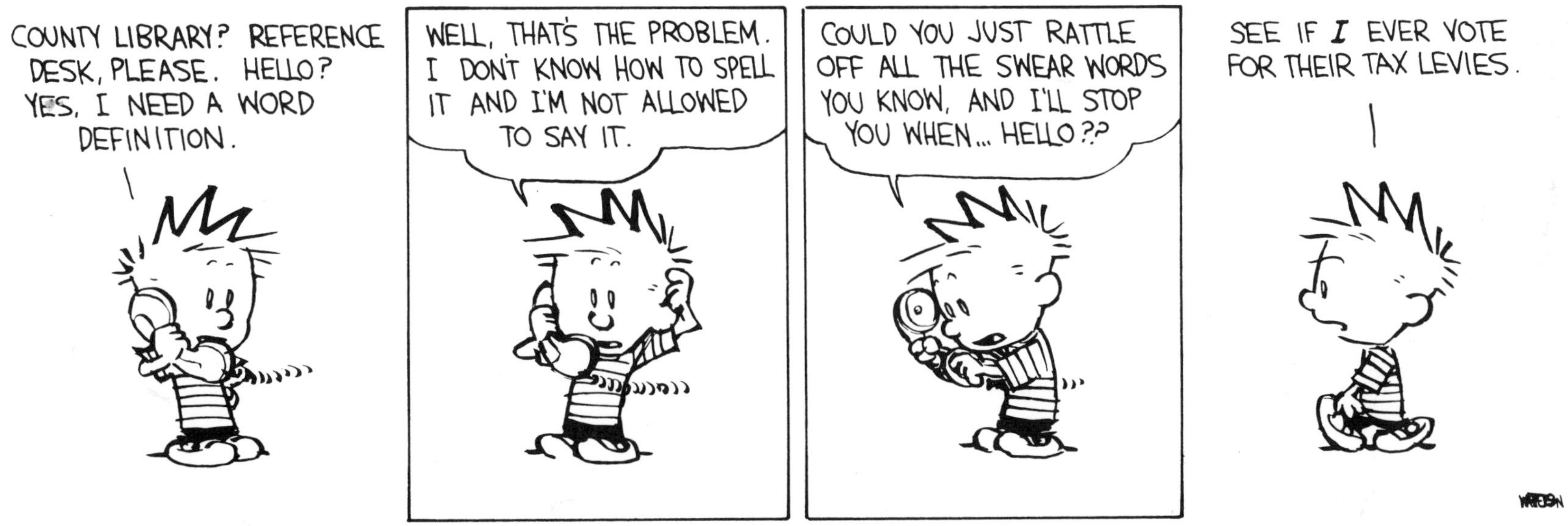
COUNTY LIBRARY? REFERENCE DESK, PLEASE. HELLO? YES, I NEED A WORD DEFINITION.
WELL, THAT'S THE PROBLEM. I DON'T KNOW HOW TO SPELL IT AND I'M NOT ALLOWED TO SAY IT.
COULD YOU JUST RATTLE OFF ALL THE SWEAR WORDS YOU KNOW, AND I'LL STOP YOU WHEN... HELLO??
SEE IF I EVER VOTE FOR THEIR TAX LEVIES.

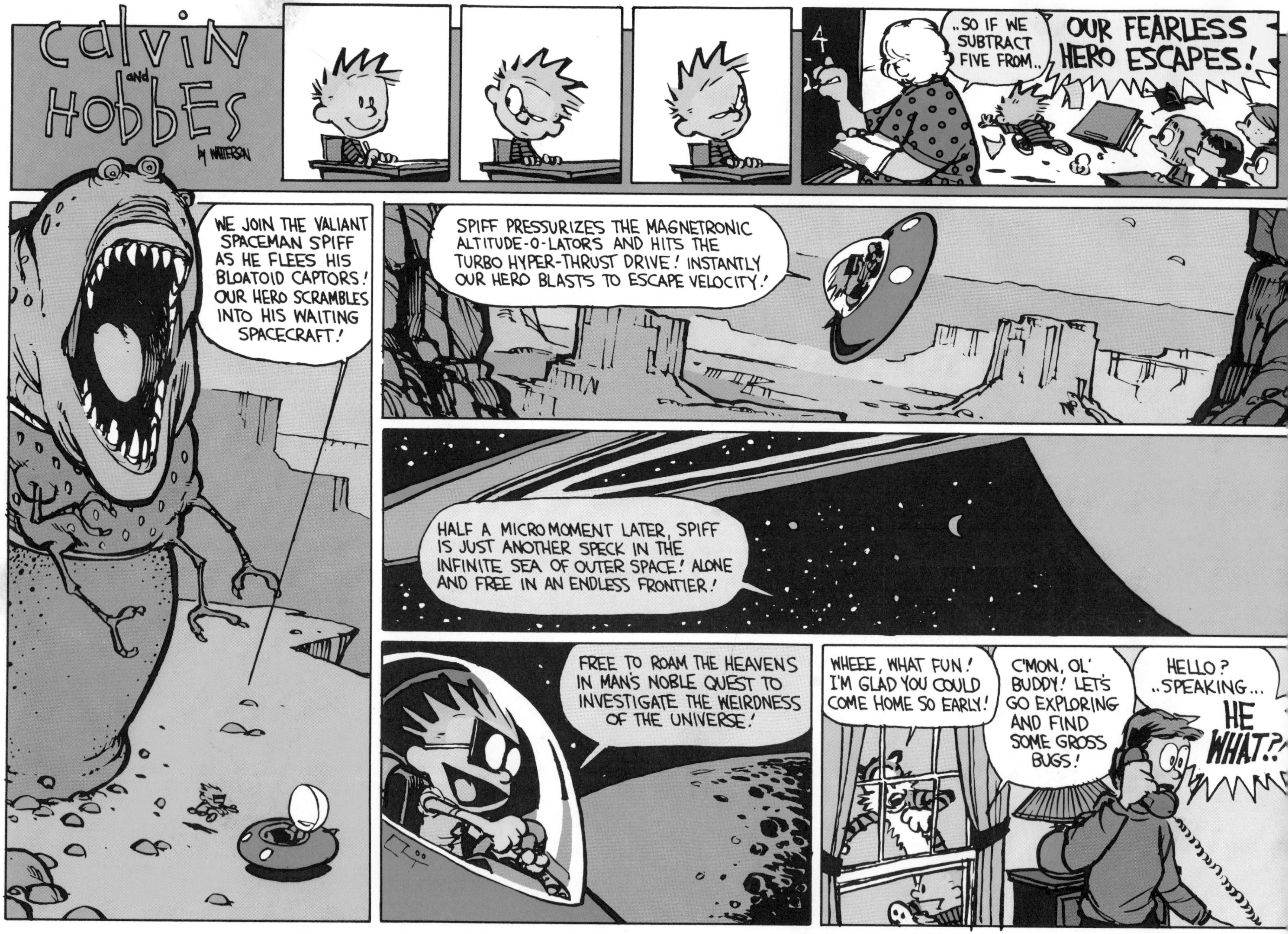
Calvin and Hobbes
by WATTERSON
..SO IF WE SUBTRACT FIVE FROM..
OUR FEARLESS HERO ESCAPES!
WE JOIN THE VALIANT SPACEMAN SPIFF AS HE FLEES HIS BLOATOID CAPTORS! OUR HERO SCRAMBLES INTO HIS WAITING SPACECRAFT!
SPIFF PRESSURIZES THE MAGNETRONIC ALTITUDE-O-LATORS AND HITS THE TURBO HYPER-THRUST DRIVE! INSTANTLY OUR HERO BLASTS TO ESCAPE VELOCITY!
HALF A MICROMOMENT LATER, SPIFF IS JUST ANOTHER SPECK IN THE INFINITE SEA OF OUTER SPACE! ALONE AND FREE IN AN ENDLESS FRONTIER!
FREE TO ROAM THE HEAVENS IN MAN'S NOBLE QUEST TO INVESTIGATE THE WEIRDNESS OF THE UNIVERSE!
WHEEE, WHAT FUN! I'M GLAD YOU COULD COME HOME SO EARLY!
C'MON, OL' BUDDY! LET'S GO EXPLORING AND FIND SOME GROSS BUGS!
HELLO? ..SPEAKING...
HE WHAT?!

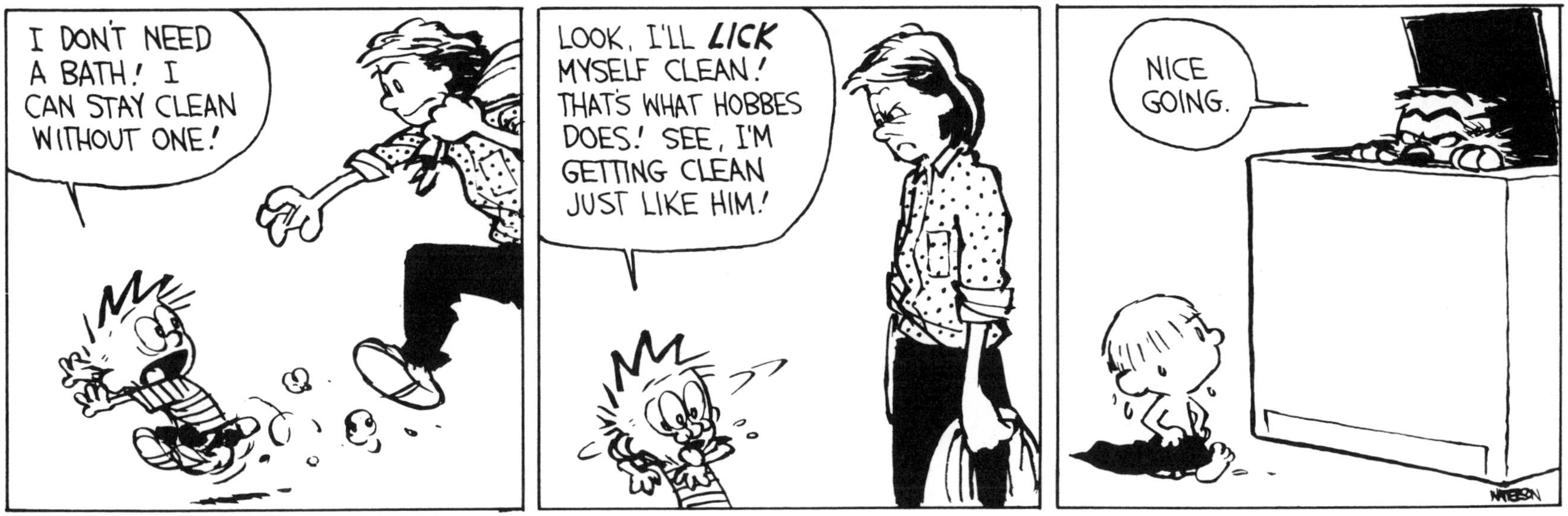
I DON'T NEED A BATH! I CAN STAY CLEAN WITHOUT ONE!
LOOK, I'LL **LICK** MYSELF CLEAN! THAT'S WHAT HOBBES DOES! SEE, I'M GETTING CLEAN JUST LIKE HIM!
NICE GOING.

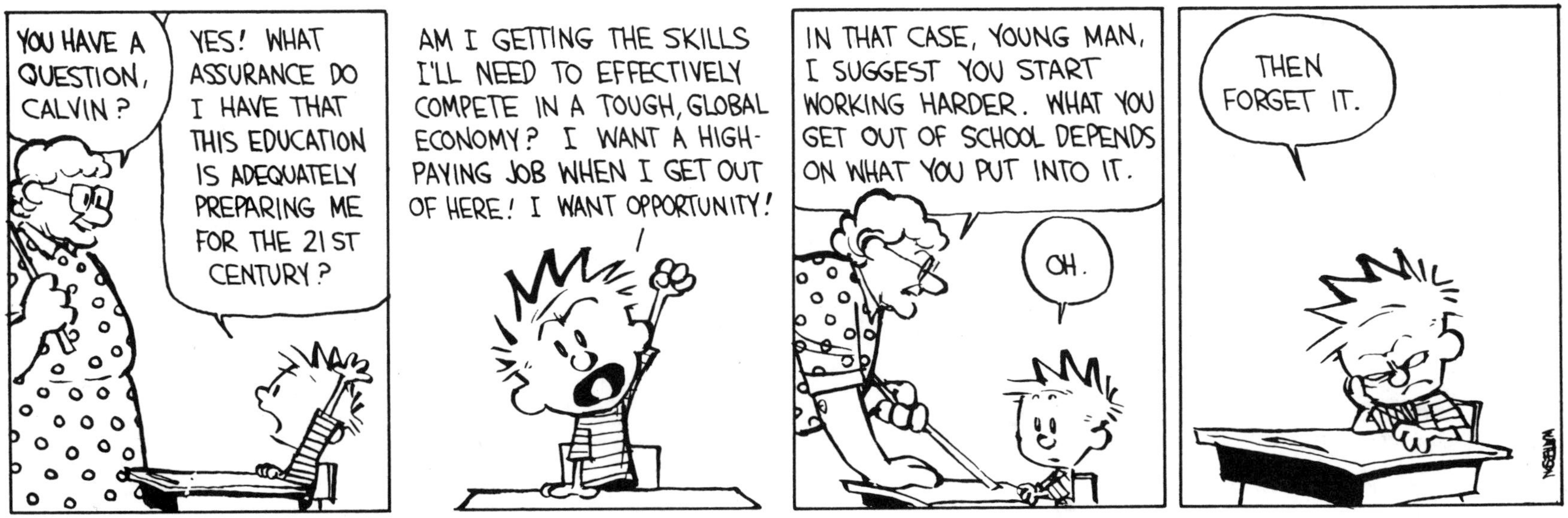
YOU HAVE A QUESTION, CALVIN?
YES! WHAT ASSURANCE DO I HAVE THAT THIS EDUCATION IS ADEQUATELY PREPARING ME FOR THE 21ST CENTURY?
AM I GETTING THE SKILLS I'LL NEED TO EFFECTIVELY COMPETE IN A TOUGH, GLOBAL ECONOMY? I WANT A HIGH-PAYING JOB WHEN I GET OUT OF HERE! I WANT OPPORTUNITY!
IN THAT CASE, YOUNG MAN, I SUGGEST YOU START WORKING HARDER. WHAT YOU GET OUT OF SCHOOL DEPENDS ON WHAT YOU PUT INTO IT.
OH.
THEN FORGET IT.

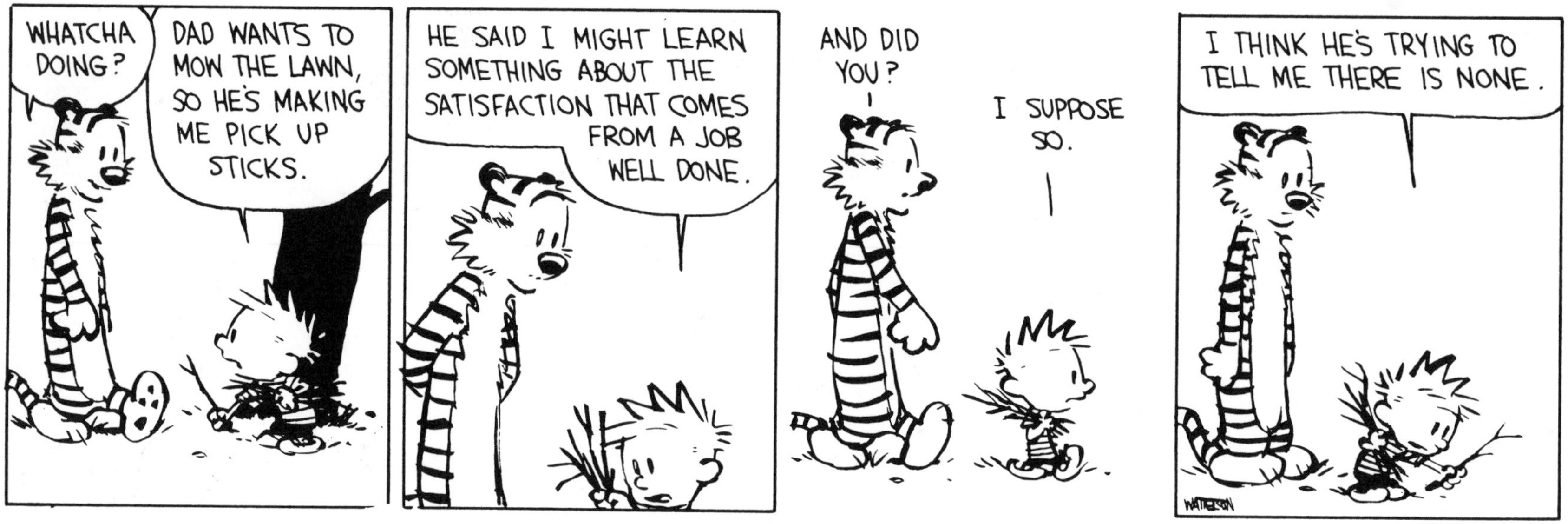
WHATCHA DOING?
DAD WANTS TO MOW THE LAWN, SO HE'S MAKING ME PICK UP STICKS.
HE SAID I MIGHT LEARN SOMETHING ABOUT THE SATISFACTION THAT COMES FROM A JOB WELL DONE.
AND DID YOU?
I SUPPOSE SO.
I THINK HE'S TRYING TO TELL ME THERE IS NONE.
WATTERSON

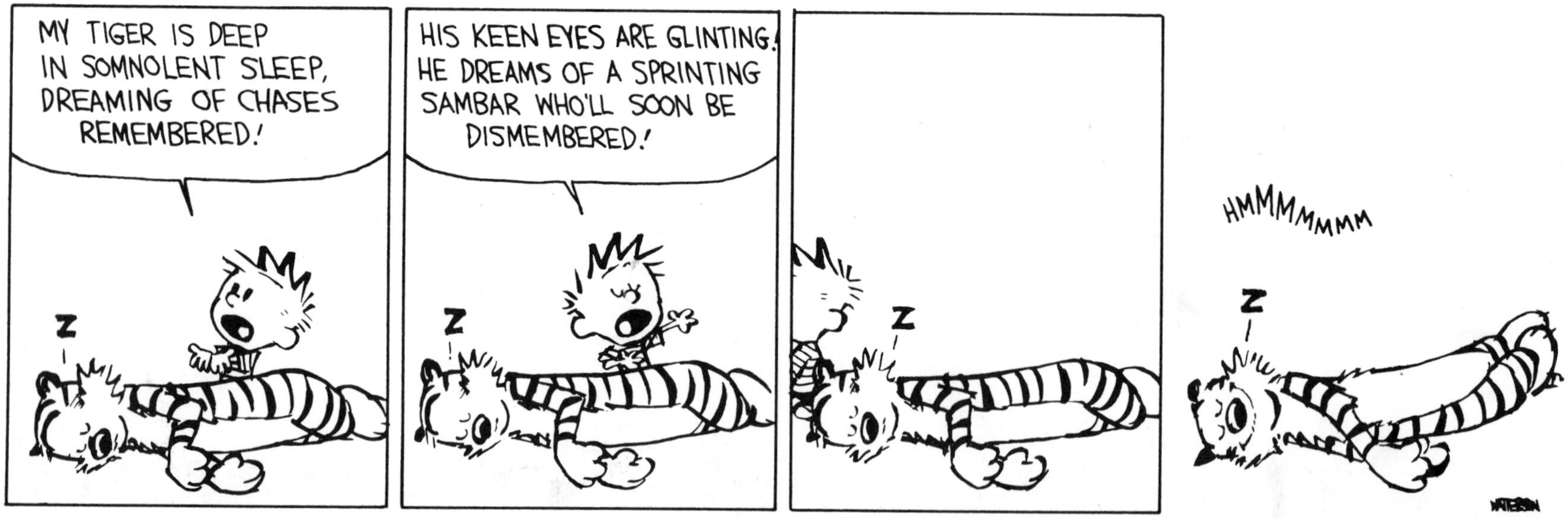
MY TIGER IS DEEP IN SOMNOLENT SLEEP, DREAMING OF CHASES REMEMBERED!
Z
HIS KEEN EYES ARE GLINTING! HE DREAMS OF A SPRINTING SAMBAR WHO'LL SOON BE DISMEMBERED!
Z
Z
HMMMMMMM
Z
WATTERSON

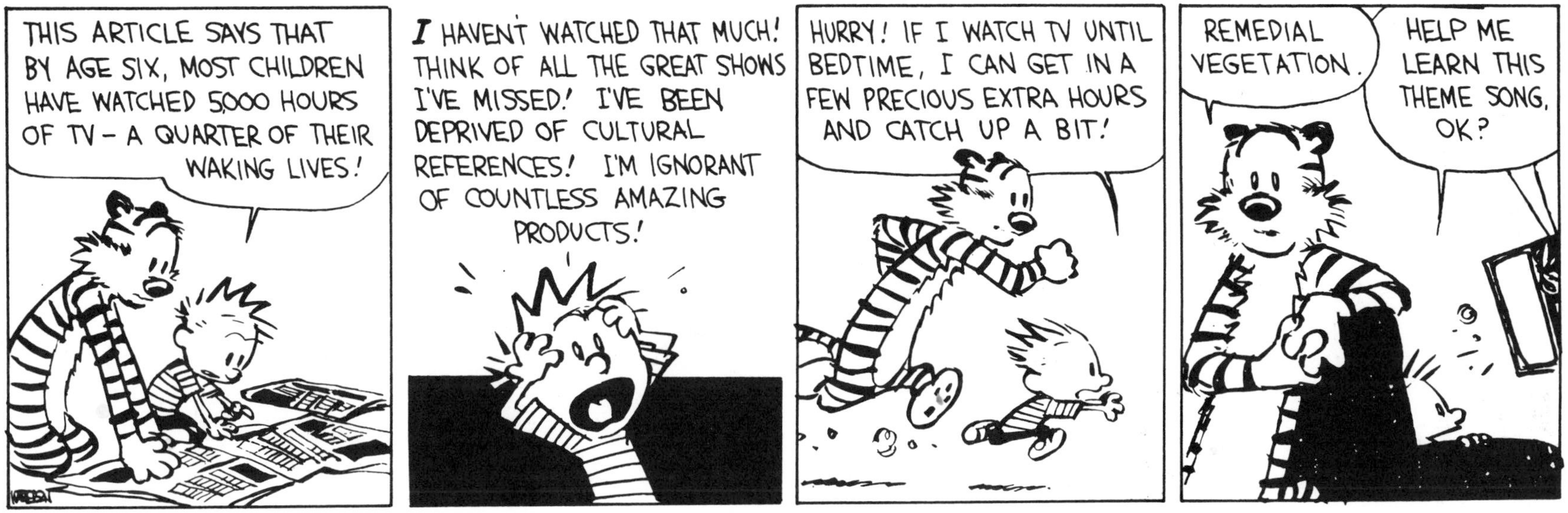
THIS ARTICLE SAYS THAT BY AGE SIX, MOST CHILDREN HAVE WATCHED 5,000 HOURS OF TV – A QUARTER OF THEIR WAKING LIVES!
I HAVEN'T WATCHED THAT MUCH! THINK OF ALL THE GREAT SHOWS I'VE MISSED! I'VE BEEN DEPRIVED OF CULTURAL REFERENCES! I'M IGNORANT OF COUNTLESS AMAZING PRODUCTS!
HURRY! IF I WATCH TV UNTIL BEDTIME, I CAN GET IN A FEW PRECIOUS EXTRA HOURS AND CATCH UP A BIT!
REMEDIAL VEGETATION.
HELP ME LEARN THIS THEME SONG, OK?

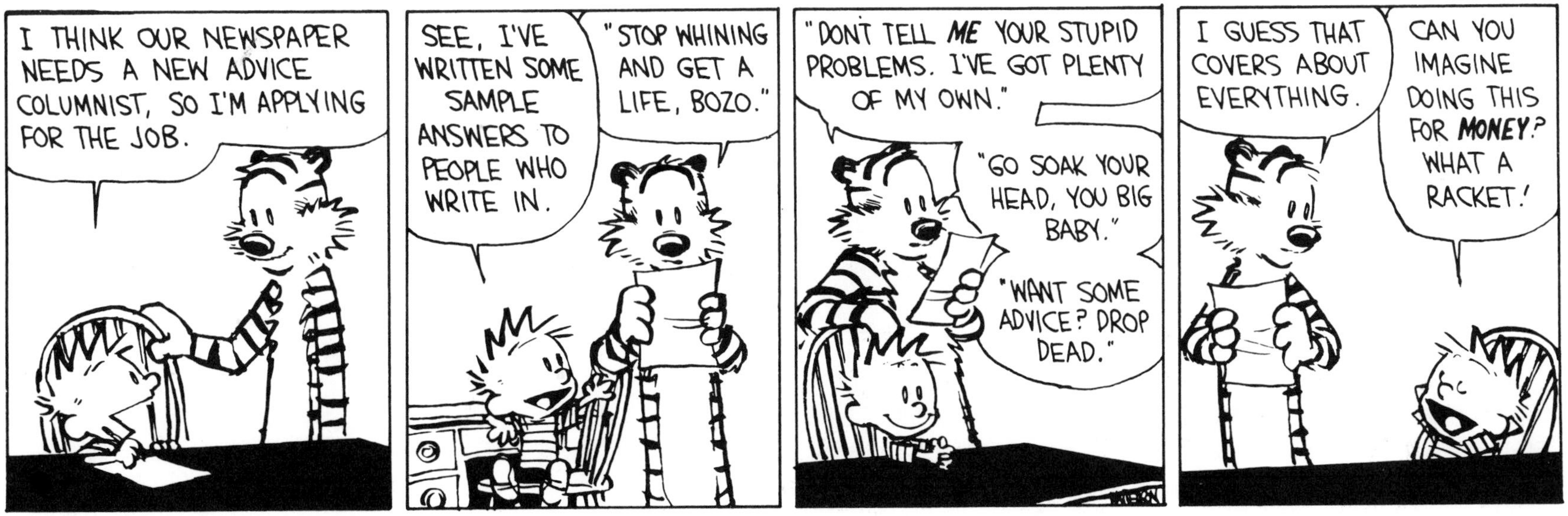
I THINK OUR NEWSPAPER NEEDS A NEW ADVICE COLUMNIST, SO I'M APPLYING FOR THE JOB.
SEE, I'VE WRITTEN SOME SAMPLE ANSWERS TO PEOPLE WHO WRITE IN.
"STOP WHINING AND GET A LIFE, BOZO."
"DON'T TELL ME YOUR STUPID PROBLEMS. I'VE GOT PLENTY OF MY OWN."
"GO SOAK YOUR HEAD, YOU BIG BABY."
"WANT SOME ADVICE? DROP DEAD."
I GUESS THAT COVERS ABOUT EVERYTHING.
CAN YOU IMAGINE DOING THIS FOR MONEY? WHAT A RACKET!

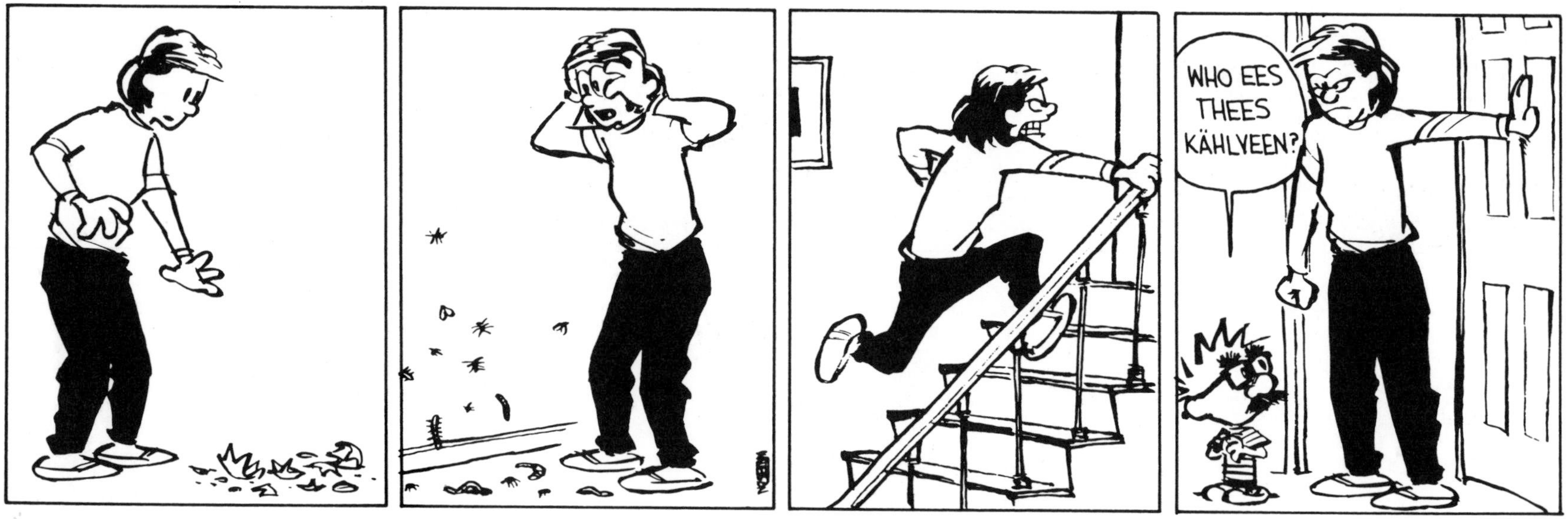
WHO EES THEES KÄHLYEEN?

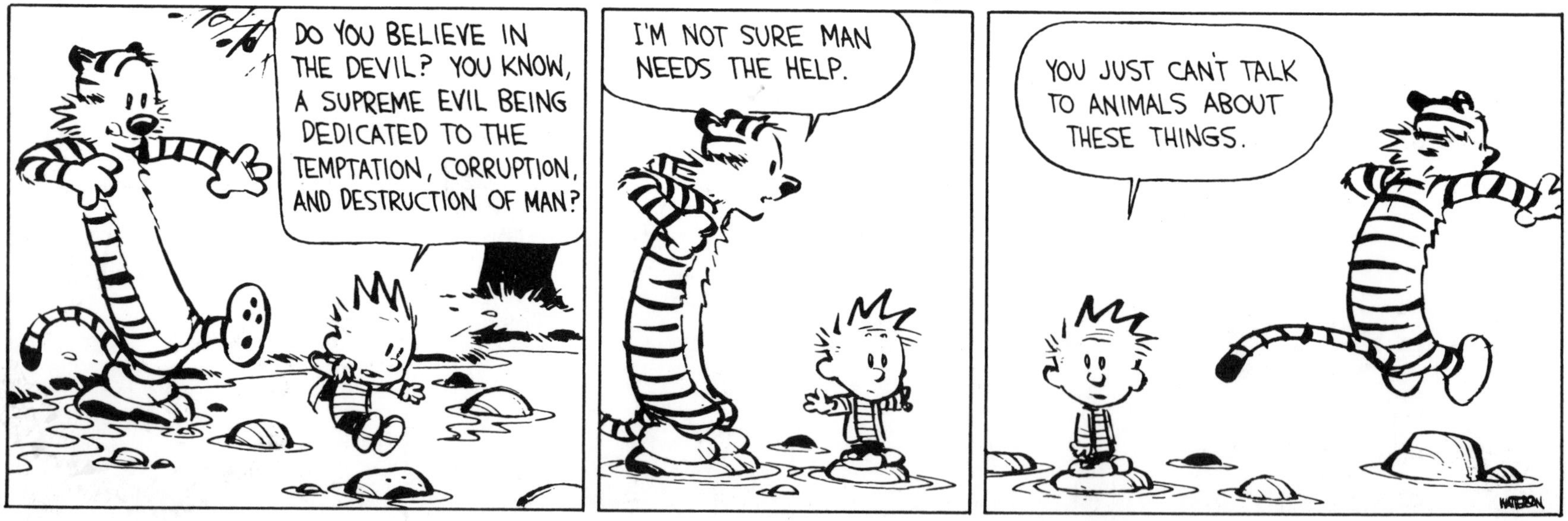
DO YOU BELIEVE IN THE DEVIL? YOU KNOW, A SUPREME EVIL BEING DEDICATED TO THE TEMPTATION, CORRUPTION, AND DESTRUCTION OF MAN?
I'M NOT SURE MAN NEEDS THE HELP.
YOU JUST CAN'T TALK TO ANIMALS ABOUT THESE THINGS.

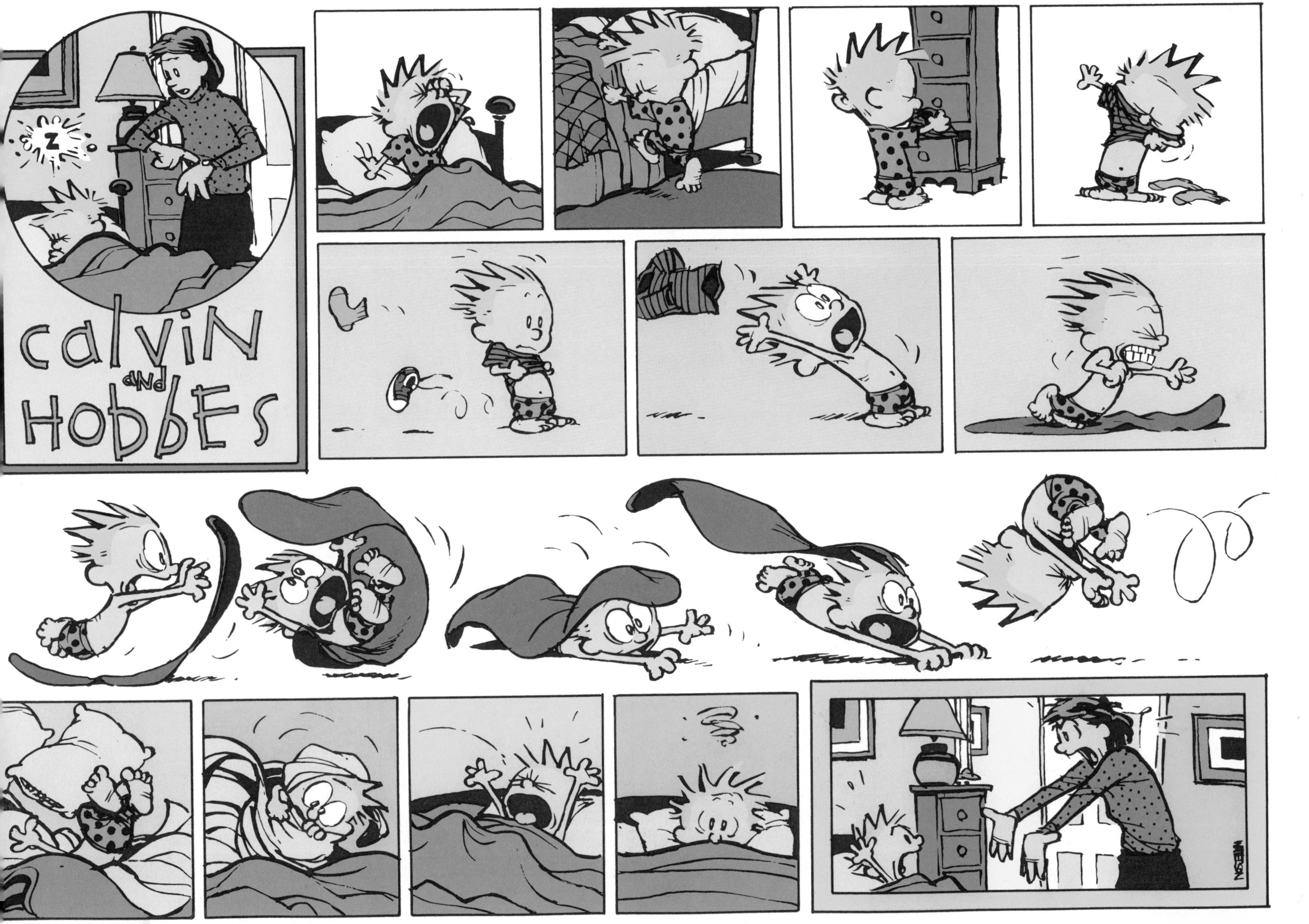
Calvin and Hobbes
Z

56

calvin and hobbes

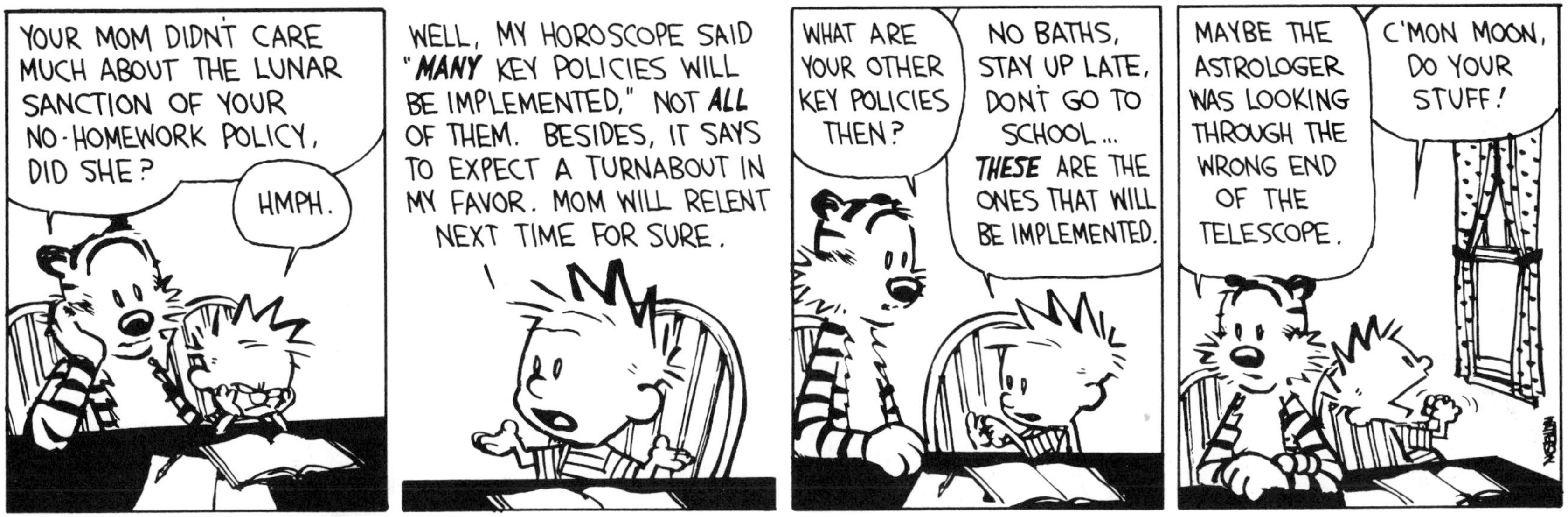
YOUR MOM DIDN'T CARE MUCH ABOUT THE LUNAR SANCTION OF YOUR NO-HOMEWORK POLICY, DID SHE?
HMPH.
WELL, MY HOROSCOPE SAID "*MANY* KEY POLICIES WILL BE IMPLEMENTED," NOT *ALL* OF THEM. BESIDES, IT SAYS TO EXPECT A TURNABOUT IN MY FAVOR. MOM WILL RELENT NEXT TIME FOR SURE.
WHAT ARE YOUR OTHER KEY POLICIES THEN?
NO BATHS, STAY UP LATE, DON'T GO TO SCHOOL... *THESE* ARE THE ONES THAT WILL BE IMPLEMENTED.
MAYBE THE ASTROLOGER WAS LOOKING THROUGH THE WRONG END OF THE TELESCOPE.
C'MON MOON, DO YOUR STUFF!

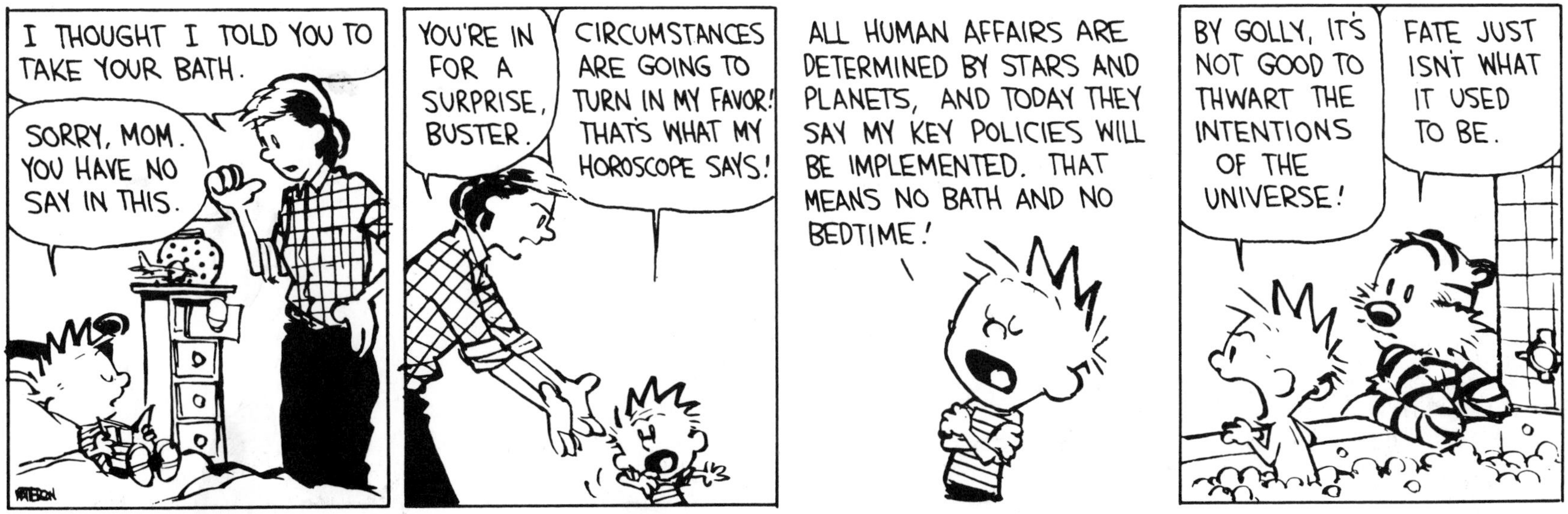
I THOUGHT I TOLD YOU TO TAKE YOUR BATH.
SORRY, MOM. YOU HAVE NO SAY IN THIS.
YOU'RE IN FOR A SURPRISE, BUSTER.
CIRCUMSTANCES ARE GOING TO TURN IN MY FAVOR! THAT'S WHAT MY HOROSCOPE SAYS!
ALL HUMAN AFFAIRS ARE DETERMINED BY STARS AND PLANETS, AND TODAY THEY SAY MY KEY POLICIES WILL BE IMPLEMENTED. THAT MEANS NO BATH AND NO BEDTIME!
BY GOLLY, IT'S NOT GOOD TO THWART THE INTENTIONS OF THE UNIVERSE!
FATE JUST ISN'T WHAT IT USED TO BE.

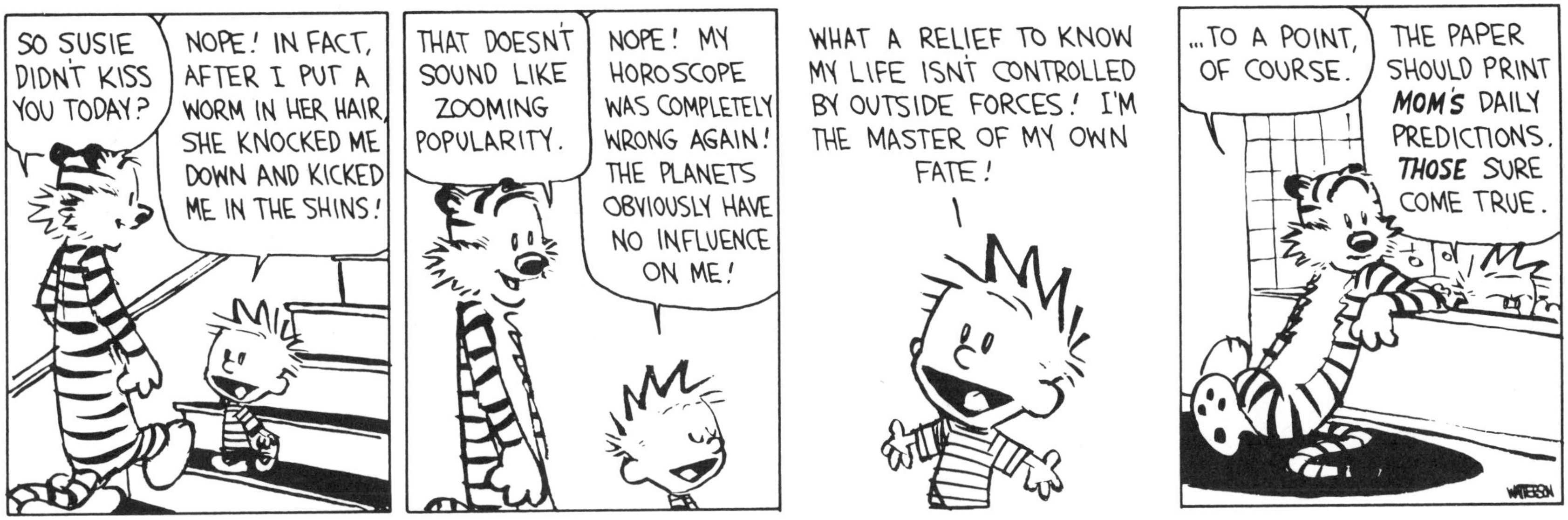
SO SUSIE DIDN'T KISS YOU TODAY?
NOPE! IN FACT, AFTER I PUT A WORM IN HER HAIR, SHE KNOCKED ME DOWN AND KICKED ME IN THE SHINS!
THAT DOESN'T SOUND LIKE ZOOMING POPULARITY.
NOPE! MY HOROSCOPE WAS COMPLETELY WRONG AGAIN! THE PLANETS OBVIOUSLY HAVE NO INFLUENCE ON ME!
WHAT A RELIEF TO KNOW MY LIFE ISN'T CONTROLLED BY OUTSIDE FORCES! I'M THE MASTER OF MY OWN FATE!
...TO A POINT, OF COURSE.
THE PAPER SHOULD PRINT **MOM'S** DAILY PREDICTIONS. **THOSE** SURE COME TRUE.
WATTERSON

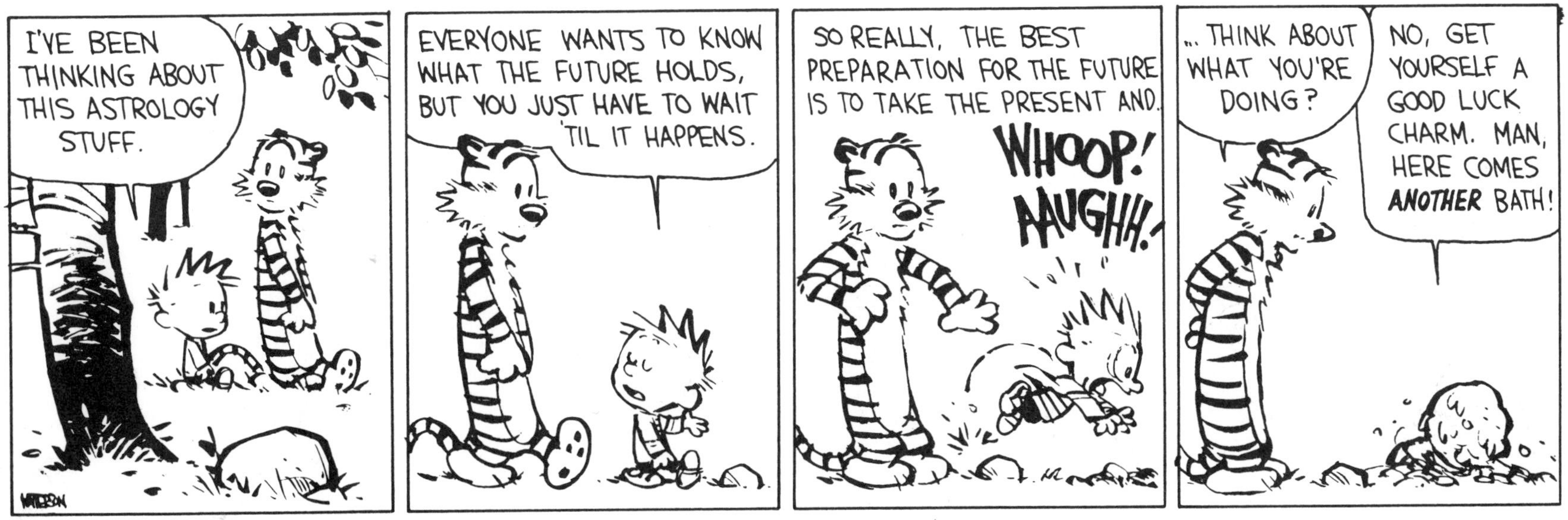
I'VE BEEN THINKING ABOUT THIS ASTROLOGY STUFF.
WATTERSON
EVERYONE WANTS TO KNOW WHAT THE FUTURE HOLDS, BUT YOU JUST HAVE TO WAIT 'TIL IT HAPPENS.
SO REALLY, THE BEST PREPARATION FOR THE FUTURE IS TO TAKE THE PRESENT AND...
WHOOP!
AAUGHH!
...THINK ABOUT WHAT YOU'RE DOING?
NO, GET YOURSELF A GOOD LUCK CHARM. MAN, HERE COMES **ANOTHER** BATH!

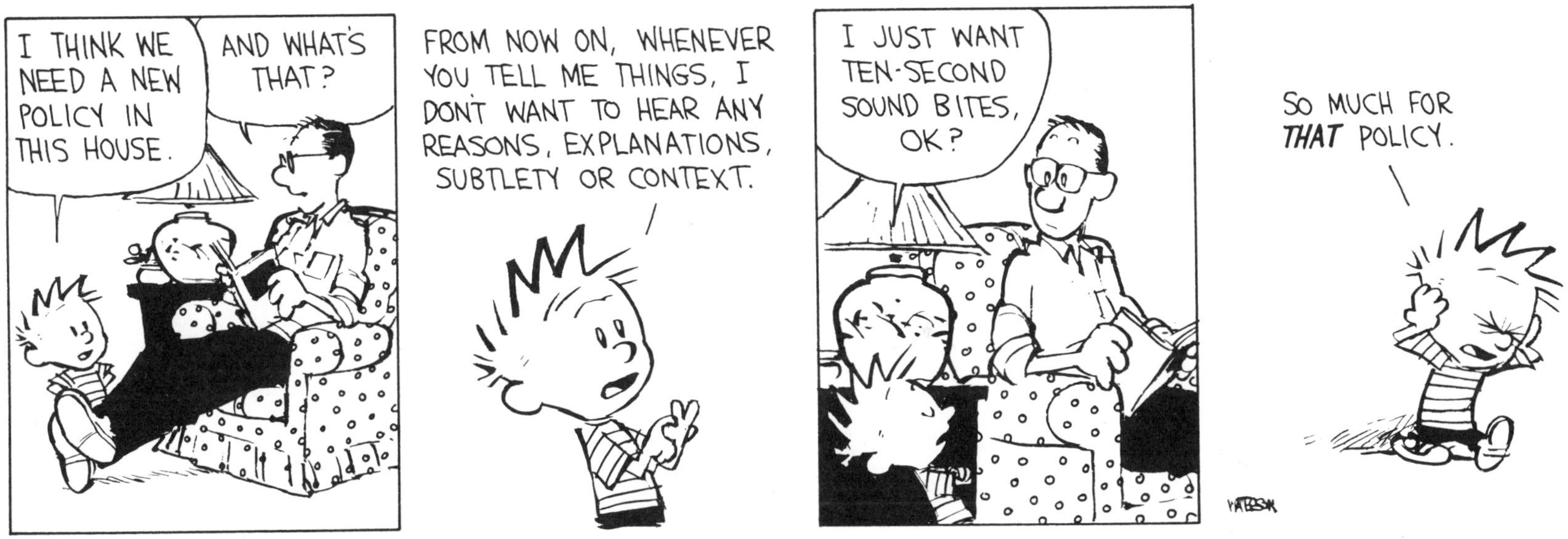
I THINK WE NEED A NEW POLICY IN THIS HOUSE.
AND WHAT'S THAT?
FROM NOW ON, WHENEVER YOU TELL ME THINGS, I DON'T WANT TO HEAR ANY REASONS, EXPLANATIONS, SUBTLETY OR CONTEXT.
I JUST WANT TEN-SECOND SOUND BITES, OK?
SO MUCH FOR *THAT* POLICY.

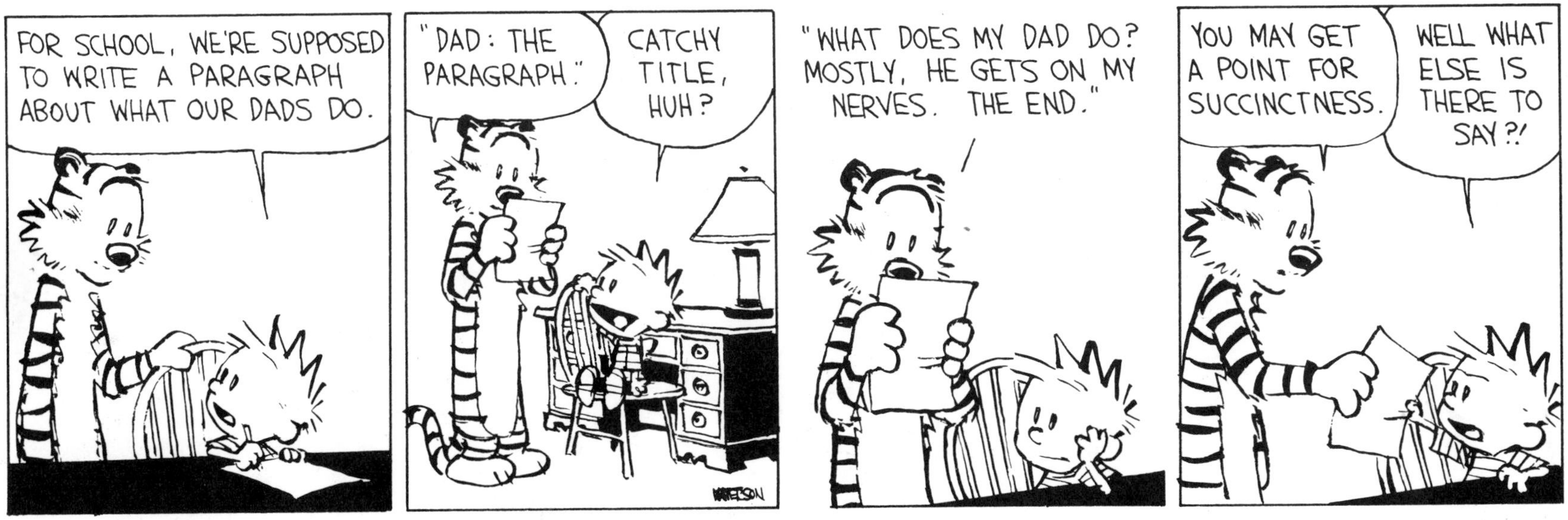
FOR SCHOOL, WE'RE SUPPOSED TO WRITE A PARAGRAPH ABOUT WHAT OUR DADS DO.
"DAD: THE PARAGRAPH."
CATCHY TITLE, HUH?
"WHAT DOES MY DAD DO? MOSTLY, HE GETS ON MY NERVES. THE END."
YOU MAY GET A POINT FOR SUCCINCTNESS.
WELL WHAT ELSE IS THERE TO SAY?!

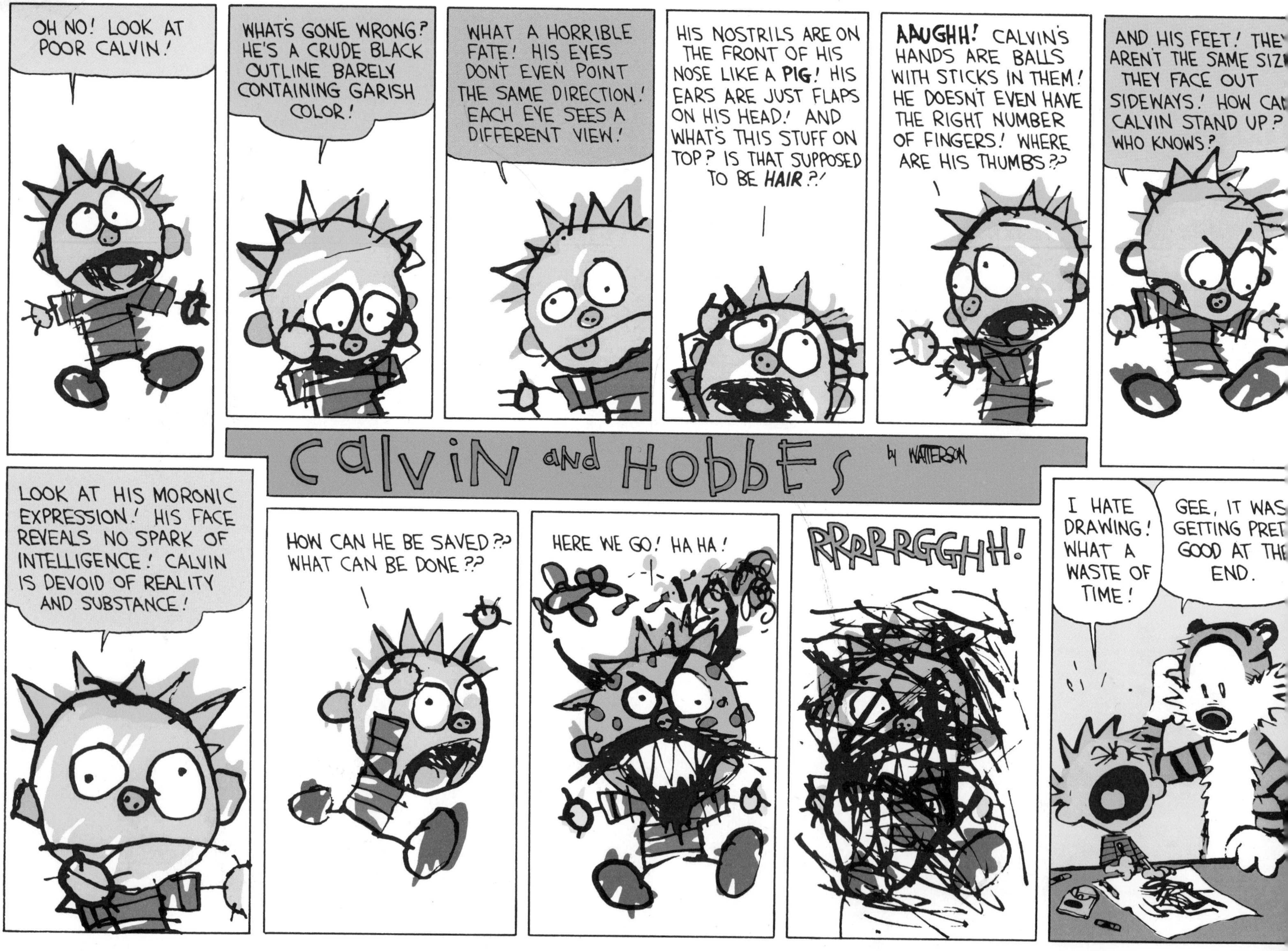

OH NO! LOOK AT POOR CALVIN!
WHAT'S GONE WRONG? HE'S A CRUDE BLACK OUTLINE BARELY CONTAINING GARISH COLOR!
WHAT A HORRIBLE FATE! HIS EYES DON'T EVEN POINT THE SAME DIRECTION! EACH EYE SEES A DIFFERENT VIEW!
HIS NOSTRILS ARE ON THE FRONT OF HIS NOSE LIKE A PIG! HIS EARS ARE JUST FLAPS ON HIS HEAD! AND WHAT'S THIS STUFF ON TOP? IS THAT SUPPOSED TO BE HAIR?!
AAUGHH! CALVIN'S HANDS ARE BALLS WITH STICKS IN THEM! HE DOESN'T EVEN HAVE THE RIGHT NUMBER OF FINGERS! WHERE ARE HIS THUMBS??
AND HIS FEET! THE ARENT THE SAME SIZ THEY FACE OUT SIDEWAYS! HOW CA CALVIN STAND UP? WHO KNOWS?
Calvin and Hobbes
by WATTERSON
LOOK AT HIS MORONIC EXPRESSION! HIS FACE REVEALS NO SPARK OF INTELLIGENCE! CALVIN IS DEVOID OF REALITY AND SUBSTANCE!
HOW CAN HE BE SAVED?? WHAT CAN BE DONE??
HERE WE GO! HA HA!
RRRRRGGHH!
I HATE DRAWING! WHAT A WASTE OF TIME!
GEE, IT WAS GETTING PRET GOOD AT TH END.

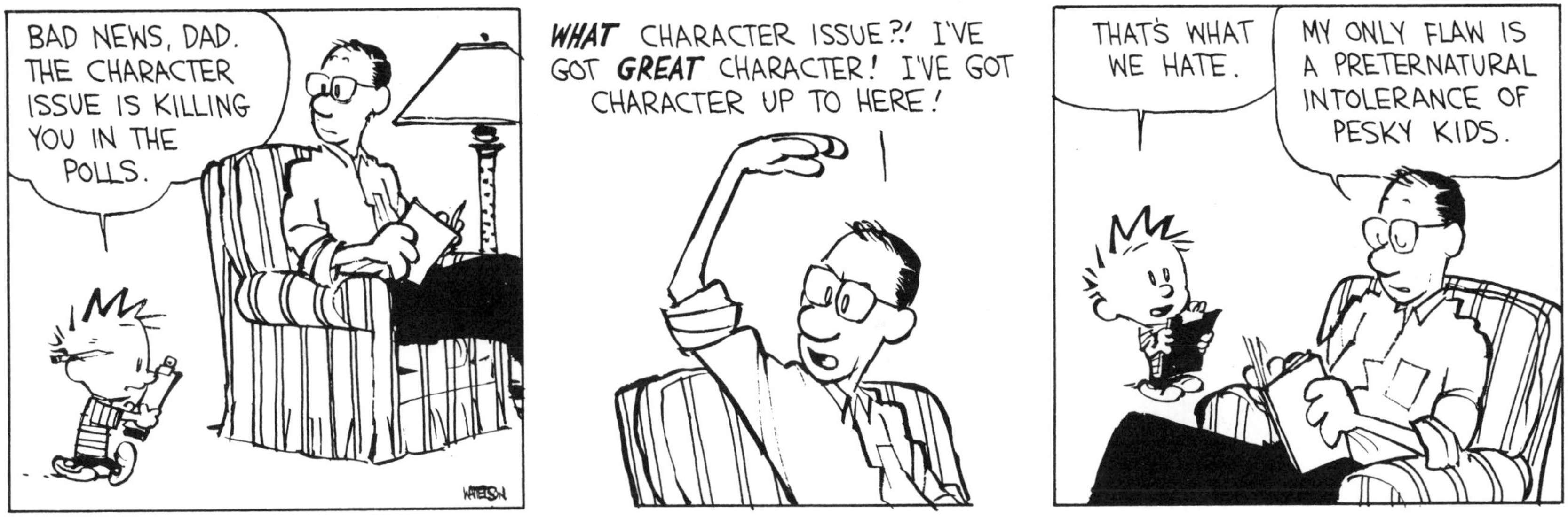
BAD NEWS, DAD. THE CHARACTER ISSUE IS KILLING YOU IN THE POLLS.
WHAT CHARACTER ISSUE?! I'VE GOT GREAT CHARACTER! I'VE GOT CHARACTER UP TO HERE!
THAT'S WHAT WE HATE.
MY ONLY FLAW IS A PRETERNATURAL INTOLERANCE OF PESKY KIDS.

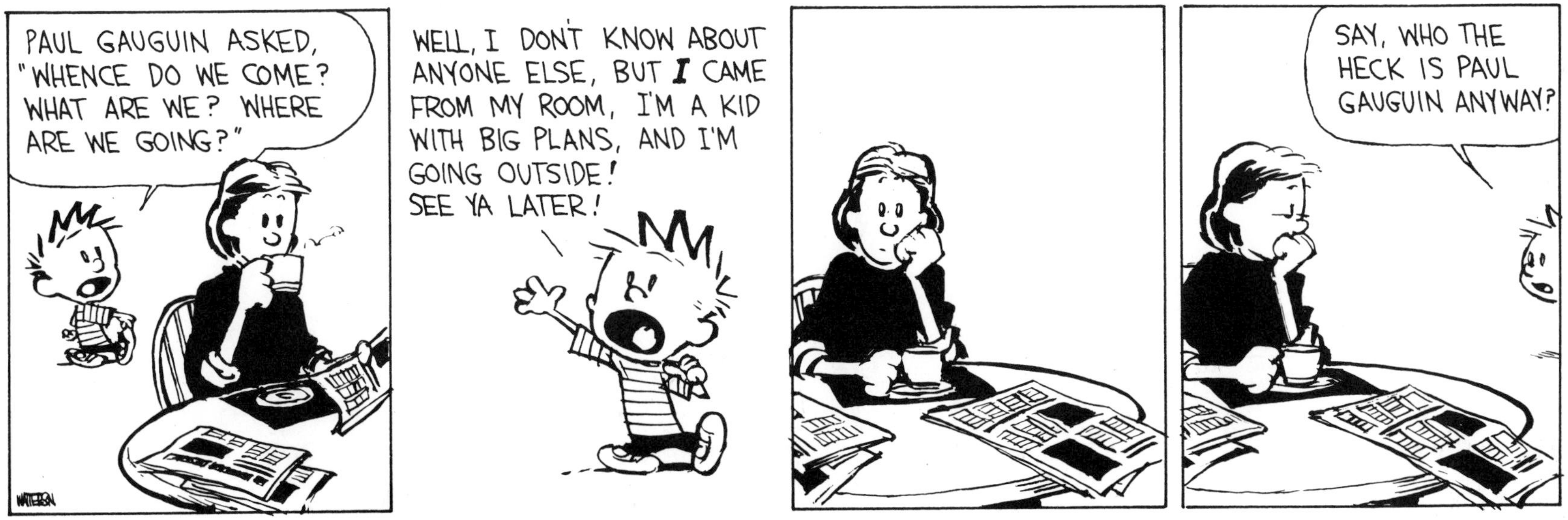
PAUL GAUGUIN ASKED, "WHENCE DO WE COME? WHAT ARE WE? WHERE ARE WE GOING?"
WELL, I DON'T KNOW ABOUT ANYONE ELSE, BUT I CAME FROM MY ROOM, I'M A KID WITH BIG PLANS, AND I'M GOING OUTSIDE! SEE YA LATER!
SAY, WHO THE HECK IS PAUL GAUGUIN ANYWAY?

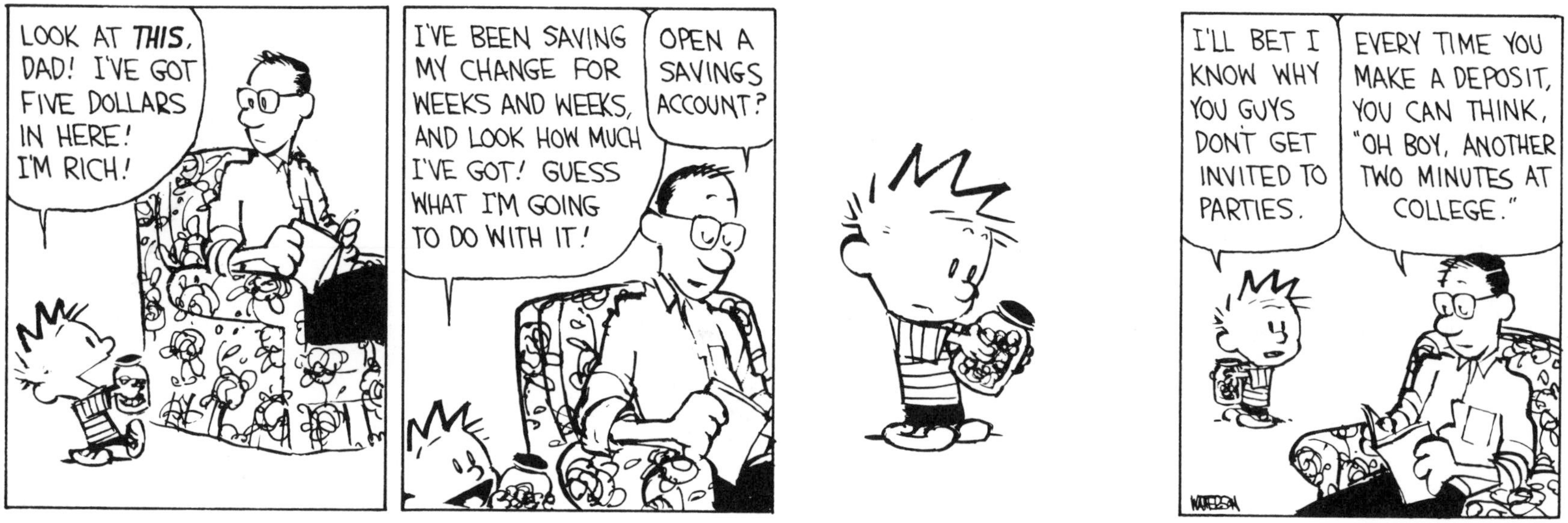
LOOK AT THIS, DAD! I'VE GOT FIVE DOLLARS IN HERE! I'M RICH!
I'VE BEEN SAVING MY CHANGE FOR WEEKS AND WEEKS, AND LOOK HOW MUCH I'VE GOT! GUESS WHAT I'M GOING TO DO WITH IT!
OPEN A SAVINGS ACCOUNT?
I'LL BET I KNOW WHY YOU GUYS DON'T GET INVITED TO PARTIES.
EVERY TIME YOU MAKE A DEPOSIT, YOU CAN THINK, "OH BOY, ANOTHER TWO MINUTES AT COLLEGE."

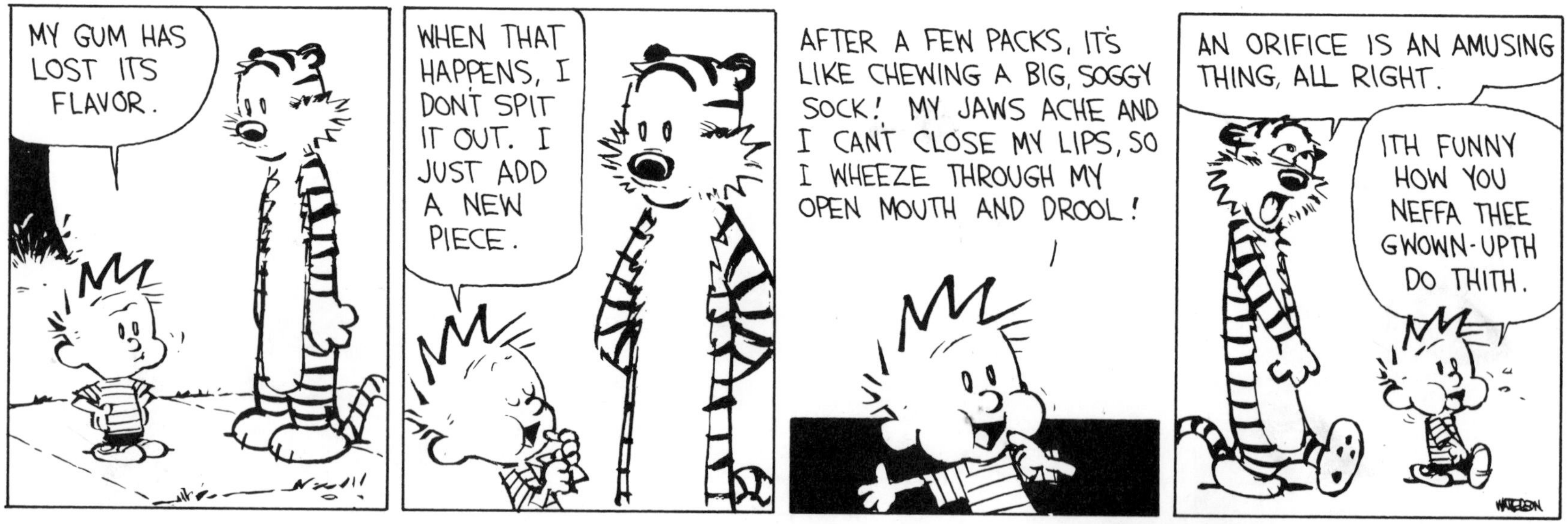
MY GUM HAS LOST ITS FLAVOR.
WHEN THAT HAPPENS, I DON'T SPIT IT OUT. I JUST ADD A NEW PIECE.
AFTER A FEW PACKS, IT'S LIKE CHEWING A BIG, SOGGY SOCK! MY JAWS ACHE AND I CAN'T CLOSE MY LIPS, SO I WHEEZE THROUGH MY OPEN MOUTH AND DROOL!
AN ORIFICE IS AN AMUSING THING, ALL RIGHT.
ITH FUNNY HOW YOU NEFFA THEE GWOWN-UPTH DO THITH.

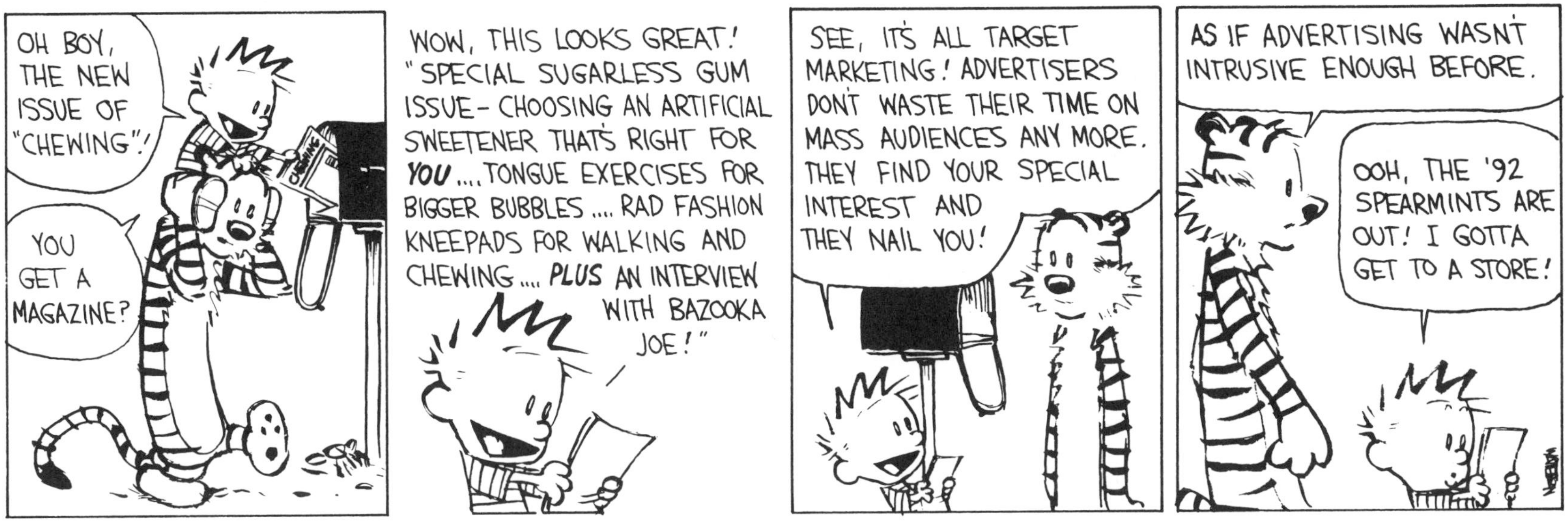
OH BOY, THE NEW ISSUE OF "CHEWING"!
YOU GET A MAGAZINE?
WOW, THIS LOOKS GREAT! "SPECIAL SUGARLESS GUM ISSUE- CHOOSING AN ARTIFICIAL SWEETENER THAT'S RIGHT FOR YOU.... TONGUE EXERCISES FOR BIGGER BUBBLES.... RAD FASHION KNEEPADS FOR WALKING AND CHEWING.... PLUS AN INTERVIEW WITH BAZOOKA JOE!"
SEE, IT'S ALL TARGET MARKETING! ADVERTISERS DON'T WASTE THEIR TIME ON MASS AUDIENCES ANY MORE. THEY FIND YOUR SPECIAL INTEREST AND THEY NAIL YOU!
AS IF ADVERTISING WASN'T INTRUSIVE ENOUGH BEFORE.
OOH, THE '92 SPEARMINTS ARE OUT! I GOTTA GET TO A STORE!

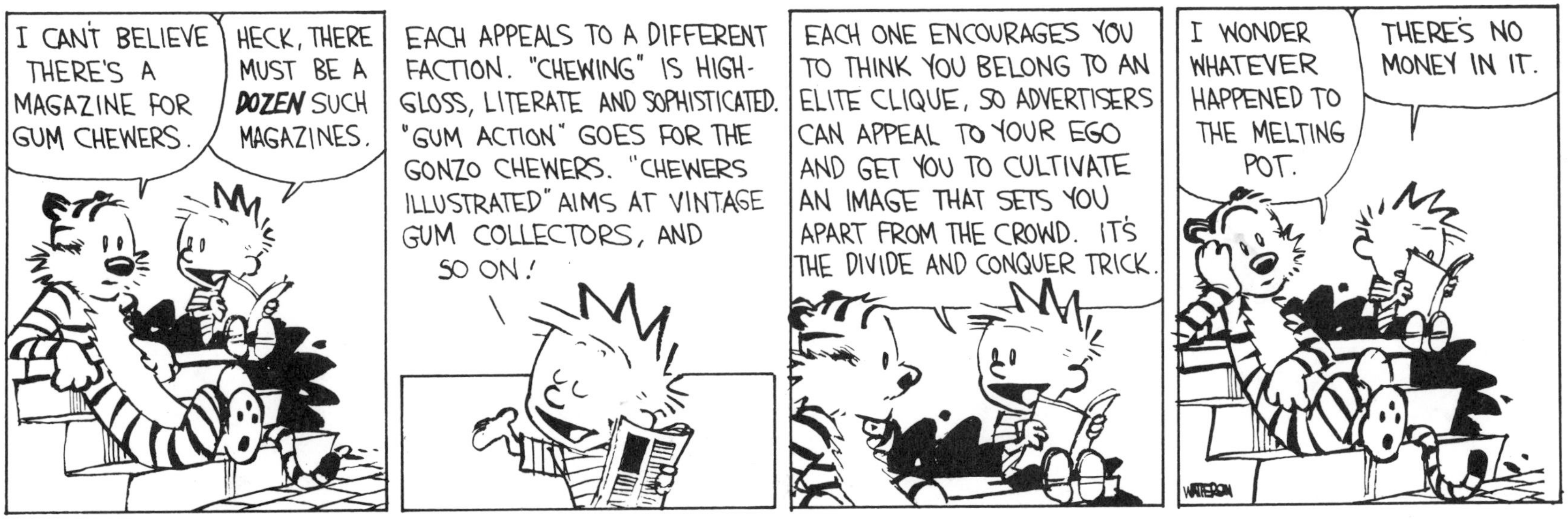
I CAN'T BELIEVE THERE'S A MAGAZINE FOR GUM CHEWERS.
HECK, THERE MUST BE A DOZEN SUCH MAGAZINES.
EACH APPEALS TO A DIFFERENT FACTION. "CHEWING" IS HIGH-GLOSS, LITERATE AND SOPHISTICATED. "GUM ACTION" GOES FOR THE GONZO CHEWERS. "CHEWERS ILLUSTRATED" AIMS AT VINTAGE GUM COLLECTORS, AND SO ON!
EACH ONE ENCOURAGES YOU TO THINK YOU BELONG TO AN ELITE CLIQUE, SO ADVERTISERS CAN APPEAL TO YOUR EGO AND GET YOU TO CULTIVATE AN IMAGE THAT SETS YOU APART FROM THE CROWD. IT'S THE DIVIDE AND CONQUER TRICK.
I WONDER WHATEVER HAPPENED TO THE MELTING POT.
THERE'S NO MONEY IN IT.

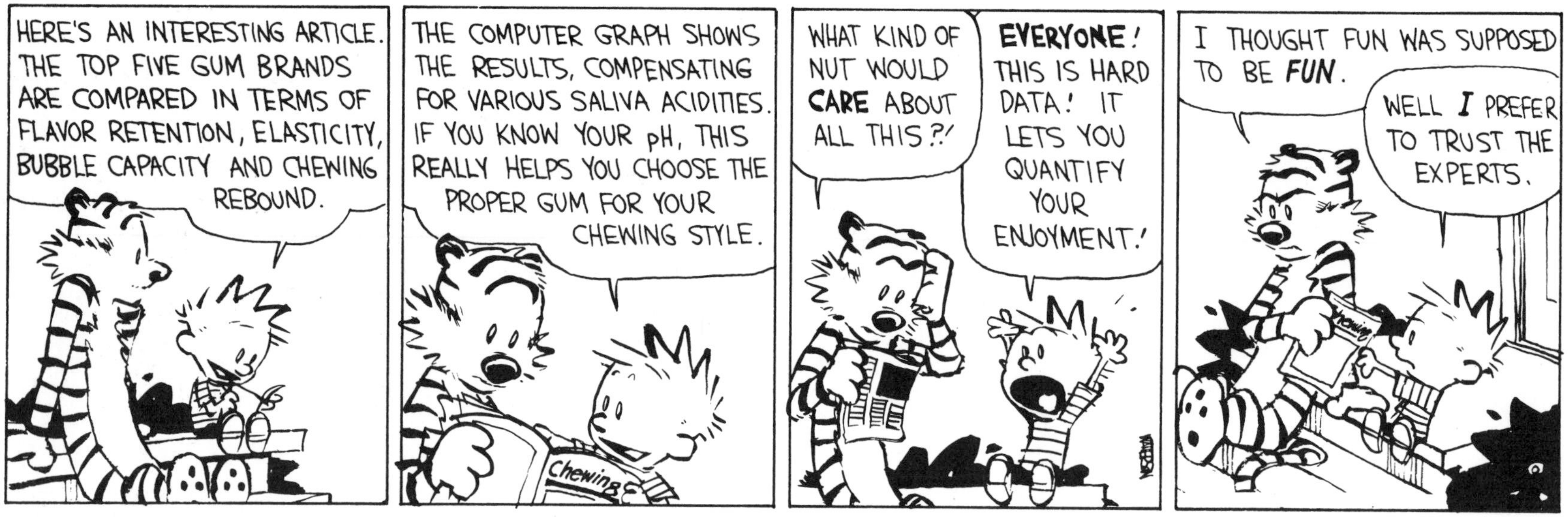
HERE'S AN INTERESTING ARTICLE. THE TOP FIVE GUM BRANDS ARE COMPARED IN TERMS OF FLAVOR RETENTION, ELASTICITY, BUBBLE CAPACITY AND CHEWING REBOUND.
THE COMPUTER GRAPH SHOWS THE RESULTS, COMPENSATING FOR VARIOUS SALIVA ACIDITIES. IF YOU KNOW YOUR pH, THIS REALLY HELPS YOU CHOOSE THE PROPER GUM FOR YOUR CHEWING STYLE.
Chewing
WHAT KIND OF NUT WOULD **CARE** ABOUT ALL THIS ?!
EVERYONE! THIS IS HARD DATA! IT LETS YOU QUANTIFY YOUR ENJOYMENT!
I THOUGHT FUN WAS SUPPOSED TO BE ***FUN***.
WELL ***I*** PREFER TO TRUST THE EXPERTS.

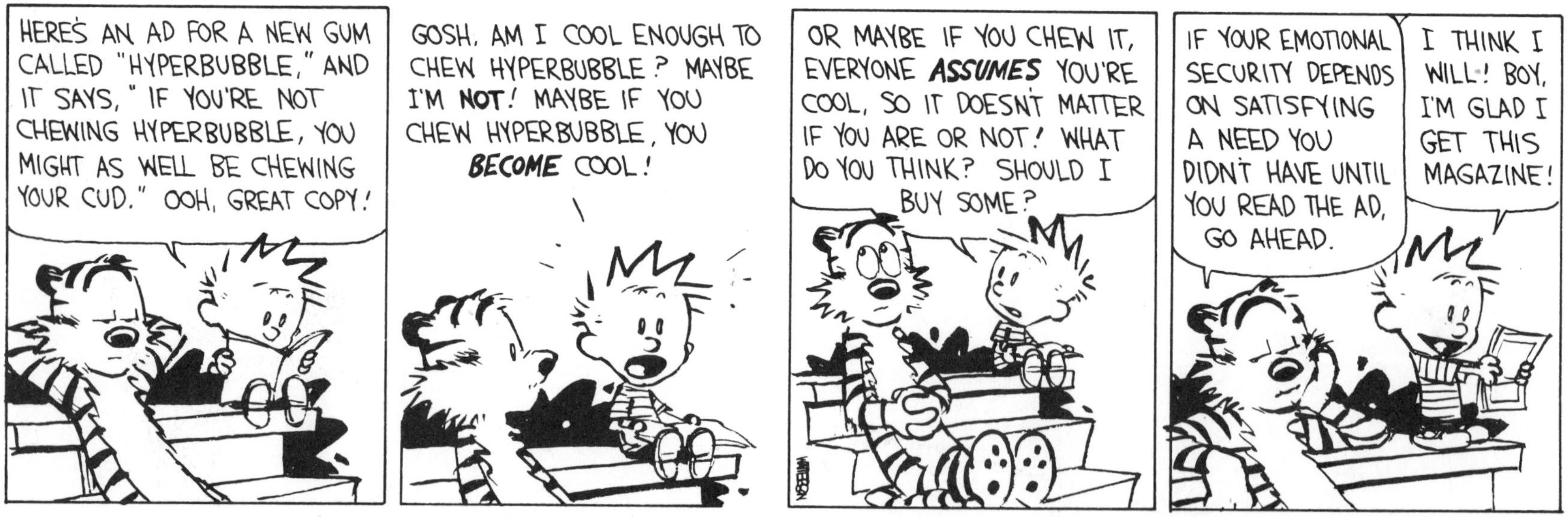
HERE'S AN AD FOR A NEW GUM CALLED "HYPERBUBBLE," AND IT SAYS, "IF YOU'RE NOT CHEWING HYPERBUBBLE, YOU MIGHT AS WELL BE CHEWING YOUR CUD." OOH, GREAT COPY!
GOSH, AM I COOL ENOUGH TO CHEW HYPERBUBBLE? MAYBE I'M **NOT**! MAYBE IF YOU CHEW HYPERBUBBLE, YOU ***BECOME*** COOL!
OR MAYBE IF YOU CHEW IT, EVERYONE ***ASSUMES*** YOU'RE COOL, SO IT DOESN'T MATTER IF YOU ARE OR NOT! WHAT DO YOU THINK? SHOULD I BUY SOME?
IF YOUR EMOTIONAL SECURITY DEPENDS ON SATISFYING A NEED YOU DIDN'T HAVE UNTIL YOU READ THE AD, GO AHEAD.
I THINK I WILL! BOY, I'M GLAD I GET THIS MAGAZINE!

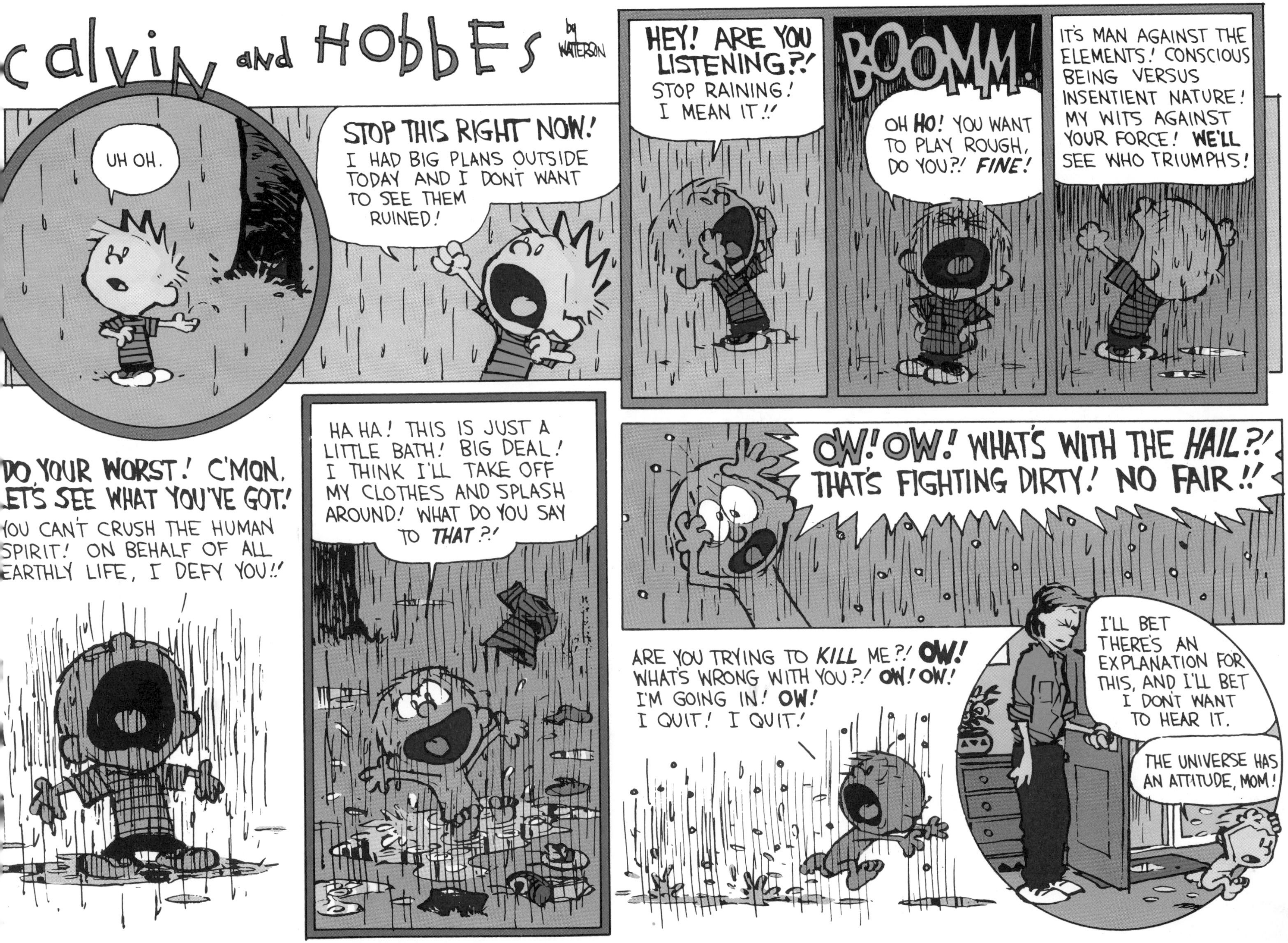

calvin and HOBBES by WATTERSON
UH OH.
STOP THIS RIGHT NOW! I HAD BIG PLANS OUTSIDE TODAY AND I DON'T WANT TO SEE THEM RUINED!
HEY! ARE YOU LISTENING?! STOP RAINING! I MEAN IT!!
BOOMM!
OH HO! YOU WANT TO PLAY ROUGH, DO YOU?! FINE!
IT'S MAN AGAINST THE ELEMENTS! CONSCIOUS BEING VERSUS INSENTIENT NATURE! MY WITS AGAINST YOUR FORCE! WE'LL SEE WHO TRIUMPHS!
DO YOUR WORST! C'MON. LET'S SEE WHAT YOU'VE GOT! YOU CAN'T CRUSH THE HUMAN SPIRIT! ON BEHALF OF ALL EARTHLY LIFE, I DEFY YOU!!
HA HA! THIS IS JUST A LITTLE BATH! BIG DEAL! I THINK I'LL TAKE OFF MY CLOTHES AND SPLASH AROUND! WHAT DO YOU SAY TO THAT?!
OW! OW! WHAT'S WITH THE HAIL?! THAT'S FIGHTING DIRTY! NO FAIR!!
ARE YOU TRYING TO KILL ME?! OW! WHAT'S WRONG WITH YOU?! OW! OW! I'M GOING IN! OW! I QUIT! I QUIT!
I'LL BET THERE'S AN EXPLANATION FOR THIS, AND I'LL BET I DON'T WANT TO HEAR IT.
THE UNIVERSE HAS AN ATTITUDE, MOM!

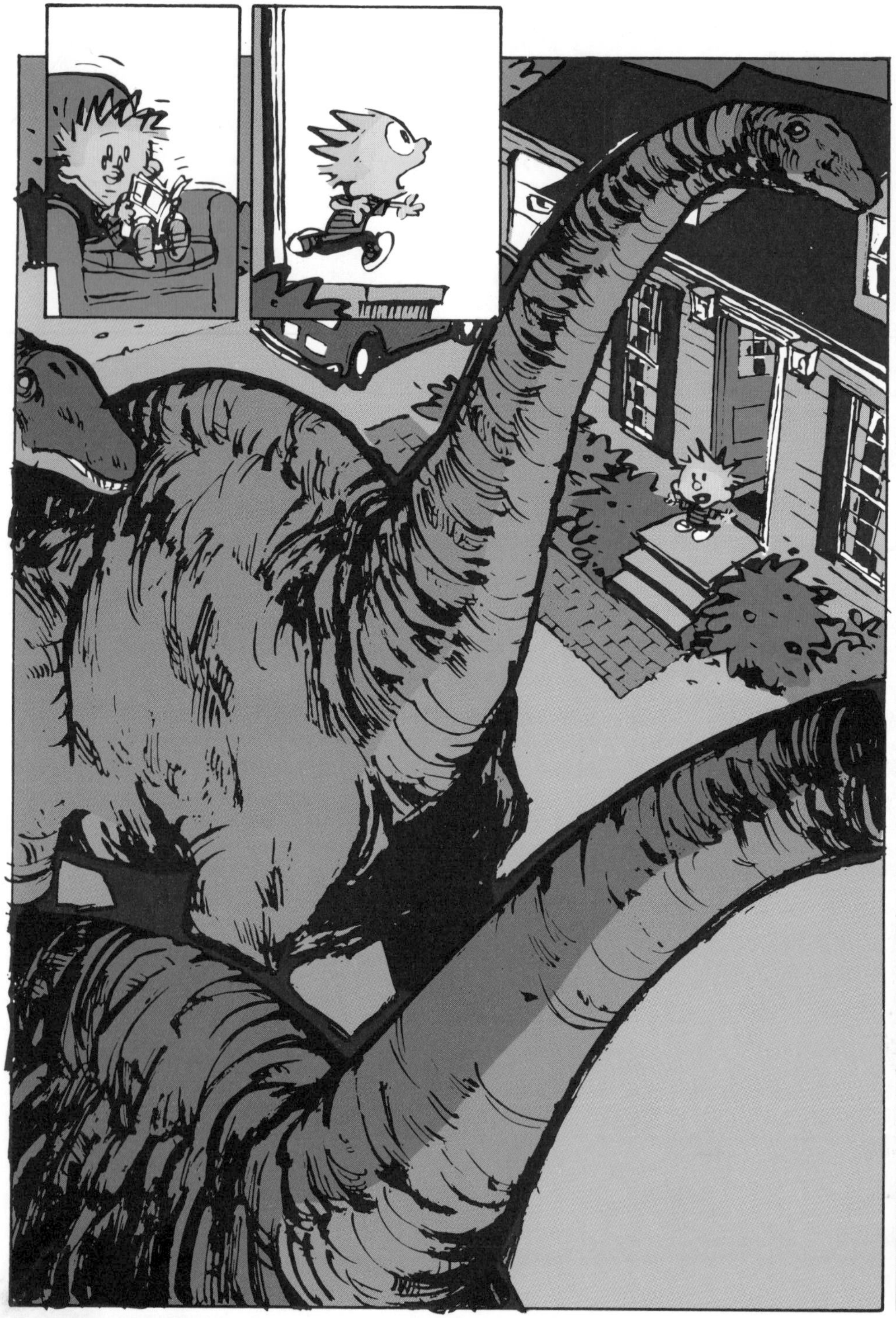

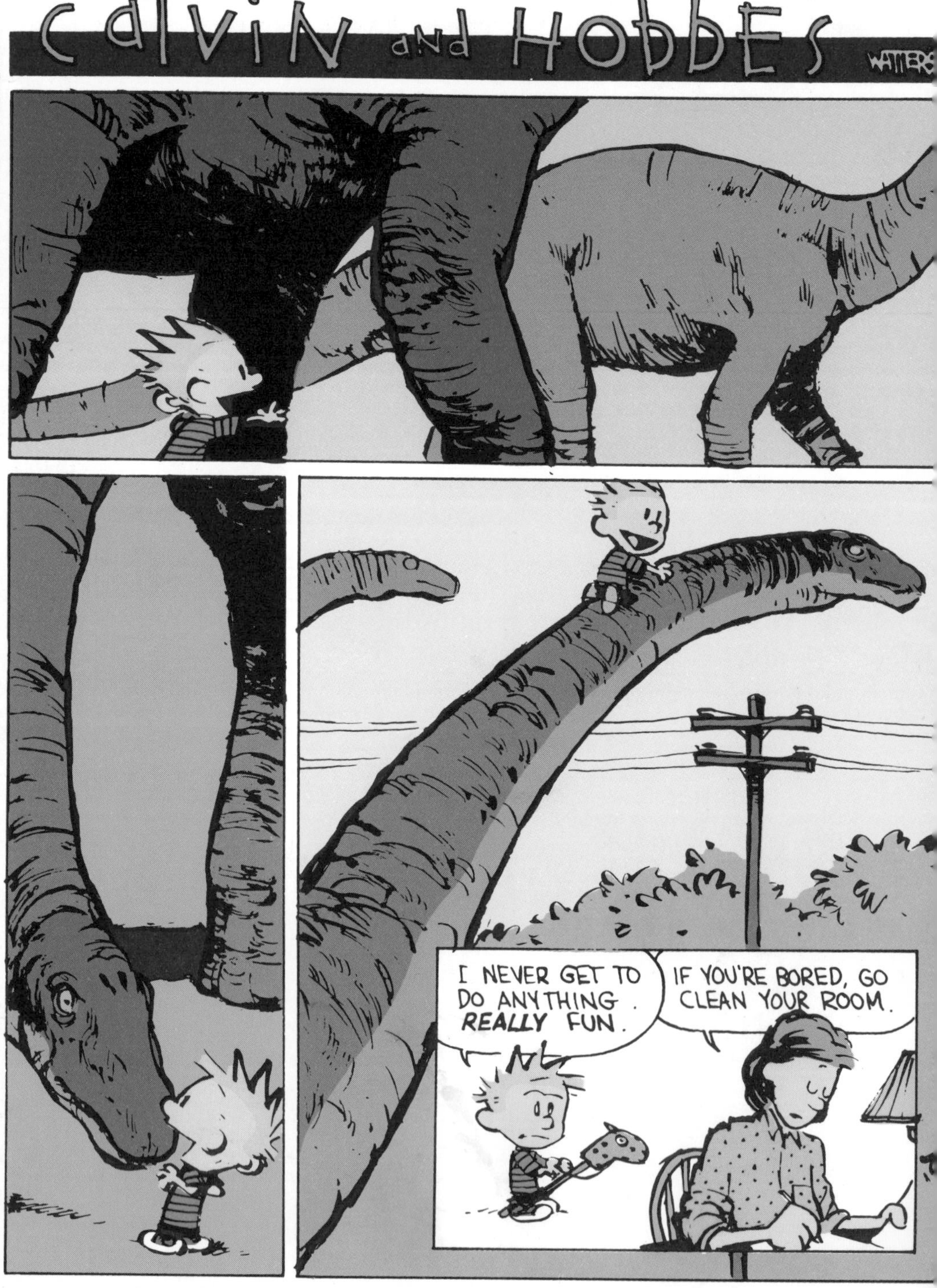

Calvin and HOBBES
WATTERS
I NEVER GET TO DO ANYTHING. *REALLY* FUN.
IF YOU'RE BORED, GO CLEAN YOUR ROOM.

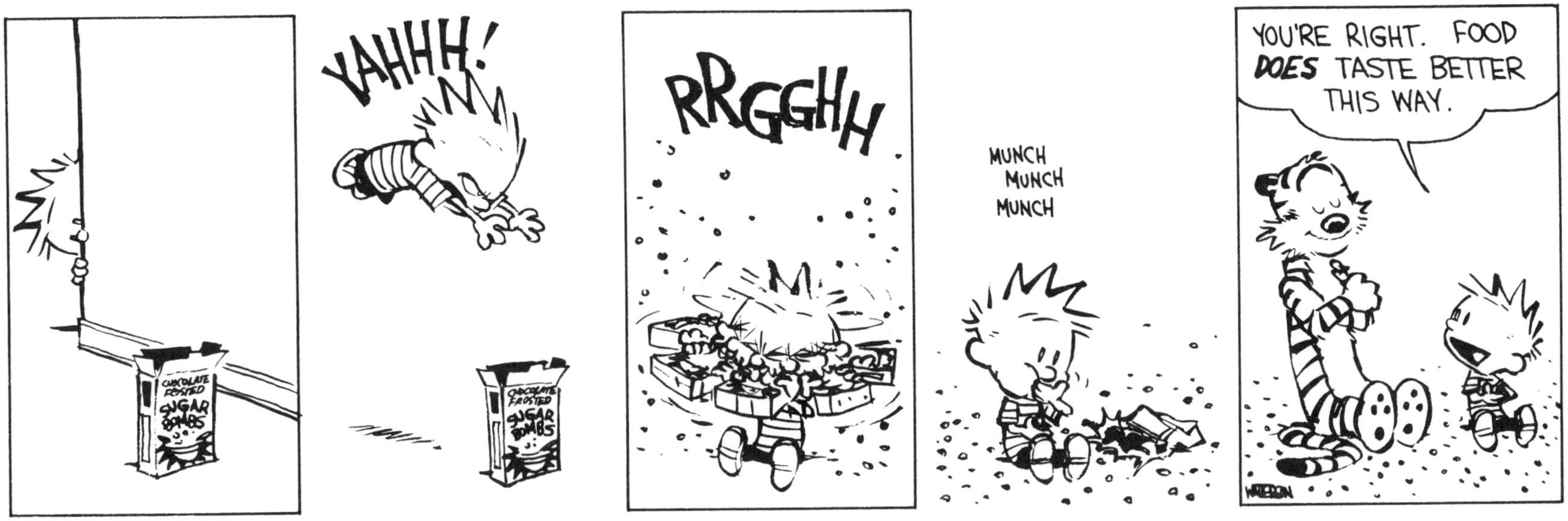
CHOCOLATE FROSTED SUGAR BOMBS
YAHHH!
RRGGHH
MUNCH MUNCH MUNCH
YOU'RE RIGHT. FOOD **DOES** TASTE BETTER THIS WAY.

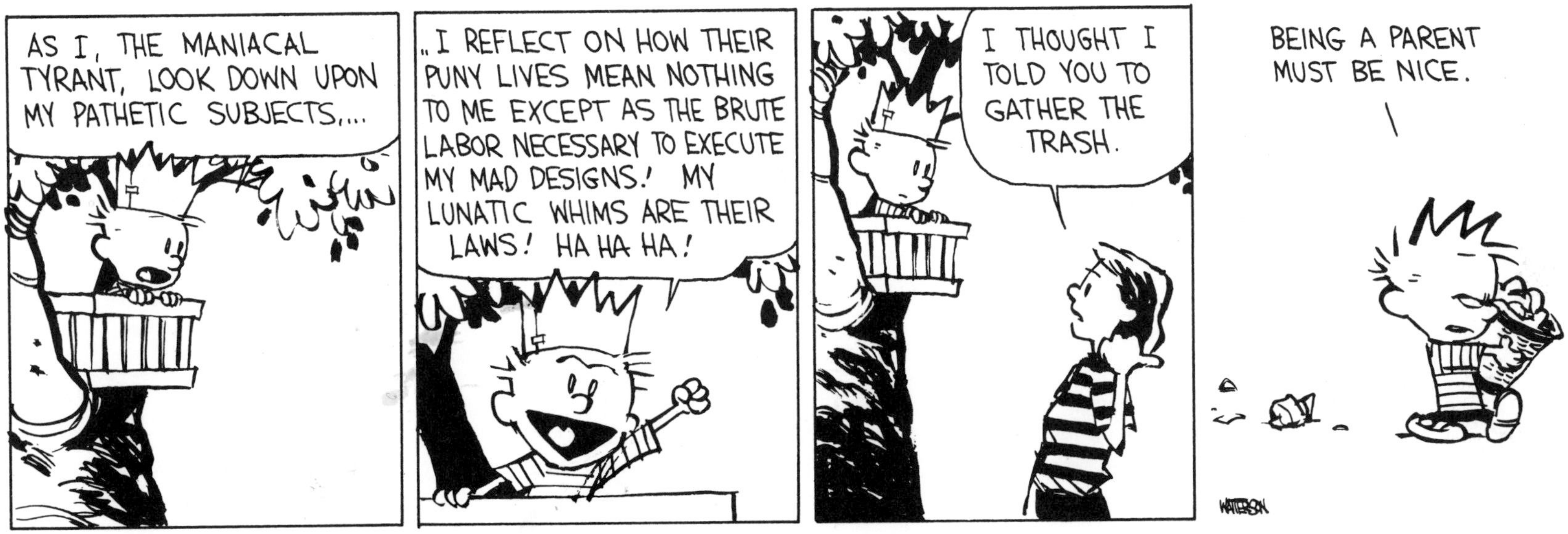
AS I, THE MANIACAL TYRANT, LOOK DOWN UPON MY PATHETIC SUBJECTS,...
..I REFLECT ON HOW THEIR PUNY LIVES MEAN NOTHING TO ME EXCEPT AS THE BRUTE LABOR NECESSARY TO EXECUTE MY MAD DESIGNS! MY LUNATIC WHIMS ARE THEIR LAWS! HA HA HA!
I THOUGHT I TOLD YOU TO GATHER THE TRASH.
BEING A PARENT MUST BE NICE.

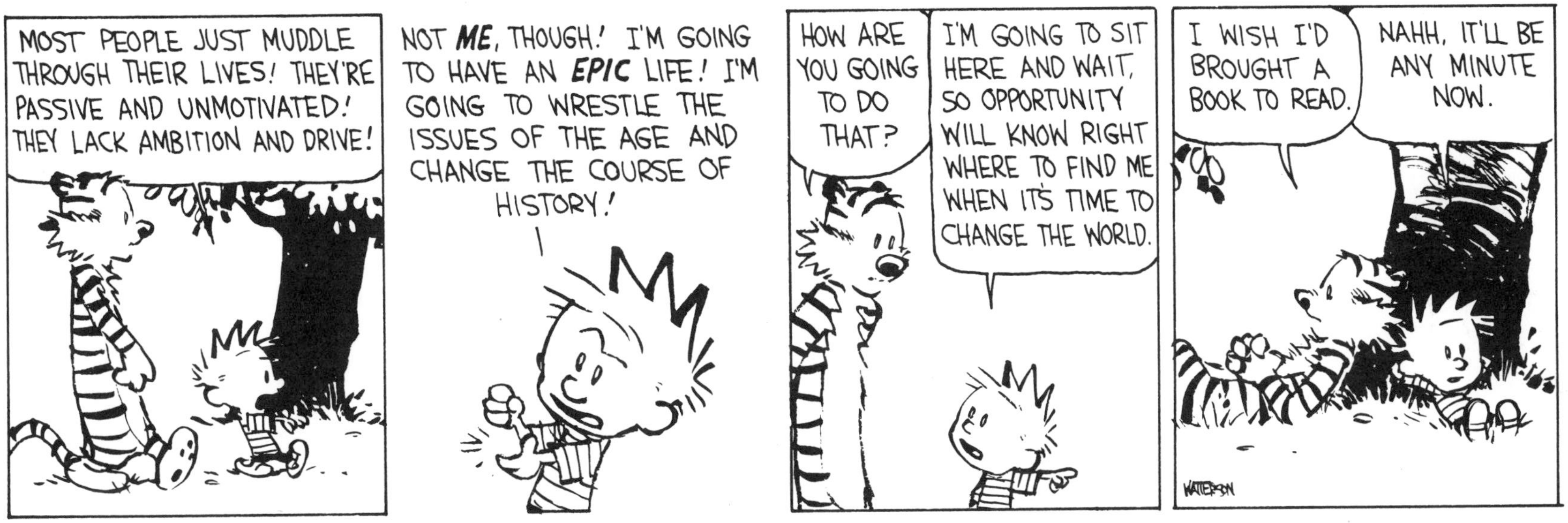
MOST PEOPLE JUST MUDDLE THROUGH THEIR LIVES! THEY'RE PASSIVE AND UNMOTIVATED! THEY LACK AMBITION AND DRIVE!
NOT ME, THOUGH! I'M GOING TO HAVE AN EPIC LIFE! I'M GOING TO WRESTLE THE ISSUES OF THE AGE AND CHANGE THE COURSE OF HISTORY!
HOW ARE YOU GOING TO DO THAT?
I'M GOING TO SIT HERE AND WAIT, SO OPPORTUNITY WILL KNOW RIGHT WHERE TO FIND ME WHEN IT'S TIME TO CHANGE THE WORLD.
I WISH I'D BROUGHT A BOOK TO READ.
NAHH, IT'LL BE ANY MINUTE NOW.

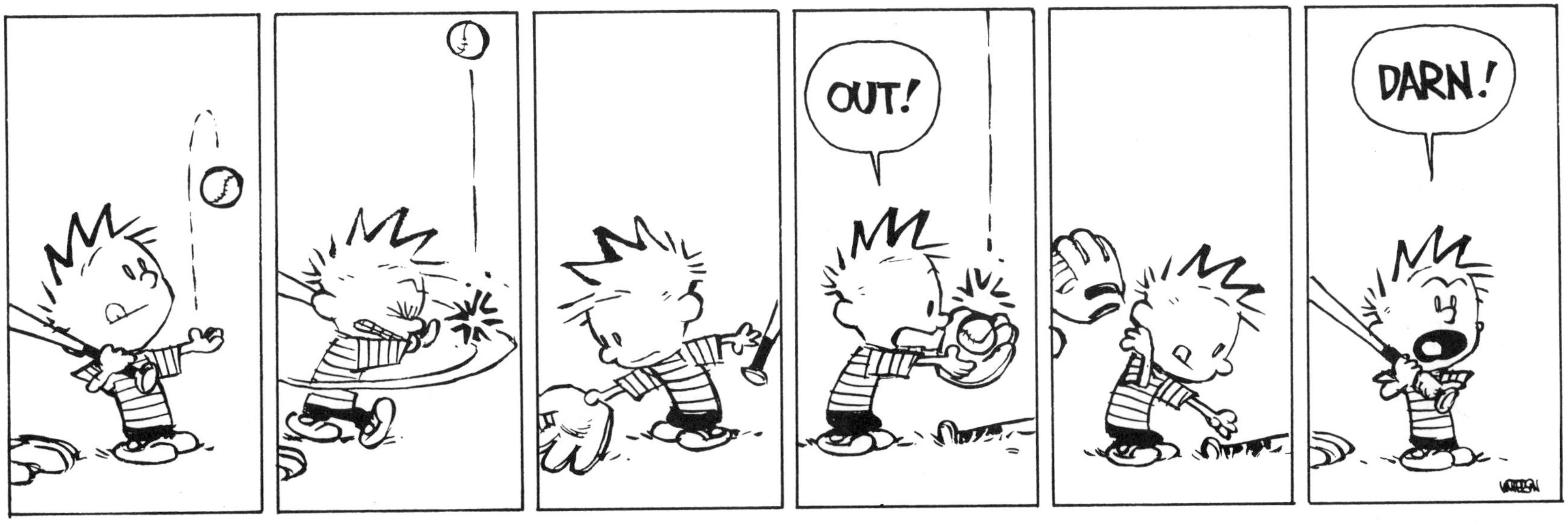
OUT!
DARN!

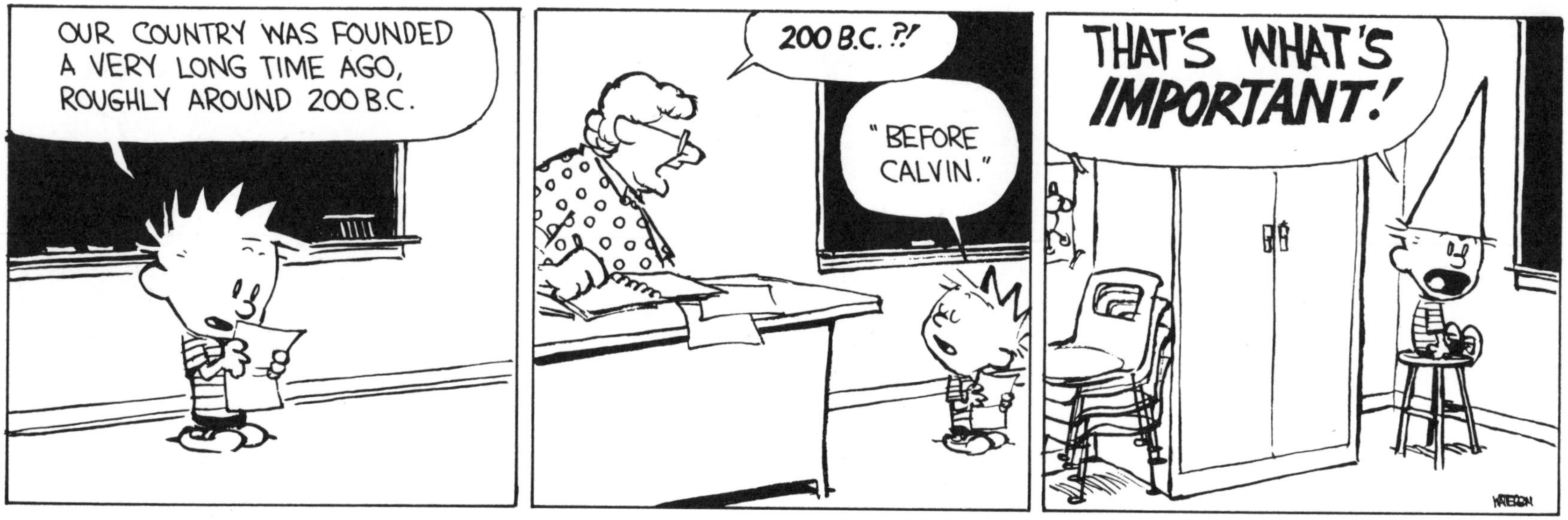
OUR COUNTRY WAS FOUNDED A VERY LONG TIME AGO, ROUGHLY AROUND 200 B.C.
200 B.C.?!
"BEFORE CALVIN."
THAT'S WHAT'S IMPORTANT!

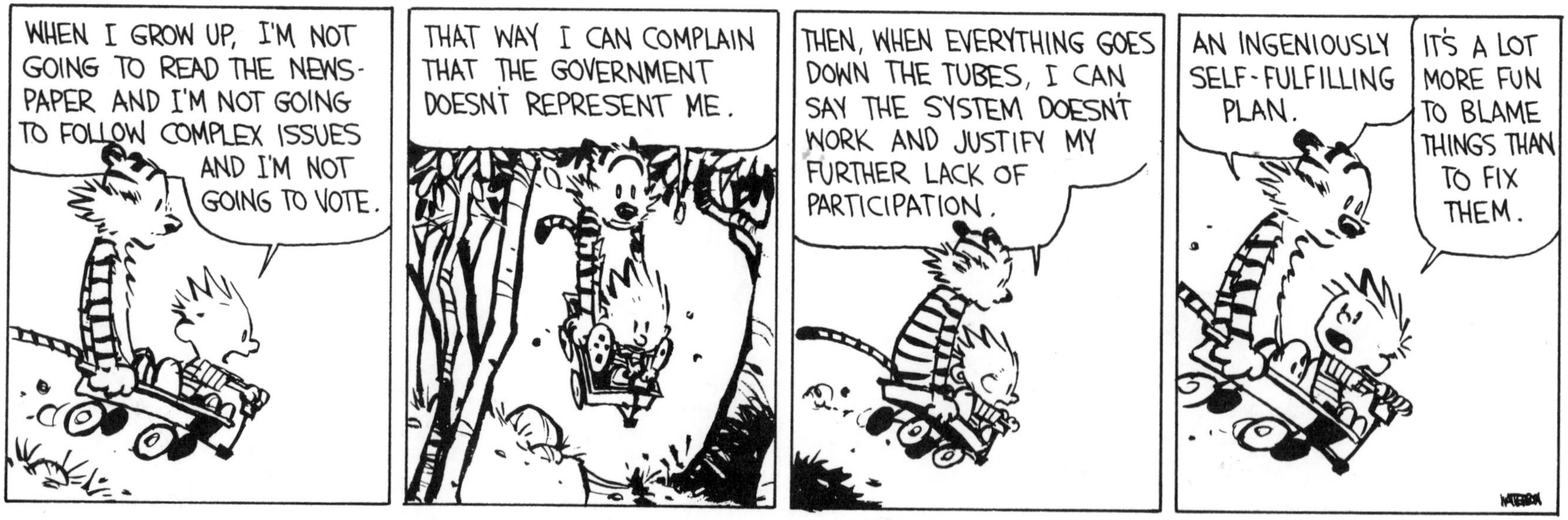
WHEN I GROW UP, I'M NOT GOING TO READ THE NEWSPAPER AND I'M NOT GOING TO FOLLOW COMPLEX ISSUES AND I'M NOT GOING TO VOTE.
THAT WAY I CAN COMPLAIN THAT THE GOVERNMENT DOESN'T REPRESENT ME.
THEN, WHEN EVERYTHING GOES DOWN THE TUBES, I CAN SAY THE SYSTEM DOESN'T WORK AND JUSTIFY MY FURTHER LACK OF PARTICIPATION.
AN INGENIOUSLY SELF-FULFILLING PLAN.
IT'S A LOT MORE FUN TO BLAME THINGS THAN TO FIX THEM.

It's true, Hobbes, ignorance *is* bliss!

Once you know things, you start seeing problems everywhere...

..and once you see problems, you feel like you ought to try to fix them...

..and fixing problems always seems to require personal change..

..and change means doing things that aren't fun! I say phooey to that!

But if you're willfully stupid, you don't know any better, so you can keep doing whatever you like!

The secret to happiness is short-term, stupid self-interest!

We're heading for that cliff!

I don't want to know about it.

WAAAUGGHH!

I'm not sure I can stand so much bliss.

Careful! We don't want to learn anything from this.

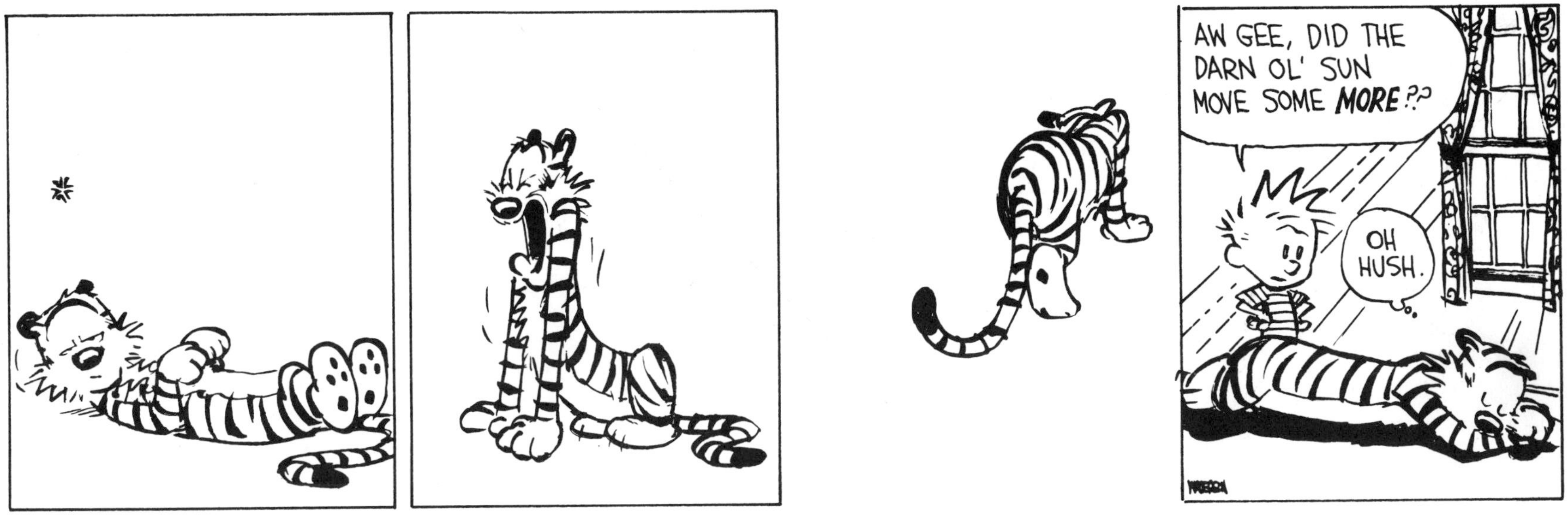
AW GEE, DID THE DARN OL' SUN MOVE SOME **MORE** ?!?
OH HUSH.

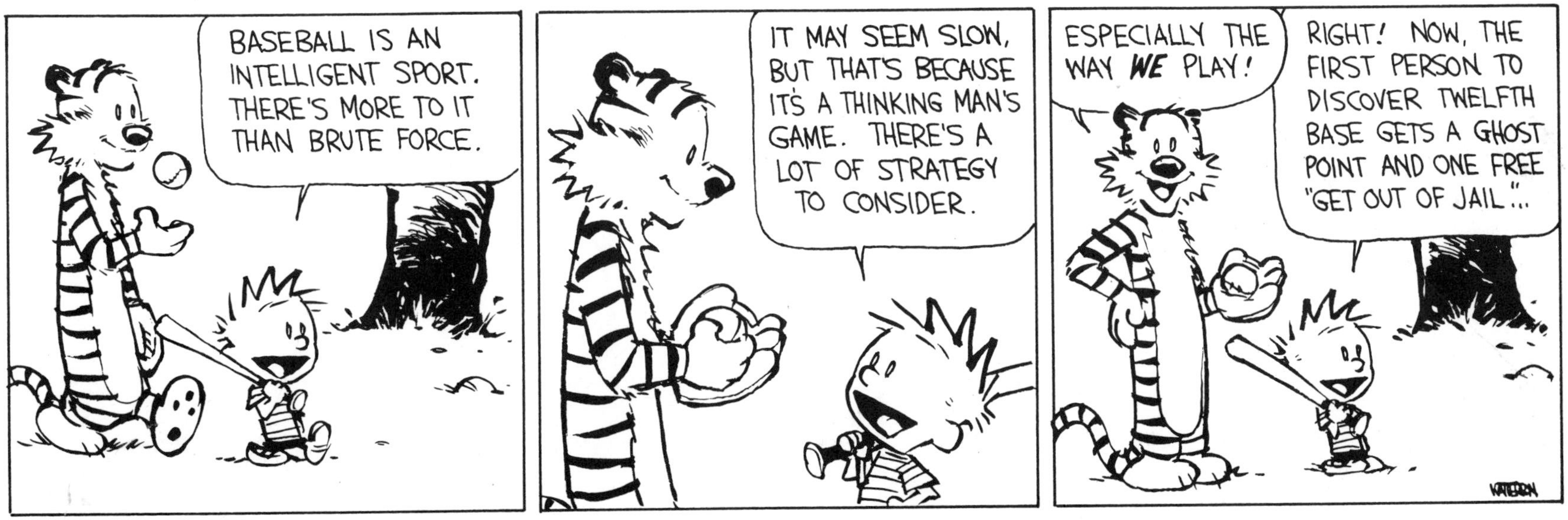
BASEBALL IS AN INTELLIGENT SPORT. THERE'S MORE TO IT THAN BRUTE FORCE.
IT MAY SEEM SLOW, BUT THAT'S BECAUSE IT'S A THINKING MAN'S GAME. THERE'S A LOT OF STRATEGY TO CONSIDER.
ESPECIALLY THE WAY **WE** PLAY!
RIGHT! NOW, THE FIRST PERSON TO DISCOVER TWELFTH BASE GETS A GHOST POINT AND ONE FREE "GET OUT OF JAIL"...

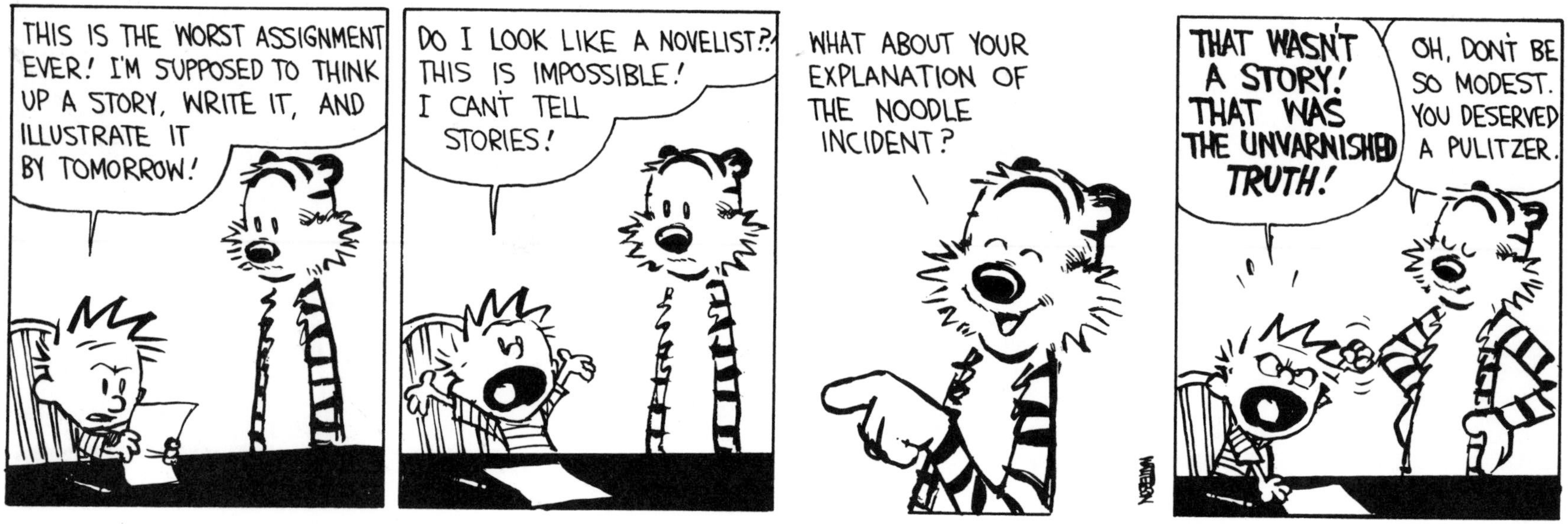
THIS IS THE WORST ASSIGNMENT EVER! I'M SUPPOSED TO THINK UP A STORY, WRITE IT, AND ILLUSTRATE IT BY TOMORROW!
DO I LOOK LIKE A NOVELIST?! THIS IS IMPOSSIBLE! I CAN'T TELL STORIES!
WHAT ABOUT YOUR EXPLANATION OF THE NOODLE INCIDENT?
THAT WASN'T A STORY! THAT WAS THE UNVARNISHED *TRUTH*!
OH, DON'T BE SO MODEST. YOU DESERVED A PULITZER.

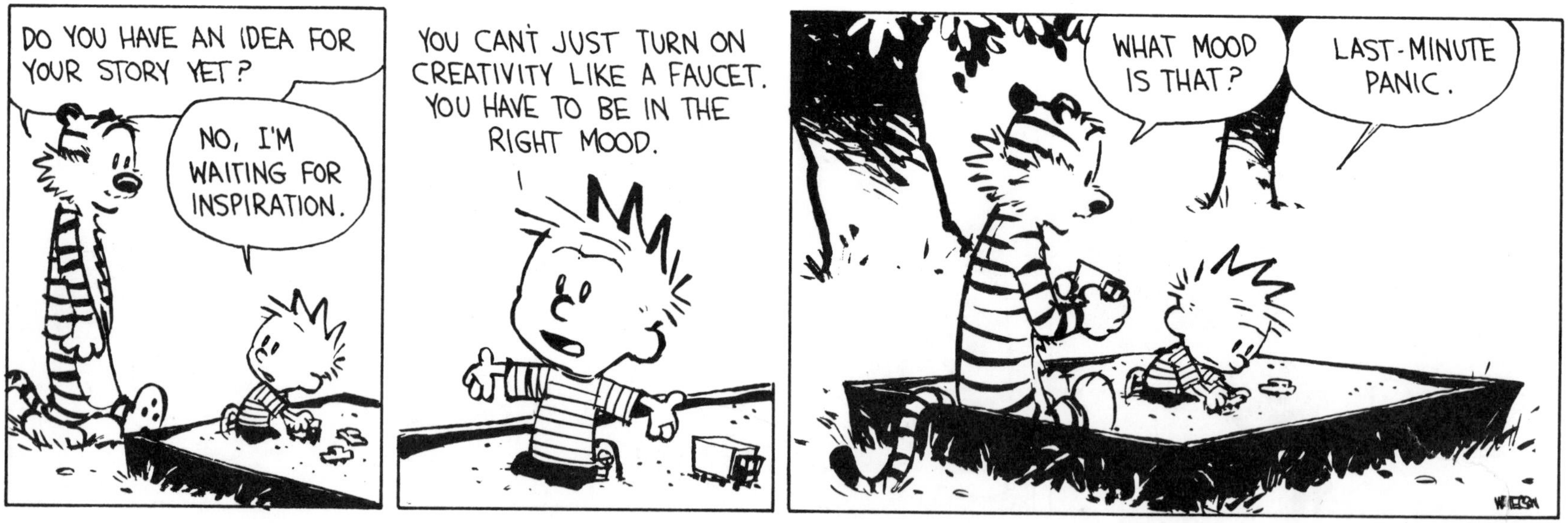
DO YOU HAVE AN IDEA FOR YOUR STORY YET?
NO, I'M WAITING FOR INSPIRATION.
YOU CAN'T JUST TURN ON CREATIVITY LIKE A FAUCET. YOU HAVE TO BE IN THE RIGHT MOOD.
WHAT MOOD IS THAT?
LAST-MINUTE PANIC.

ALL RIGHT, CALVIN, GO AHEAD. WHAT'S *YOUR* STORY ABOUT?

I DON'T KNOW YET, BUT I'M SURE IT'S GOOD!

MY STORY IS ENTITLED, "HOW HOBBES, THE HANDSOME TIGER, SAVES THE DAY...

... NO THANKS TO CALVIN, THE TIME TRAVELING CHOWDERHEAD."

WHAT?!

IS THERE A PROBLEM?

THERE *WILL* BE FOR A CERTAIN STRIPEY FURBALL WHEN I GET HOME.

OK, YOU!

ME??

THIS STORY YOU WROTE IS ABOUT *ME* TRYING TO GET *OUT* OF WRITING THE *STORY!* YOU MADE MY TIME TRAVELING SOUND LIKE *LUNACY!*

AND THE ILLUSTRATION! YOU DREW THE *THREE* OF ME FIGHTING! I WAS THE LAUGHING-STOCK OF THE WHOLE CLASS!

WHAT GRADE DID IT GET?

UM... A+. SHE WROTE, " VERY CREATIVE. THE 'TIGER' NARRATION WAS A CLEVER TOUCH. I'M GLAD YOU'RE FINALLY APPLYING YOURSELF."

..BUT EVEN SO..!!

A+?? MAYBE I SHOULD SEND THIS TO THE NEW YORKER.

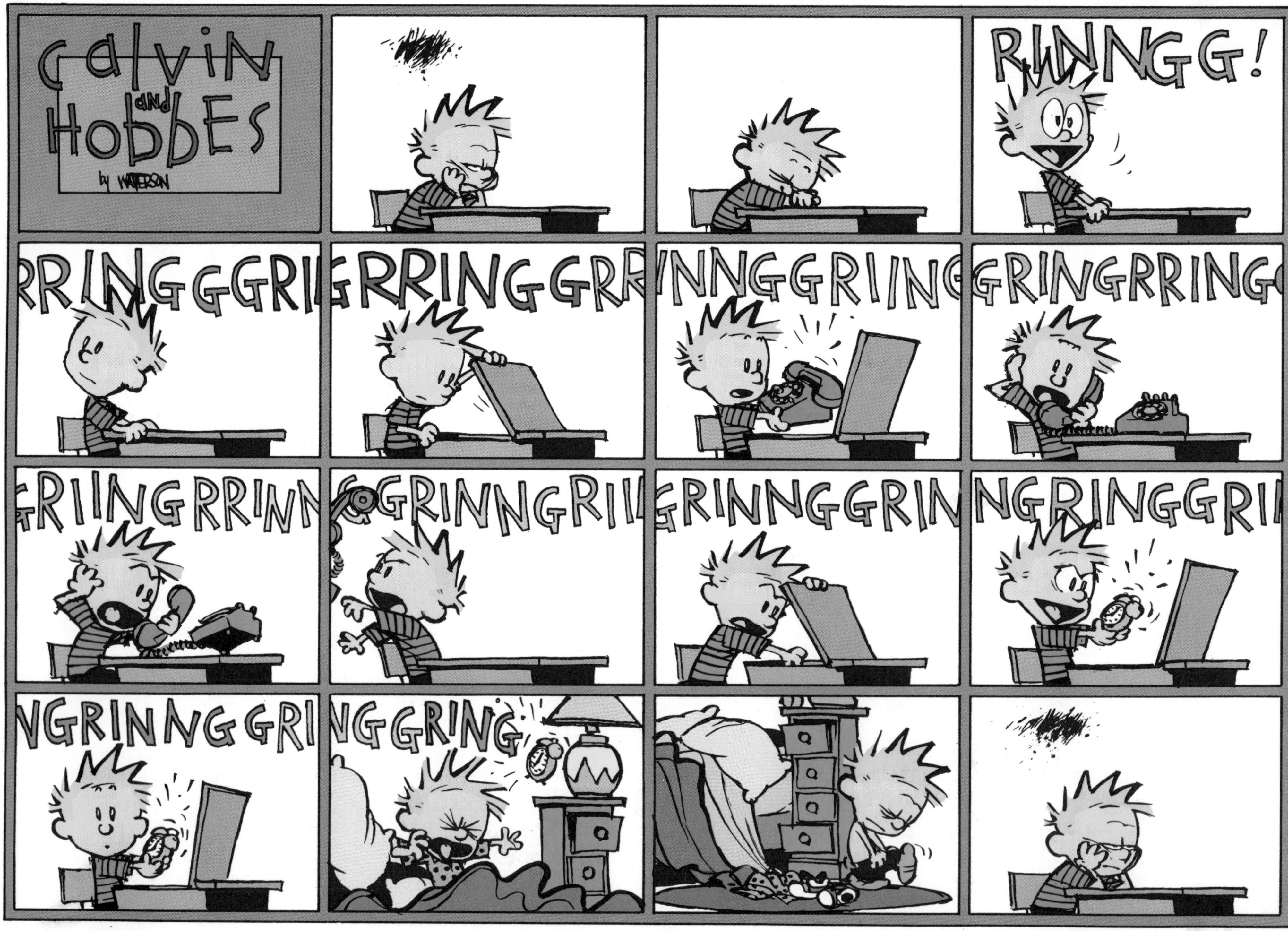
Calvin and Hobbes
by Watterson
RINNGG!
RRINGGGRI
GRRINGGGRR
INNGGRIING
GRINGRRING
GRIINGRRINN
GRINNGRII
GRINNGGRIN
NGRINGGRI
NGRINNGGRI
NGGRING

HOW DO I KNOW YOUR IDEAS ARE GREAT?

GREat IdEas $|⁰⁰

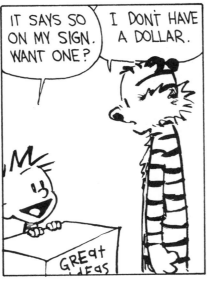

IT SAYS SO ON MY SIGN. WANT ONE?

I DON'T HAVE A DOLLAR.

GREat IdEas

NO PROBLEM! YOU CAN PUT 50 CENTS DOWN AND PAY 100% INTEREST IN DIME INSTALLMENTS OVER THE NEXT 10 DAYS!

PEOPLE JUST DON'T KNOW A GREAT IDEA WHEN THEY HEAR ONE.

GREat IdEas $|⁰⁰

I'M HAVING AN INVENTORY REDUCTION SALE! GREAT IDEAS ARE NOW JUST A QUARTER!

GREat IdEas NOW 25¢

OK, HERE. WHAT'S YOUR GREAT IDEA?

BUY SOME MORE!

GREat IdEas NOW 25¢

I'M GETTING ANOTHER GREAT IDEA RIGHT NOW.

ME TOO. SEE YA.

GREat

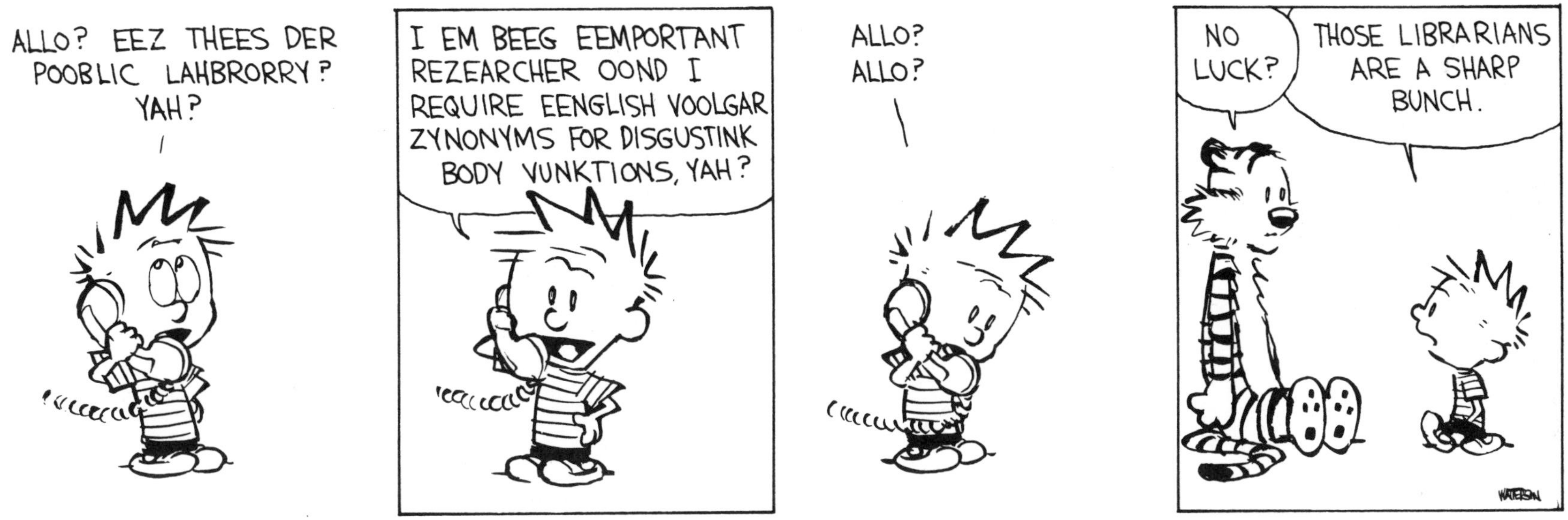
ALLO? EEZ THEES DER POOBLIC LAHBRORRY? YAH?
I EM BEEG EEMPORTANT REZEARCHER OOND I REQUIRE EENGLISH VOOLGAR ZYNONYMS FOR DISGUSTINK BODY VUNKTIONS, YAH?
ALLO? ALLO?
NO LUCK?
THOSE LIBRARIANS ARE A SHARP BUNCH.
WATTERSON

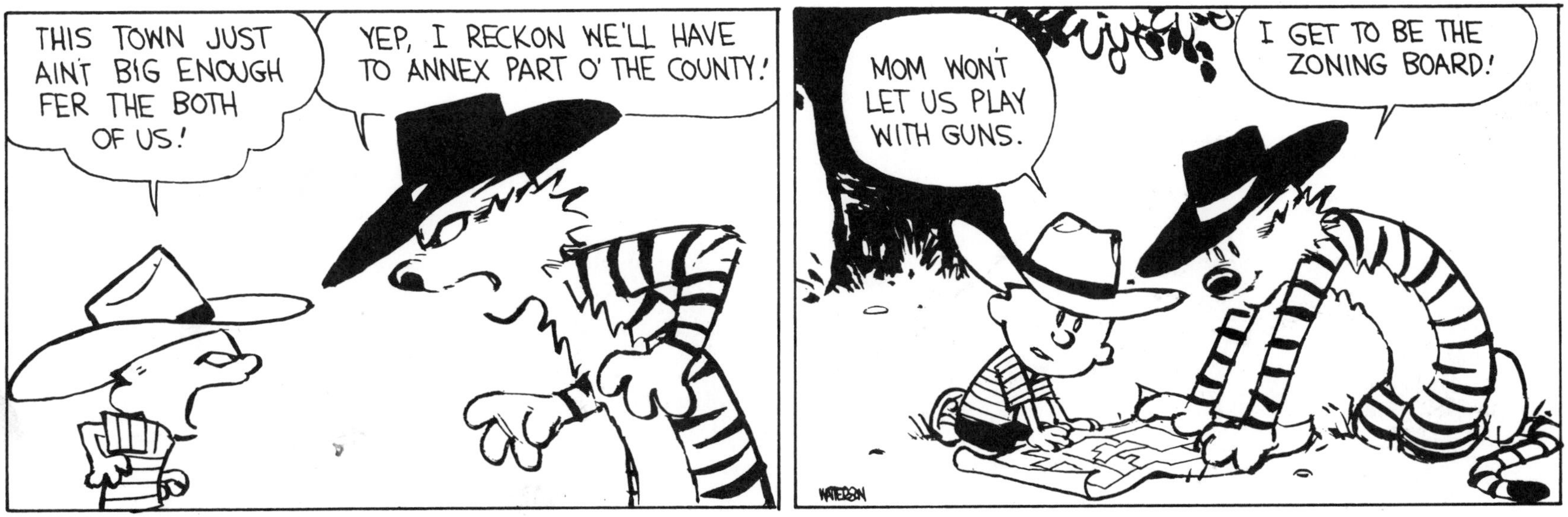
THIS TOWN JUST AIN'T BIG ENOUGH FER THE BOTH OF US!
YEP, I RECKON WE'LL HAVE TO ANNEX PART O' THE COUNTY!
WATTERSON
MOM WON'T LET US PLAY WITH GUNS.
I GET TO BE THE ZONING BOARD!

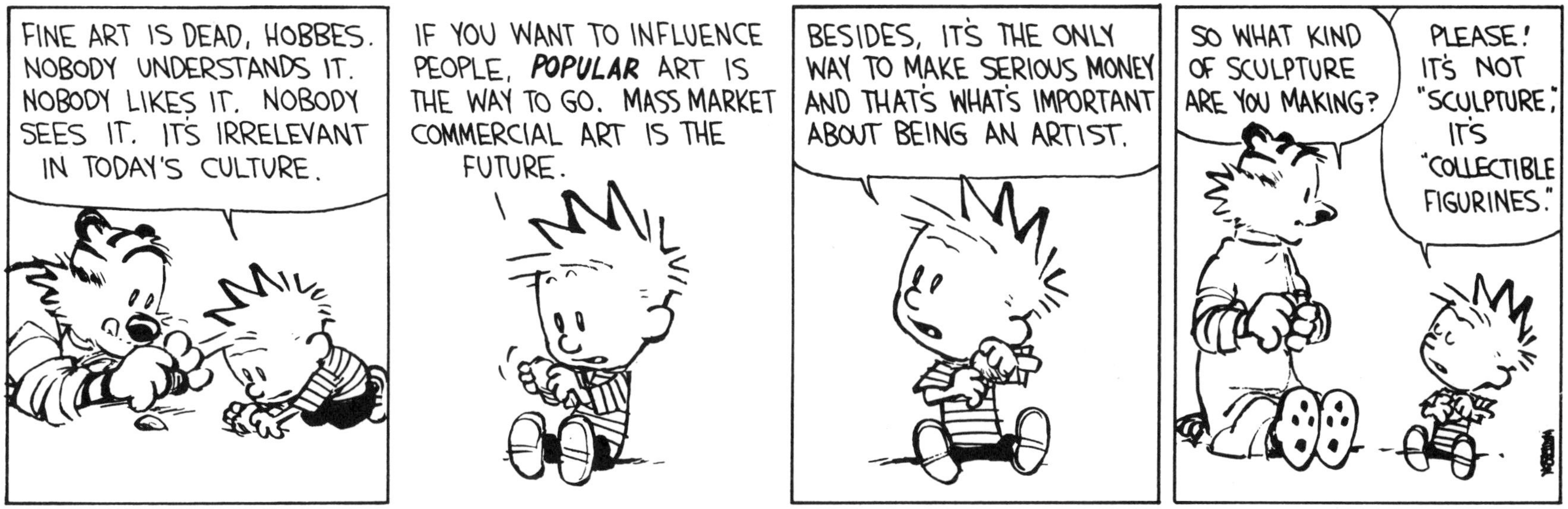
FINE ART IS DEAD, HOBBES. NOBODY UNDERSTANDS IT. NOBODY LIKES IT. NOBODY SEES IT. IT'S IRRELEVANT IN TODAY'S CULTURE.
IF YOU WANT TO INFLUENCE PEOPLE, POPULAR ART IS THE WAY TO GO. MASS MARKET COMMERCIAL ART IS THE FUTURE.
BESIDES, IT'S THE ONLY WAY TO MAKE SERIOUS MONEY AND THAT'S WHAT'S IMPORTANT ABOUT BEING AN ARTIST.
SO WHAT KIND OF SCULPTURE ARE YOU MAKING?
PLEASE! IT'S NOT "SCULPTURE," IT'S "COLLECTIBLE FIGURINES."

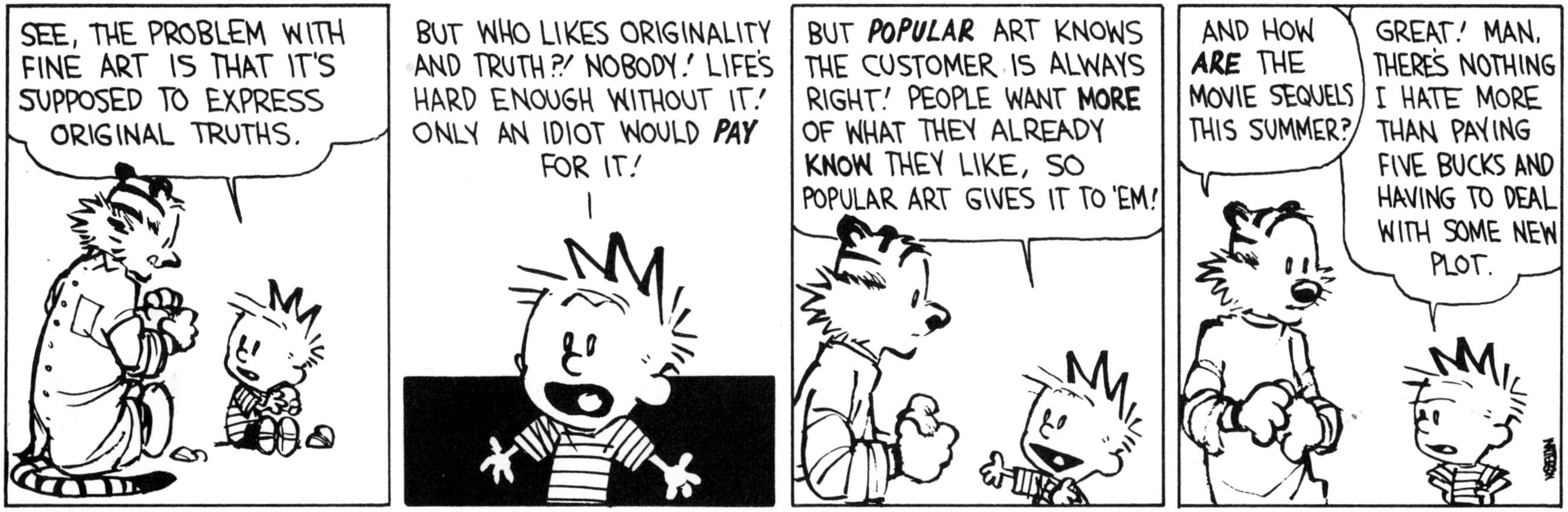
SEE, THE PROBLEM WITH FINE ART IS THAT IT'S SUPPOSED TO EXPRESS ORIGINAL TRUTHS.
BUT WHO LIKES ORIGINALITY AND TRUTH?! NOBODY! LIFE'S HARD ENOUGH WITHOUT IT! ONLY AN IDIOT WOULD PAY FOR IT!
BUT POPULAR ART KNOWS THE CUSTOMER IS ALWAYS RIGHT! PEOPLE WANT MORE OF WHAT THEY ALREADY KNOW THEY LIKE, SO POPULAR ART GIVES IT TO 'EM!
AND HOW ARE THE MOVIE SEQUELS THIS SUMMER?
GREAT! MAN, THERE'S NOTHING I HATE MORE THAN PAYING FIVE BUCKS AND HAVING TO DEAL WITH SOME NEW PLOT.

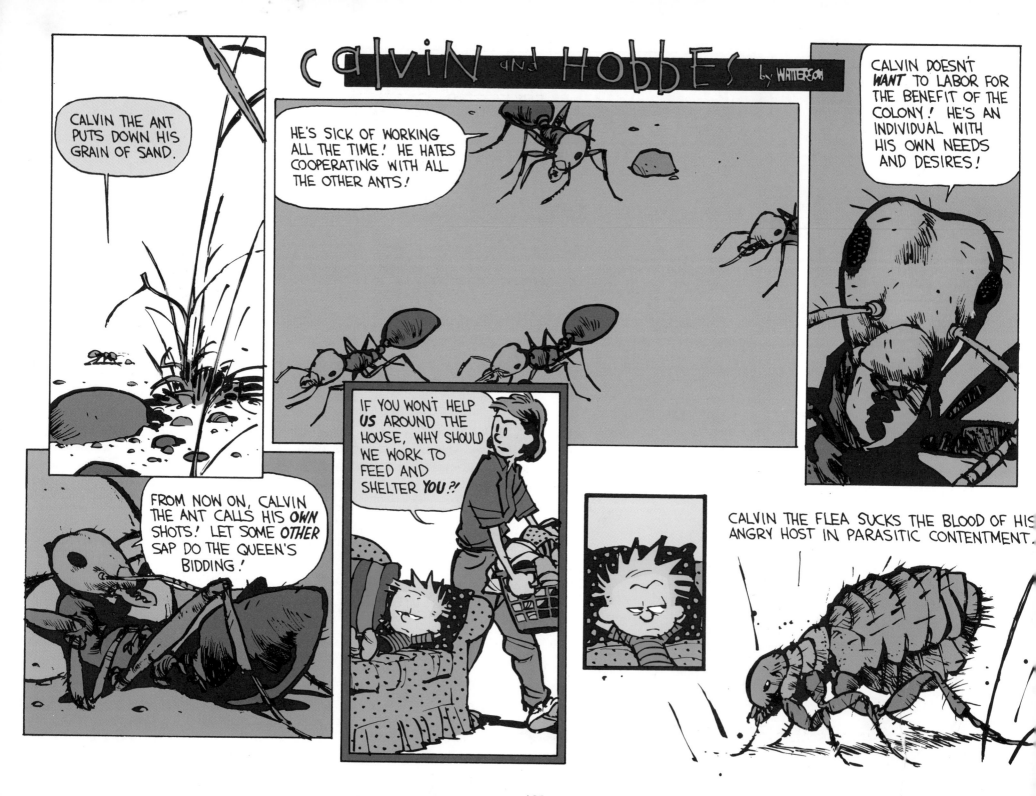

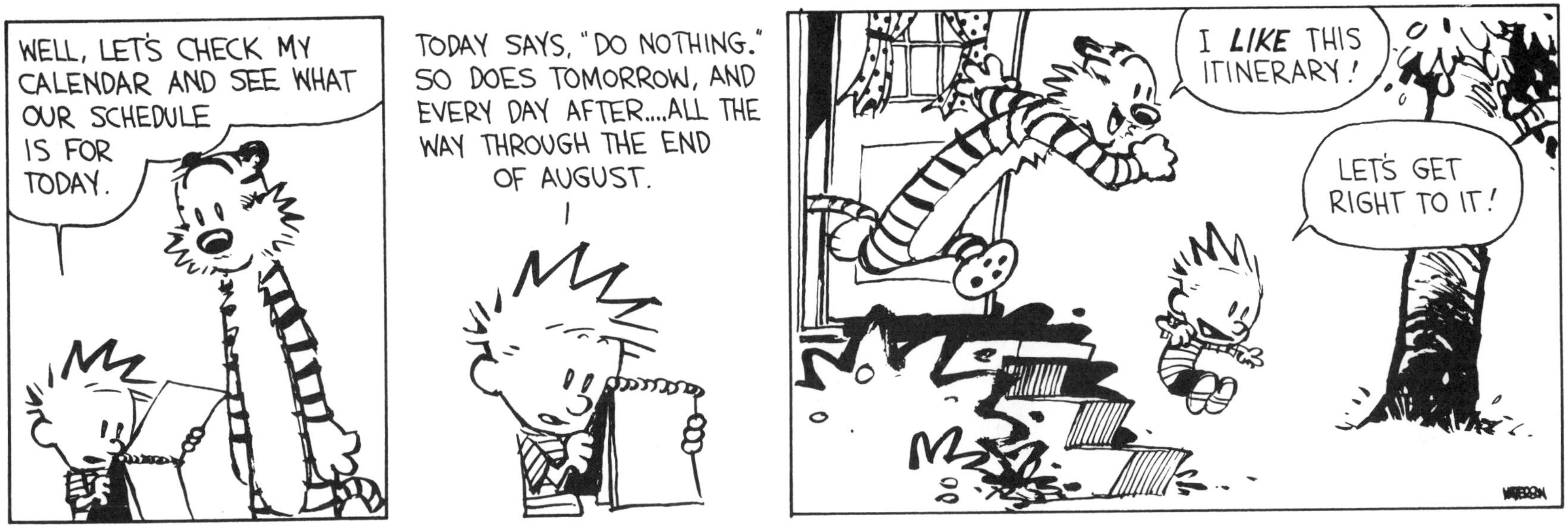
WELL, LET'S CHECK MY CALENDAR AND SEE WHAT OUR SCHEDULE IS FOR TODAY.
TODAY SAYS, "DO NOTHING." SO DOES TOMORROW, AND EVERY DAY AFTER....ALL THE WAY THROUGH THE END OF AUGUST.
I **LIKE** THIS ITINERARY!
LET'S GET RIGHT TO IT!

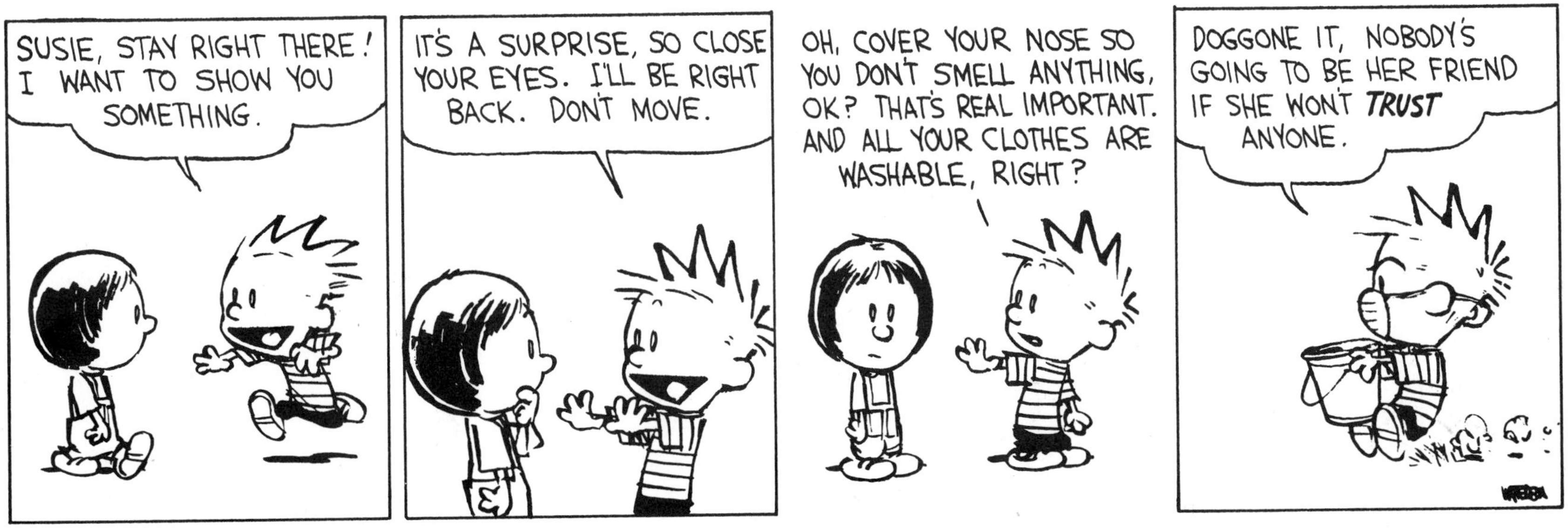
SUSIE, STAY RIGHT THERE! I WANT TO SHOW YOU SOMETHING.
IT'S A SURPRISE, SO CLOSE YOUR EYES. I'LL BE RIGHT BACK. DON'T MOVE.
OH, COVER YOUR NOSE SO YOU DON'T SMELL ANYTHING, OK? THAT'S REAL IMPORTANT. AND ALL YOUR CLOTHES ARE WASHABLE, RIGHT?
DOGGONE IT, NOBODY'S GOING TO BE HER FRIEND IF SHE WON'T ***TRUST*** ANYONE.

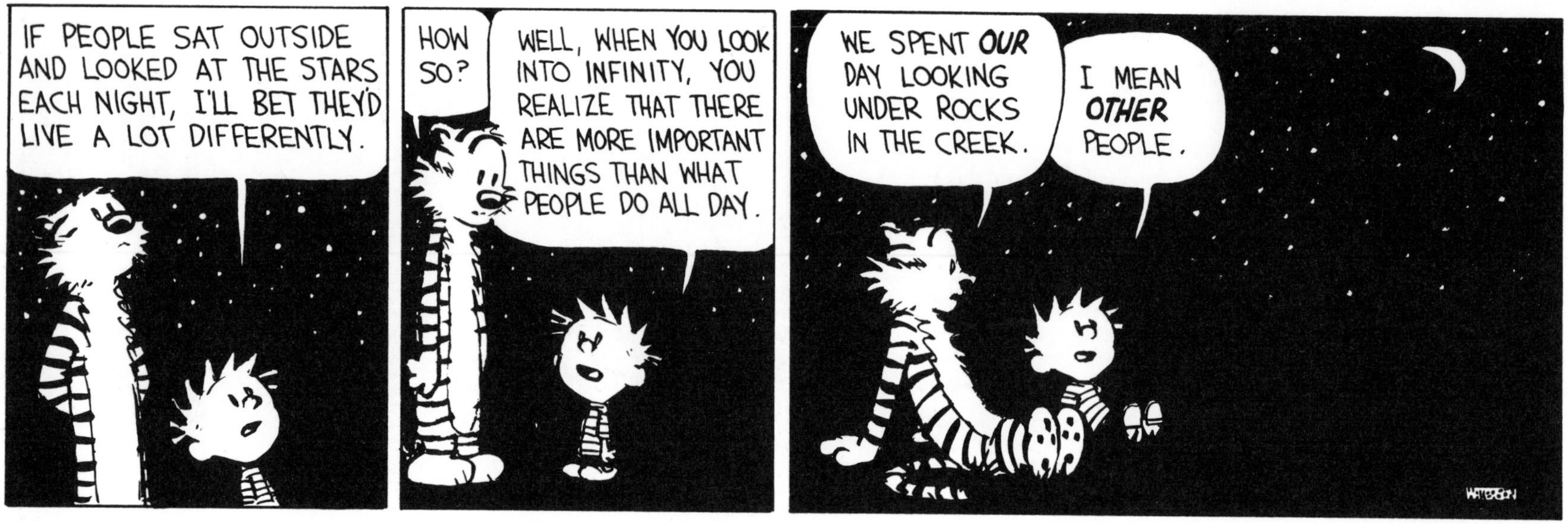
IF PEOPLE SAT OUTSIDE AND LOOKED AT THE STARS EACH NIGHT, I'LL BET THEY'D LIVE A LOT DIFFERENTLY.
HOW SO?
WELL, WHEN YOU LOOK INTO INFINITY, YOU REALIZE THAT THERE ARE MORE IMPORTANT THINGS THAN WHAT PEOPLE DO ALL DAY.
WE SPENT OUR DAY LOOKING UNDER ROCKS IN THE CREEK.
I MEAN OTHER PEOPLE.
WATTERSON

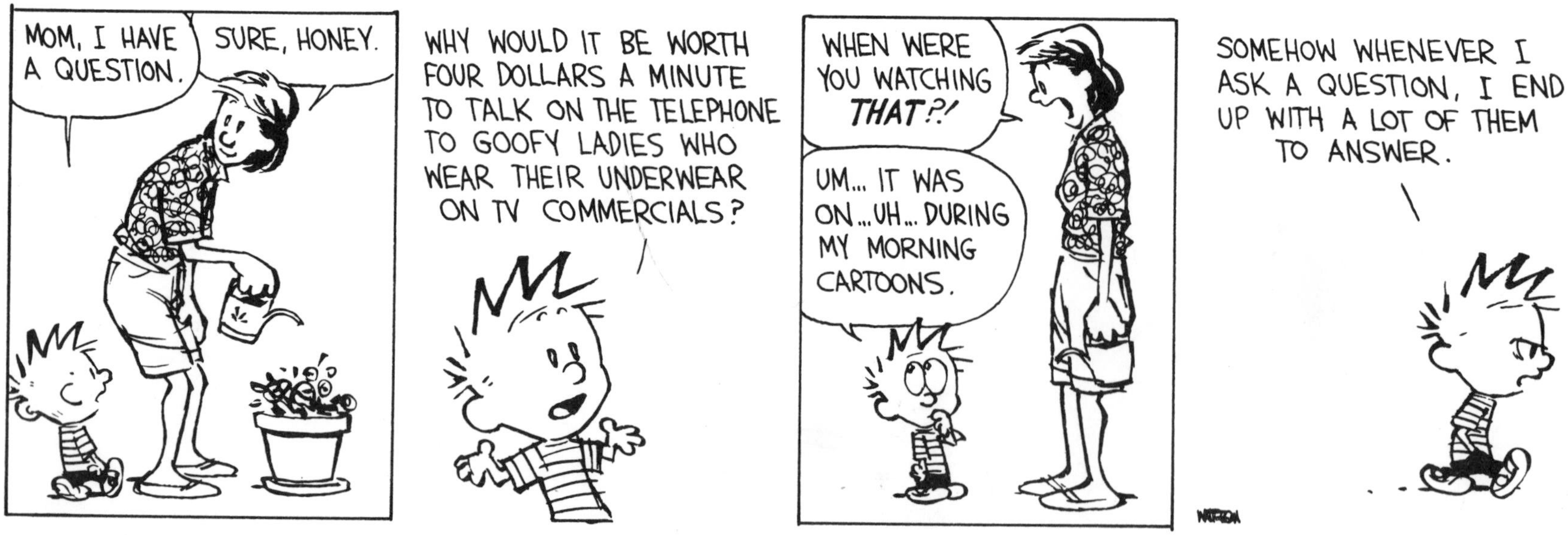
MOM, I HAVE A QUESTION.
SURE, HONEY.
WHY WOULD IT BE WORTH FOUR DOLLARS A MINUTE TO TALK ON THE TELEPHONE TO GOOFY LADIES WHO WEAR THEIR UNDERWEAR ON TV COMMERCIALS?
WHEN WERE YOU WATCHING THAT?!
UM... IT WAS ON... UH... DURING MY MORNING CARTOONS.
SOMEHOW WHENEVER I ASK A QUESTION, I END UP WITH A LOT OF THEM TO ANSWER.

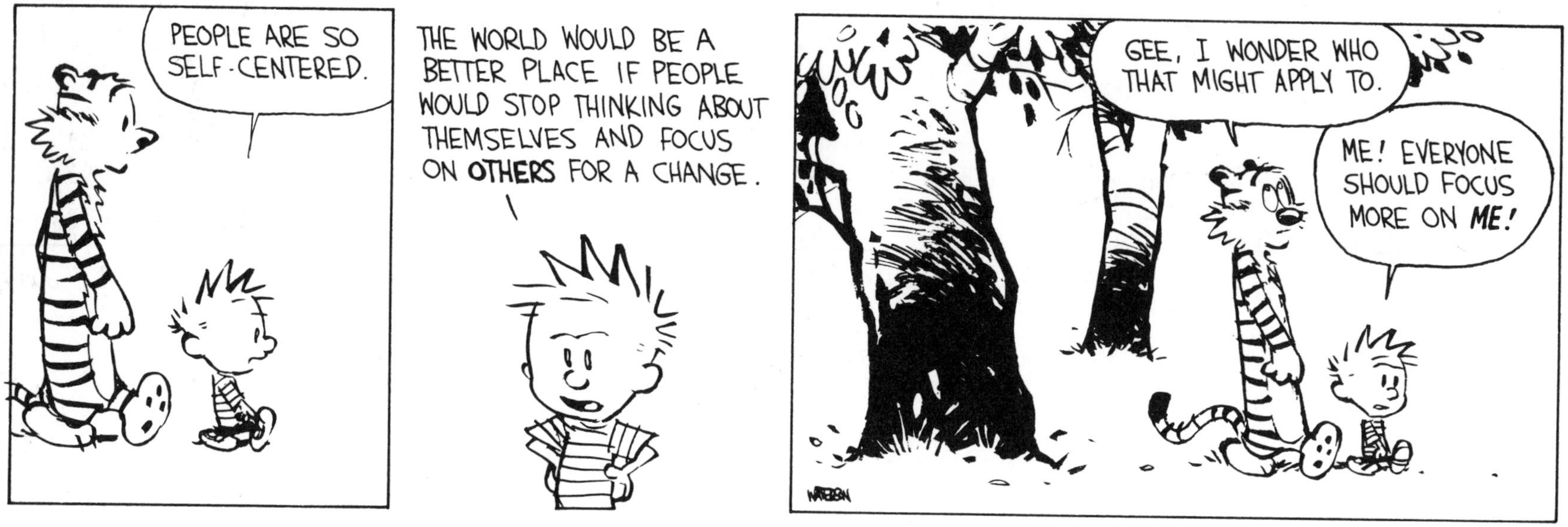
PEOPLE ARE SO SELF-CENTERED.
THE WORLD WOULD BE A BETTER PLACE IF PEOPLE WOULD STOP THINKING ABOUT THEMSELVES AND FOCUS ON **OTHERS** FOR A CHANGE.
GEE, I WONDER WHO THAT MIGHT APPLY TO.
ME! EVERYONE SHOULD FOCUS MORE ON ***ME!***
WATERSON

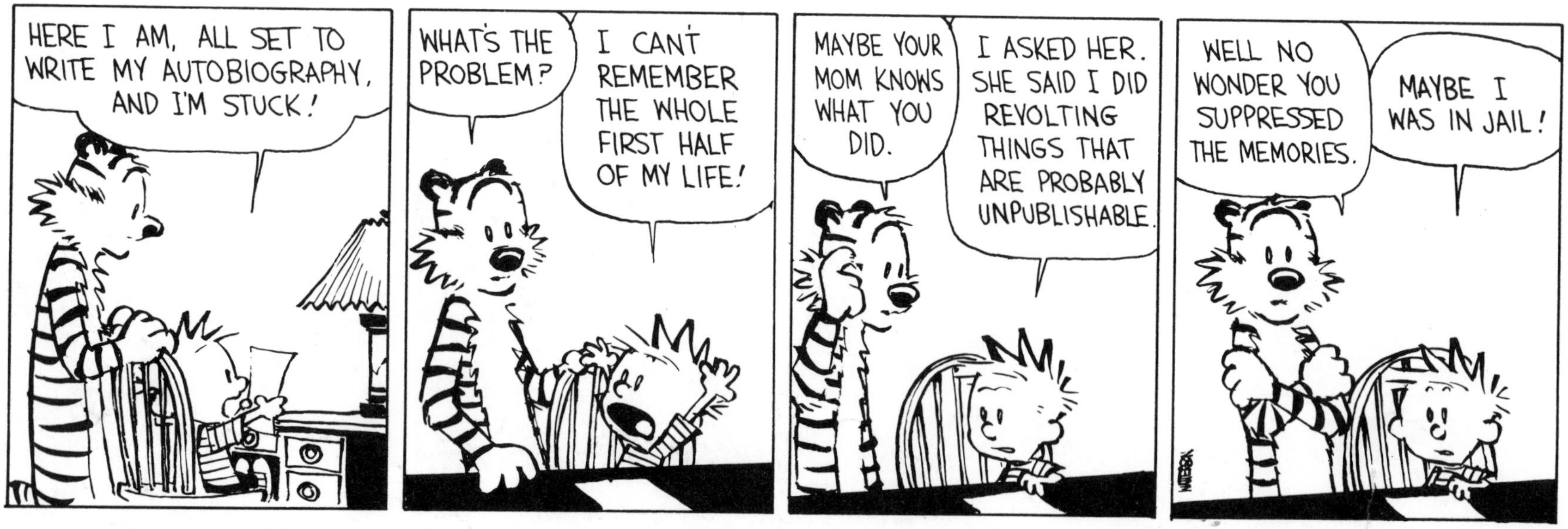
HERE I AM, ALL SET TO WRITE MY AUTOBIOGRAPHY, AND I'M STUCK!
WHAT'S THE PROBLEM?
I CAN'T REMEMBER THE WHOLE FIRST HALF OF MY LIFE!
MAYBE YOUR MOM KNOWS WHAT YOU DID.
I ASKED HER. SHE SAID I DID REVOLTING THINGS THAT ARE PROBABLY UNPUBLISHABLE.
WELL NO WONDER YOU SUPPRESSED THE MEMORIES.
MAYBE I WAS IN JAIL!
WATERSON

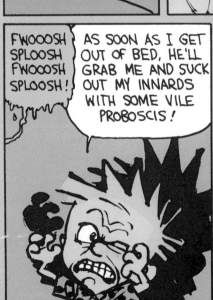

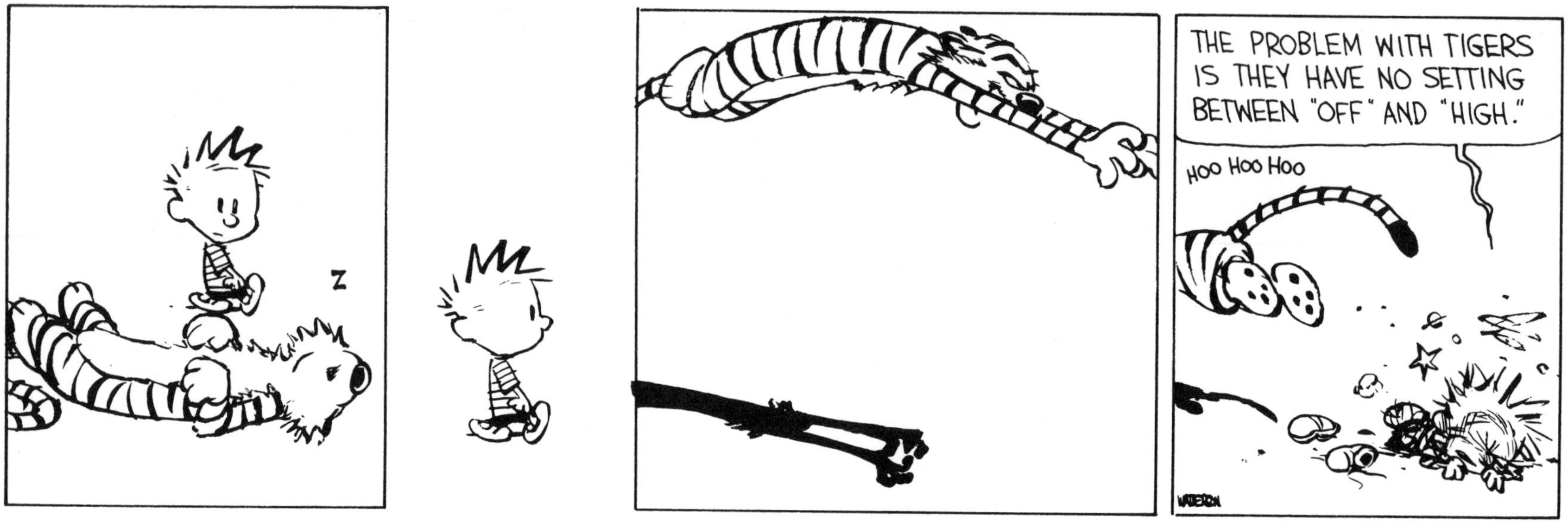
Z
THE PROBLEM WITH TIGERS IS THEY HAVE NO SETTING BETWEEN "OFF" AND "HIGH."
HOO HOO HOO

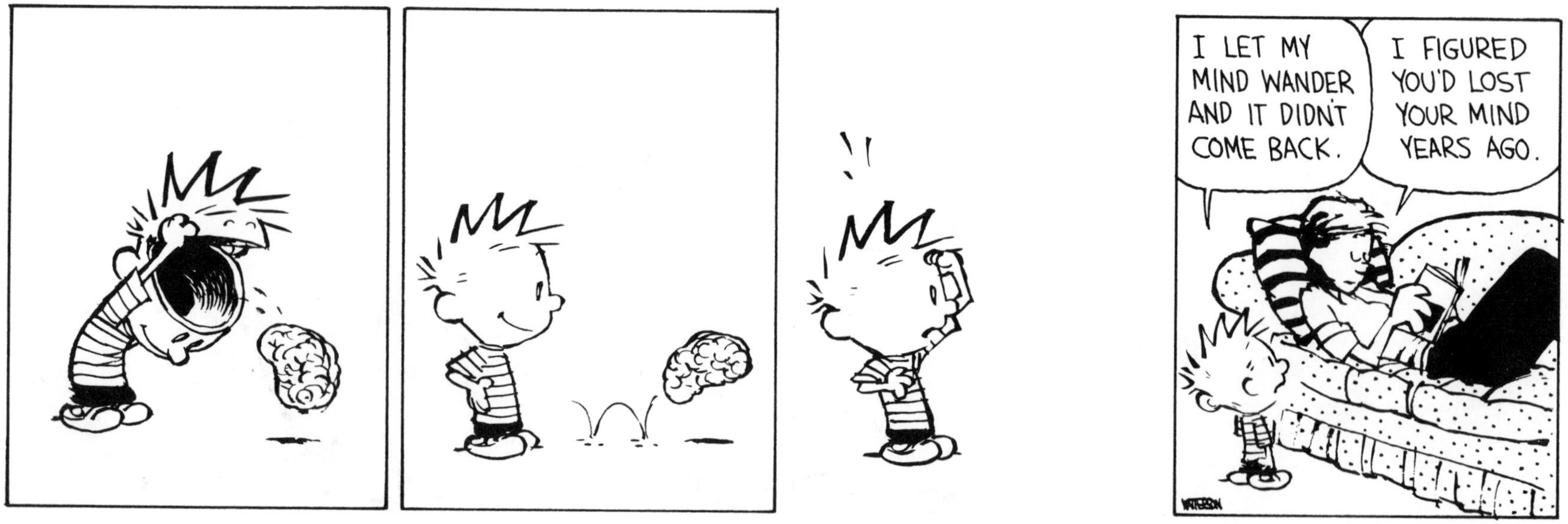
I LET MY MIND WANDER AND IT DIDN'T COME BACK.
I FIGURED YOU'D LOST YOUR MIND YEARS AGO.

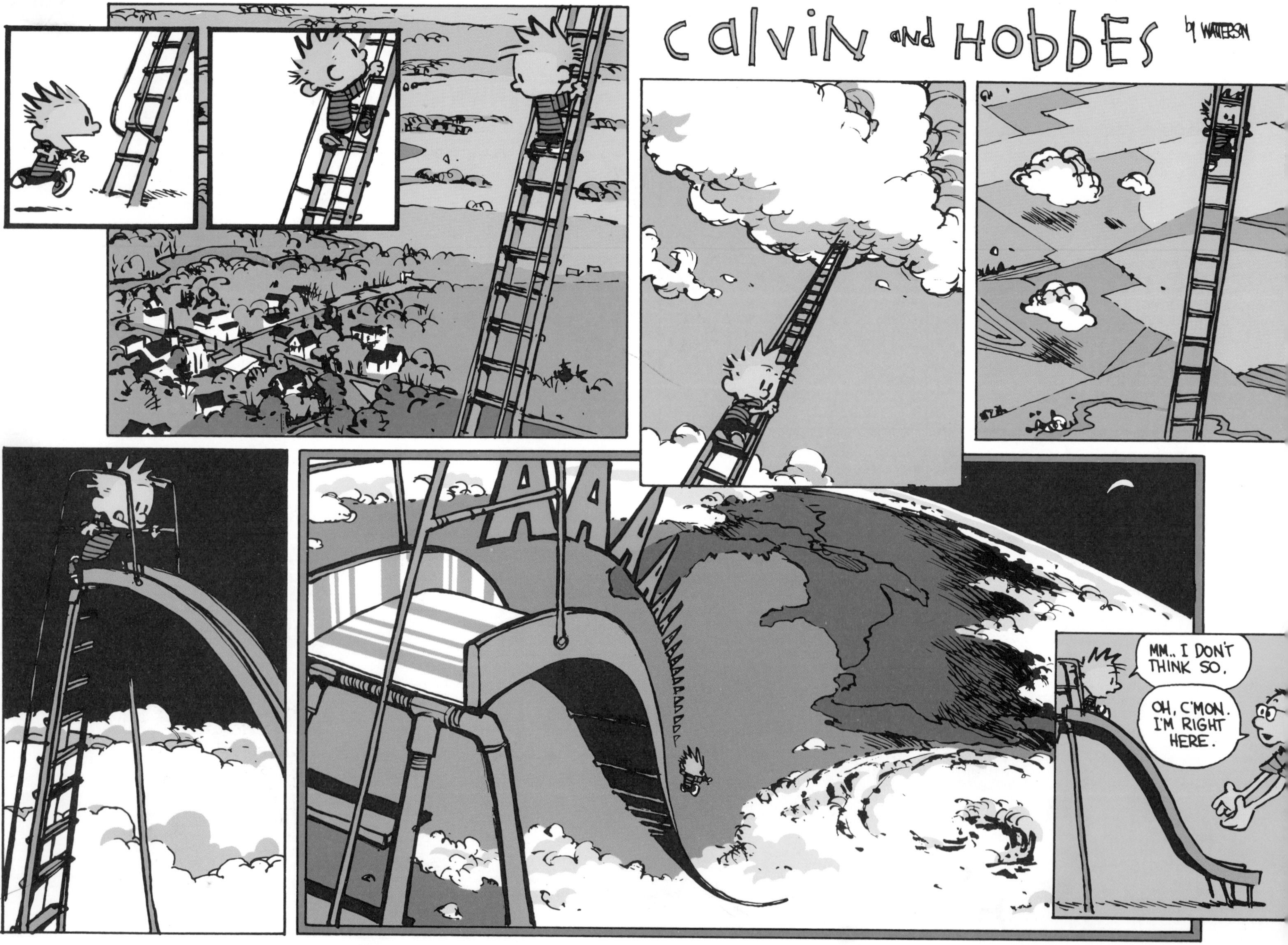
Calvin and Hobbes
by WATTERSON
MM.. I DON'T THINK SO.
OH, C'MON. I'M RIGHT HERE.

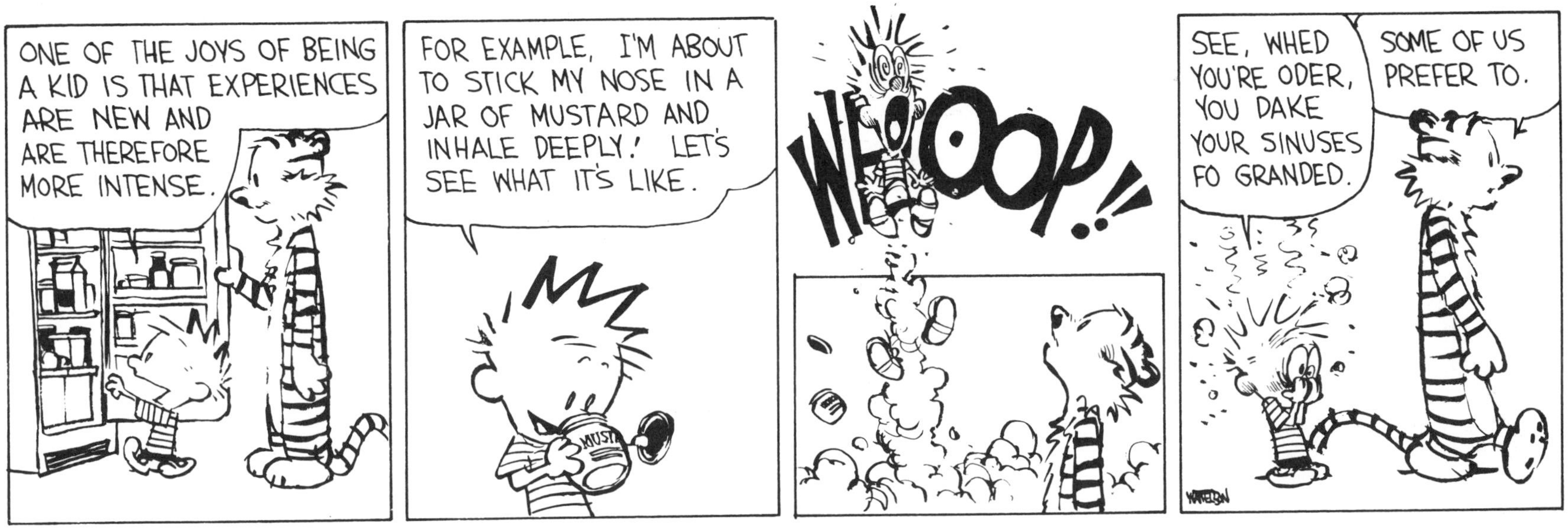
ONE OF THE JOYS OF BEING A KID IS THAT EXPERIENCES ARE NEW AND ARE THEREFORE MORE INTENSE.
FOR EXAMPLE, I'M ABOUT TO STICK MY NOSE IN A JAR OF MUSTARD AND INHALE DEEPLY! LET'S SEE WHAT IT'S LIKE.
WHOOP!!
SEE, WHED YOU'RE ODER, YOU DAKE YOUR SINUSES FO GRANDED.
SOME OF US PREFER TO.

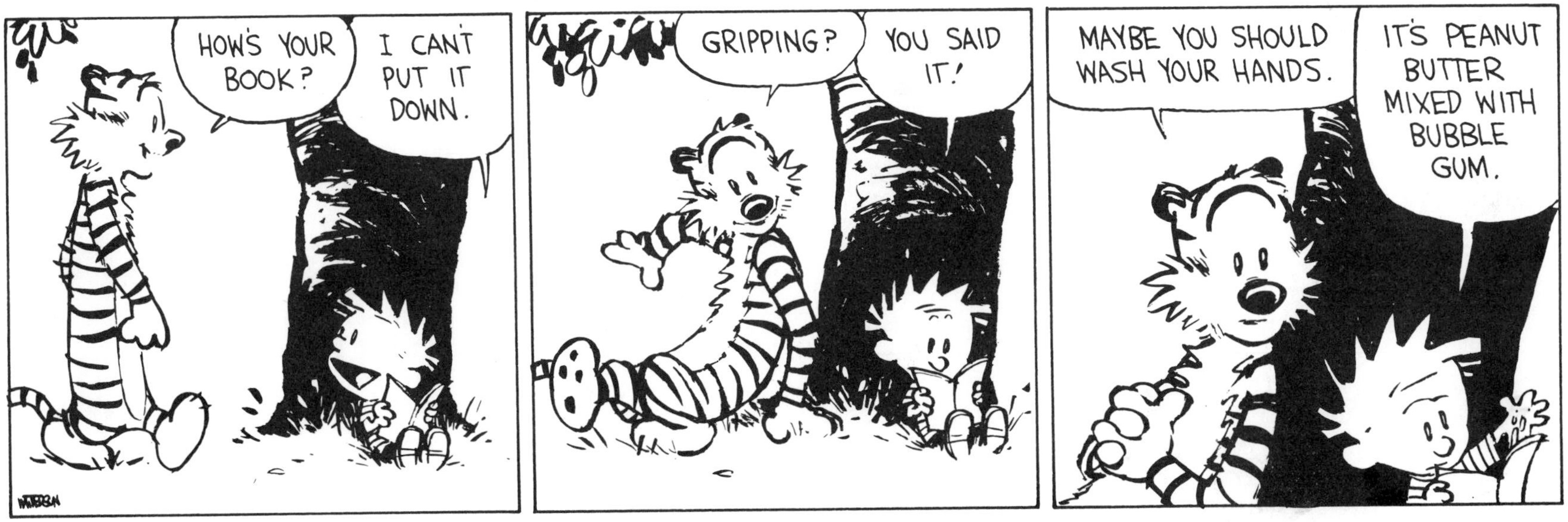
HOW'S YOUR BOOK?
I CAN'T PUT IT DOWN.
GRIPPING?
YOU SAID IT!
MAYBE YOU SHOULD WASH YOUR HANDS.
IT'S PEANUT BUTTER MIXED WITH BUBBLE GUM.

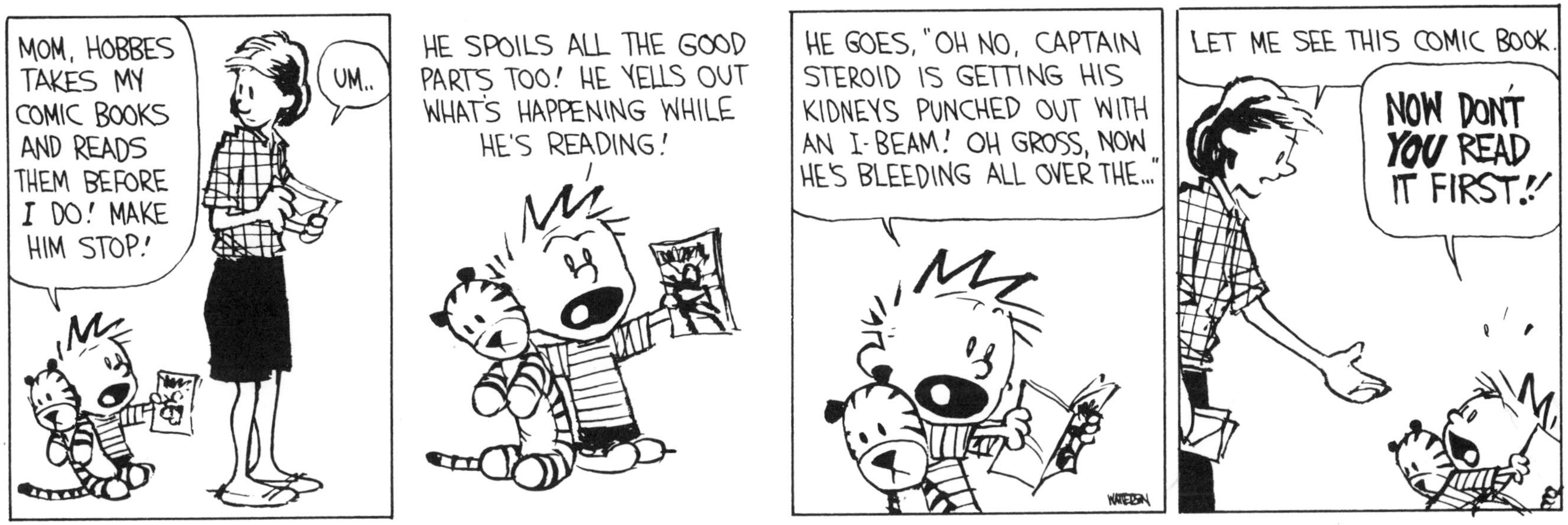
MOM, HOBBES TAKES MY COMIC BOOKS AND READS THEM BEFORE I DO! MAKE HIM STOP!
UM..
HE SPOILS ALL THE GOOD PARTS TOO! HE YELLS OUT WHAT'S HAPPENING WHILE HE'S READING!
HE GOES, "OH NO, CAPTAIN STEROID IS GETTING HIS KIDNEYS PUNCHED OUT WITH AN I-BEAM! OH GROSS, NOW HE'S BLEEDING ALL OVER THE..."
LET ME SEE THIS COMIC BOOK.
NOW DON'T YOU READ IT FIRST!!

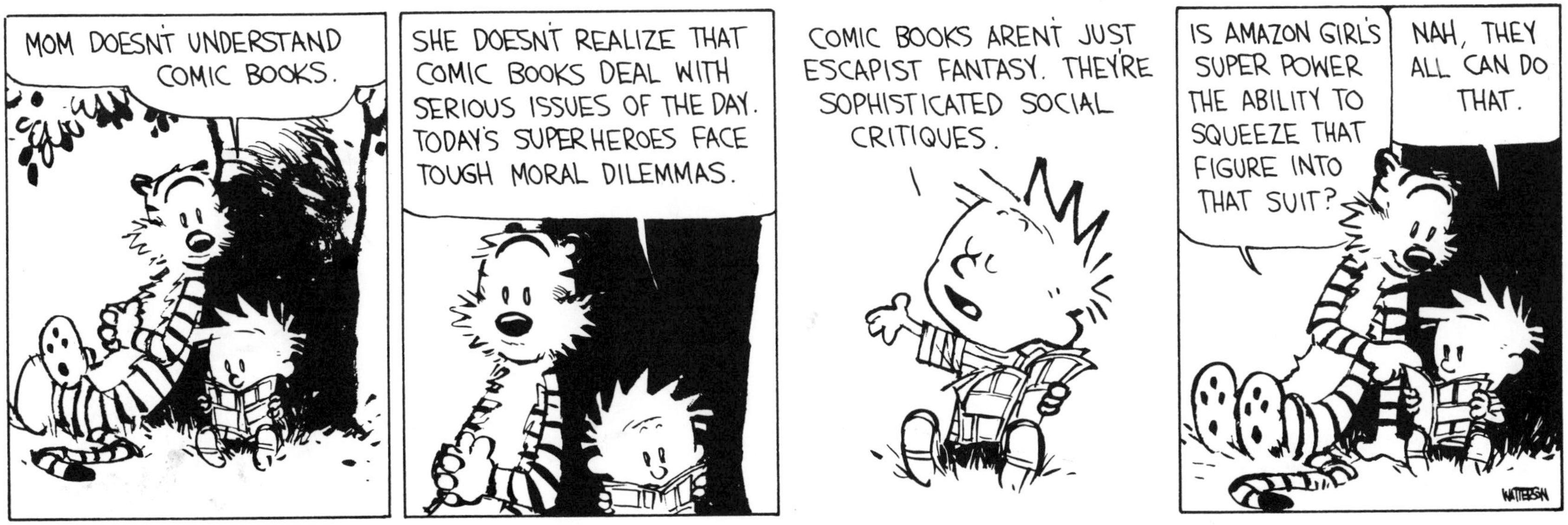
MOM DOESN'T UNDERSTAND COMIC BOOKS.
SHE DOESN'T REALIZE THAT COMIC BOOKS DEAL WITH SERIOUS ISSUES OF THE DAY. TODAY'S SUPERHEROES FACE TOUGH MORAL DILEMMAS.
COMIC BOOKS AREN'T JUST ESCAPIST FANTASY. THEY'RE SOPHISTICATED SOCIAL CRITIQUES.
IS AMAZON GIRL'S SUPER POWER THE ABILITY TO SQUEEZE THAT FIGURE INTO THAT SUIT?
NAH, THEY ALL CAN DO THAT.

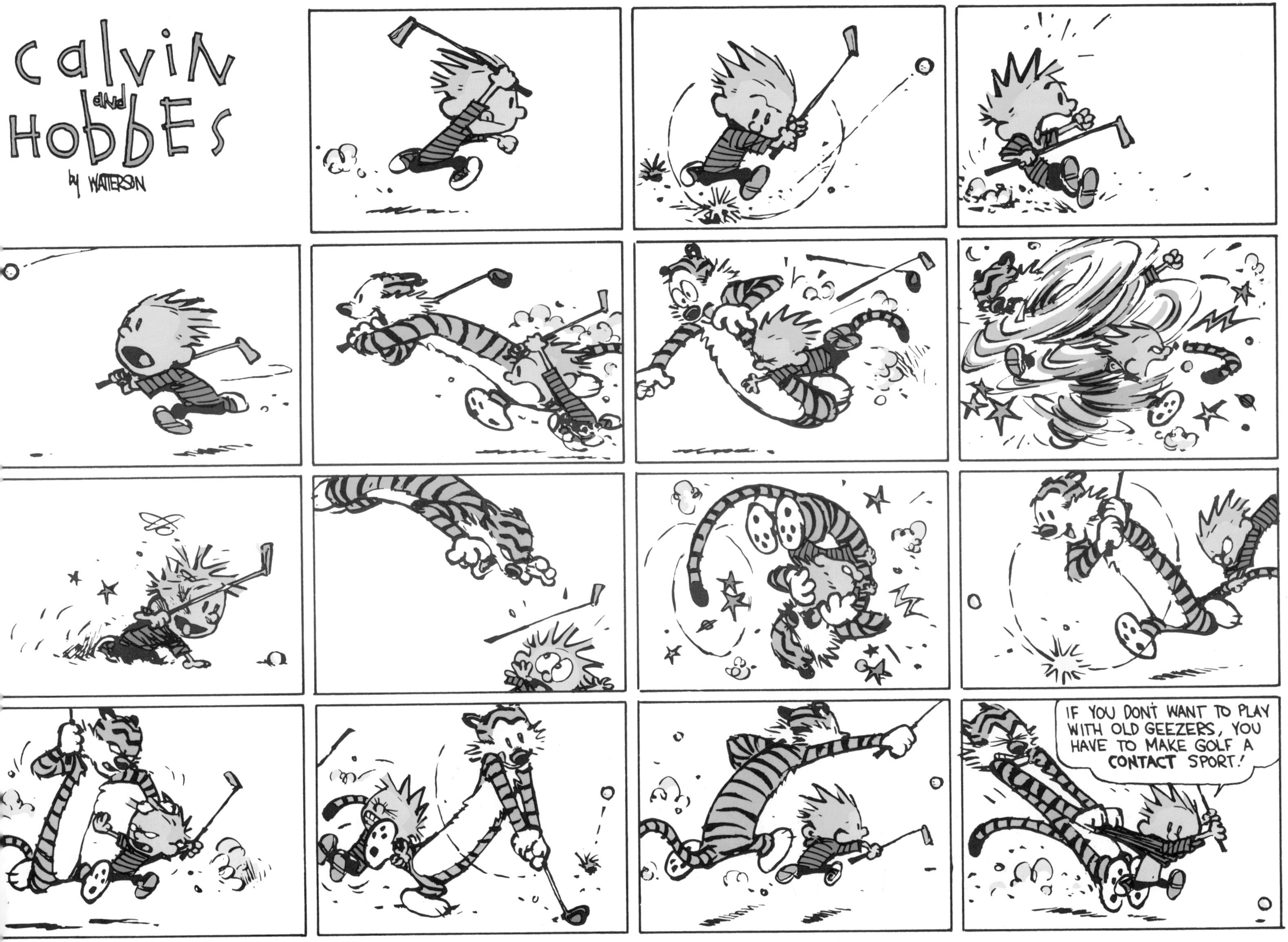
Calvin and Hobbes
by WATTERSON
IF YOU DON'T WANT TO PLAY WITH OLD GEEZERS, YOU HAVE TO MAKE GOLF A **CONTACT** SPORT!

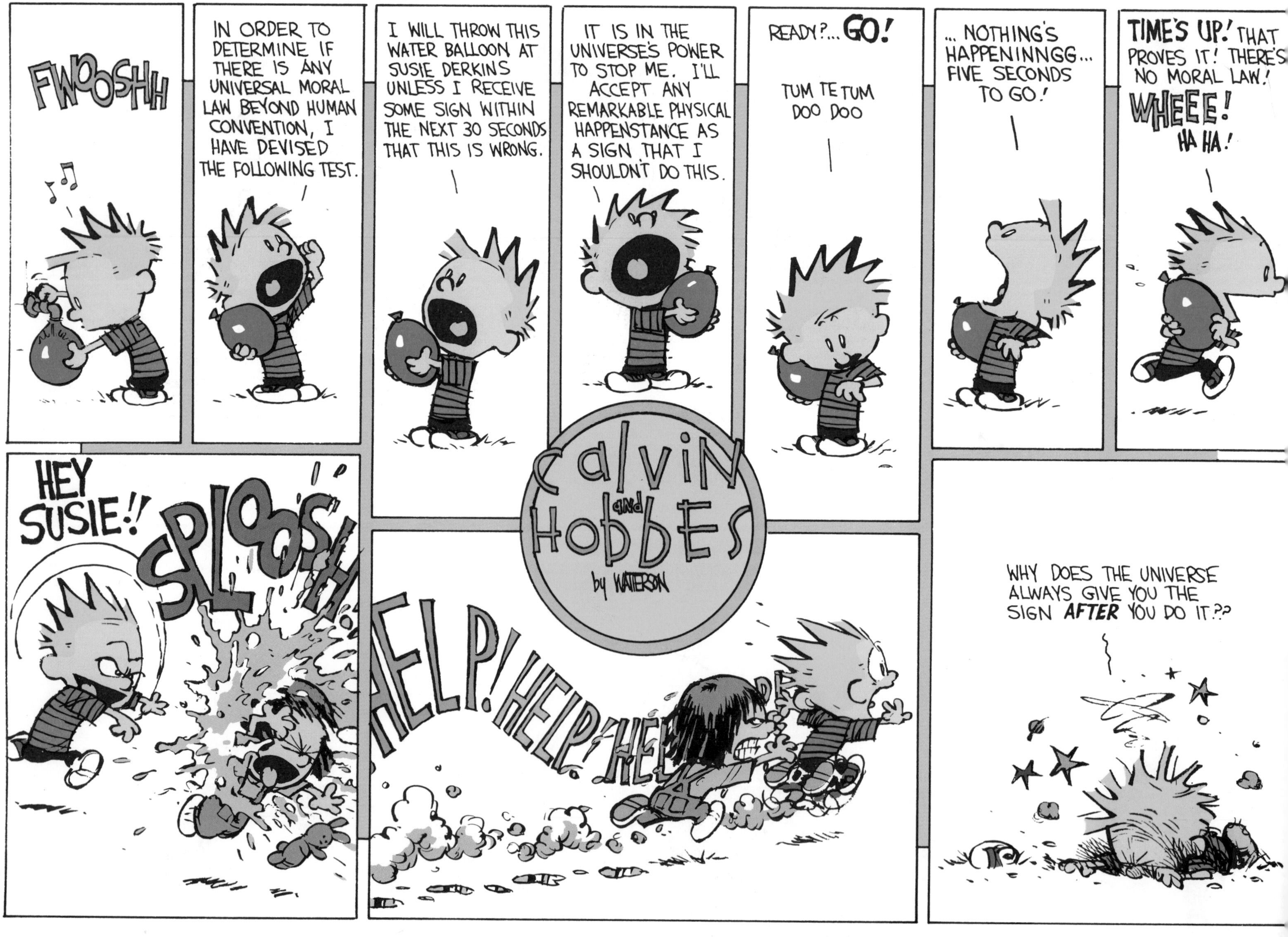

FWOOSHH
IN ORDER TO DETERMINE IF THERE IS ANY UNIVERSAL MORAL LAW BEYOND HUMAN CONVENTION, I HAVE DEVISED THE FOLLOWING TEST.
I WILL THROW THIS WATER BALLOON AT SUSIE DERKINS UNLESS I RECEIVE SOME SIGN WITHIN THE NEXT 30 SECONDS THAT THIS IS WRONG.
IT IS IN THE UNIVERSE'S POWER TO STOP ME. I'LL ACCEPT ANY REMARKABLE PHYSICAL HAPPENSTANCE AS A SIGN THAT I SHOULDN'T DO THIS.
READY?... GO!
TUM TE TUM DOO DOO
... NOTHING'S HAPPENINNGG... FIVE SECONDS TO GO!
TIME'S UP! THAT PROVES IT! THERE'S NO MORAL LAW! WHEEE! HA HA!
Calvin and Hobbes
by WATTERSON
HEY SUSIE!!
SPLOOSH
HELP! HELP! HEL
WHY DOES THE UNIVERSE ALWAYS GIVE YOU THE SIGN AFTER YOU DO IT??

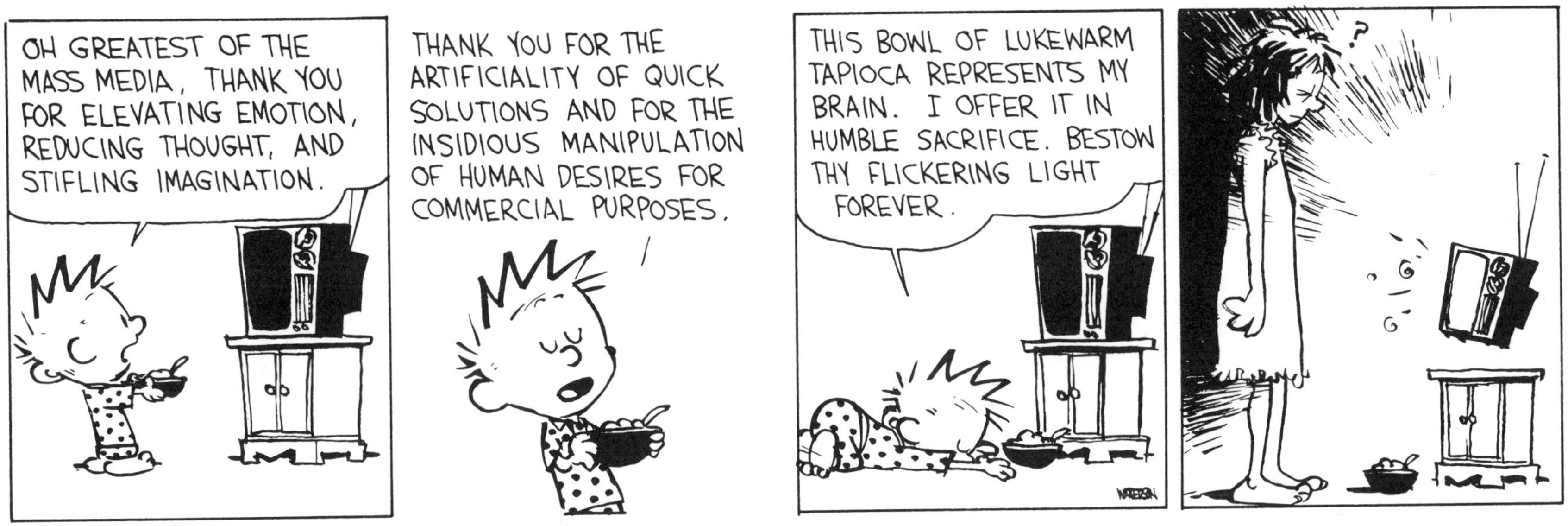
OH GREATEST OF THE MASS MEDIA, THANK YOU FOR ELEVATING EMOTION, REDUCING THOUGHT, AND STIFLING IMAGINATION.
THANK YOU FOR THE ARTIFICIALITY OF QUICK SOLUTIONS AND FOR THE INSIDIOUS MANIPULATION OF HUMAN DESIRES FOR COMMERCIAL PURPOSES.
THIS BOWL OF LUKEWARM TAPIOCA REPRESENTS MY BRAIN. I OFFER IT IN HUMBLE SACRIFICE. BESTOW THY FLICKERING LIGHT FOREVER.
?

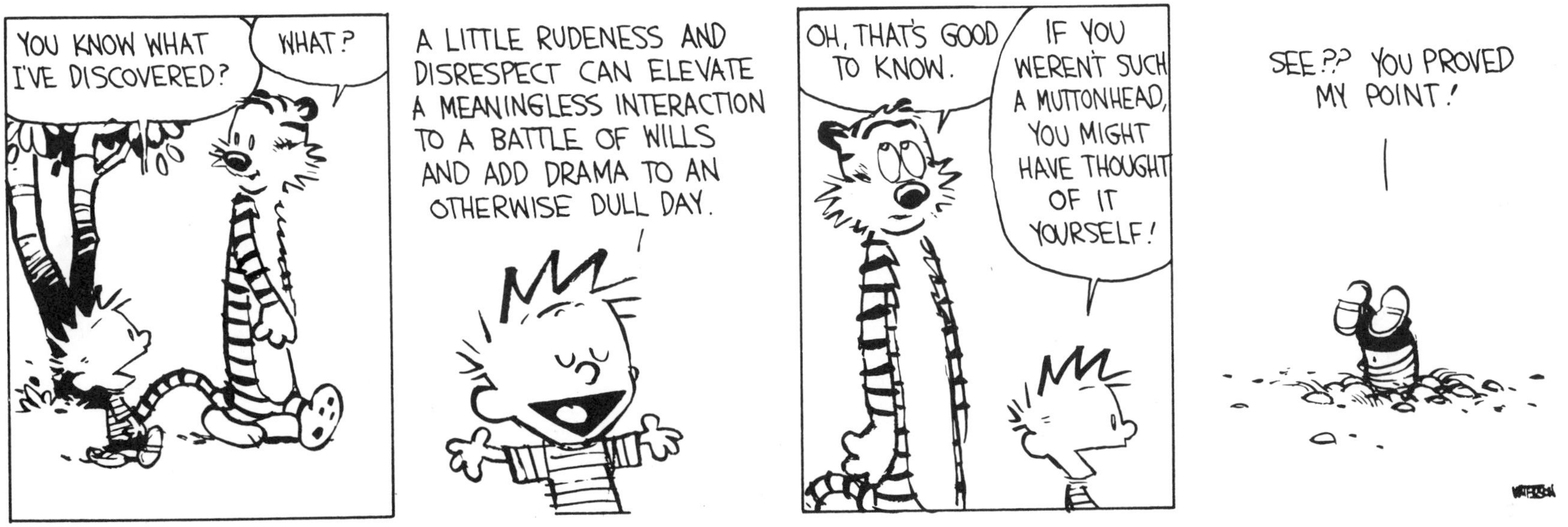
YOU KNOW WHAT I'VE DISCOVERED?
WHAT?
A LITTLE RUDENESS AND DISRESPECT CAN ELEVATE A MEANINGLESS INTERACTION TO A BATTLE OF WILLS AND ADD DRAMA TO AN OTHERWISE DULL DAY.
OH, THAT'S GOOD TO KNOW.
IF YOU WEREN'T SUCH A MUTTONHEAD, YOU MIGHT HAVE THOUGHT OF IT YOURSELF!
SEE?? YOU PROVED MY POINT!

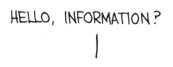

126

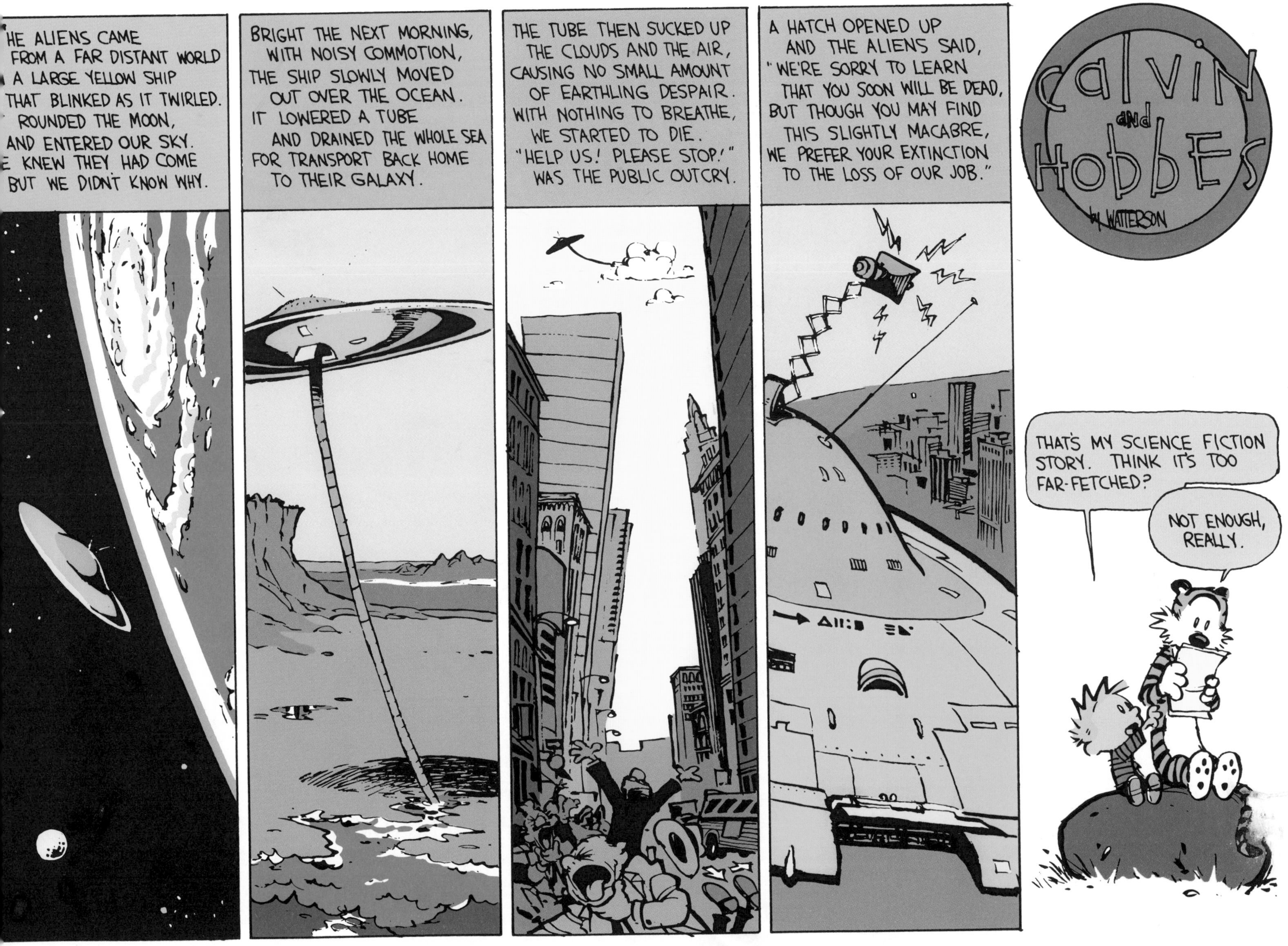
HE ALIENS CAME
FROM A FAR DISTANT WORLD
A LARGE YELLOW SHIP
THAT BLINKED AS IT TWIRLED.
ROUNDED THE MOON,
AND ENTERED OUR SKY.
E KNEW THEY HAD COME
BUT WE DIDN'T KNOW WHY.
BRIGHT THE NEXT MORNING, WITH NOISY COMMOTION, THE SHIP SLOWLY MOVED OUT OVER THE OCEAN. IT LOWERED A TUBE AND DRAINED THE WHOLE SEA FOR TRANSPORT BACK HOME TO THEIR GALAXY.
THE TUBE THEN SUCKED UP THE CLOUDS AND THE AIR, CAUSING NO SMALL AMOUNT OF EARTHLING DESPAIR. WITH NOTHING TO BREATHE, WE STARTED TO DIE. "HELP US! PLEASE STOP!" WAS THE PUBLIC OUTCRY.
A HATCH OPENED UP AND THE ALIENS SAID, "WE'RE SORRY TO LEARN THAT YOU SOON WILL BE DEAD, BUT THOUGH YOU MAY FIND THIS SLIGHTLY MACABRE, WE PREFER YOUR EXTINCTION TO THE LOSS OF OUR JOB."
Calvin and Hobbes
by WATTERSON
THAT'S MY SCIENCE FICTION STORY. THINK IT'S TOO FAR-FETCHED?
NOT ENOUGH, REALLY.

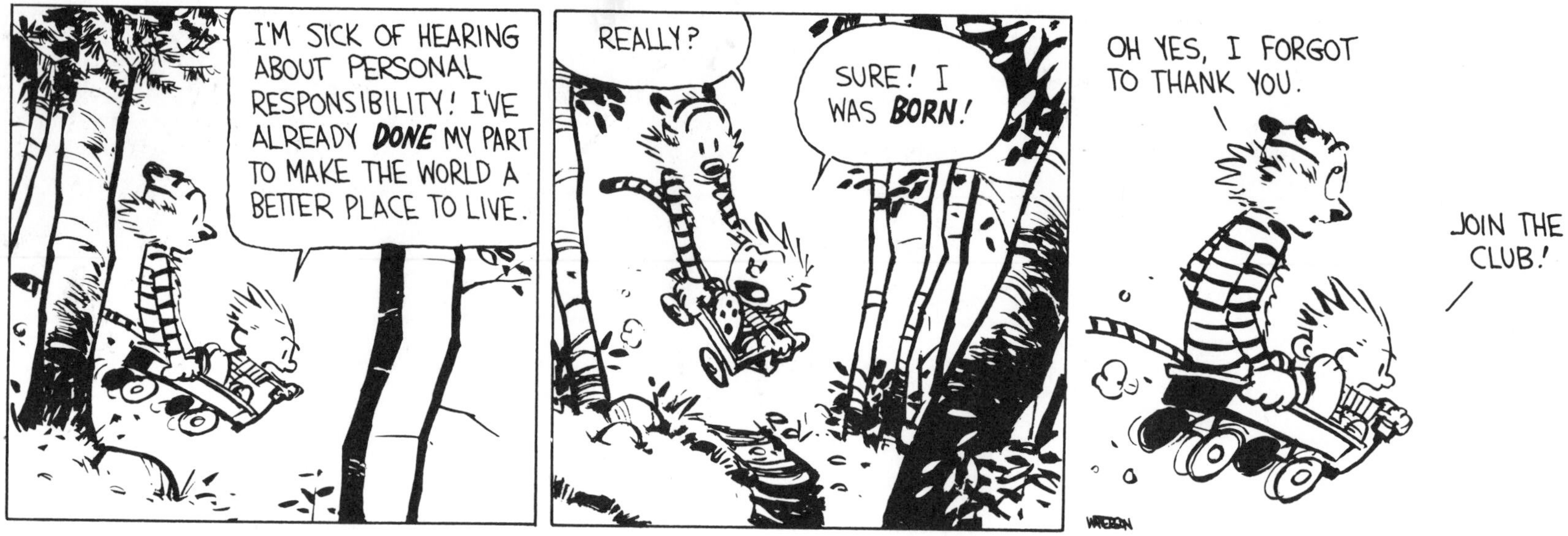
I'M SICK OF HEARING ABOUT PERSONAL RESPONSIBILITY! I'VE ALREADY **DONE** MY PART TO MAKE THE WORLD A BETTER PLACE TO LIVE.
REALLY?
SURE! I WAS **BORN**!
OH YES, I FORGOT TO THANK YOU.
JOIN THE CLUB!

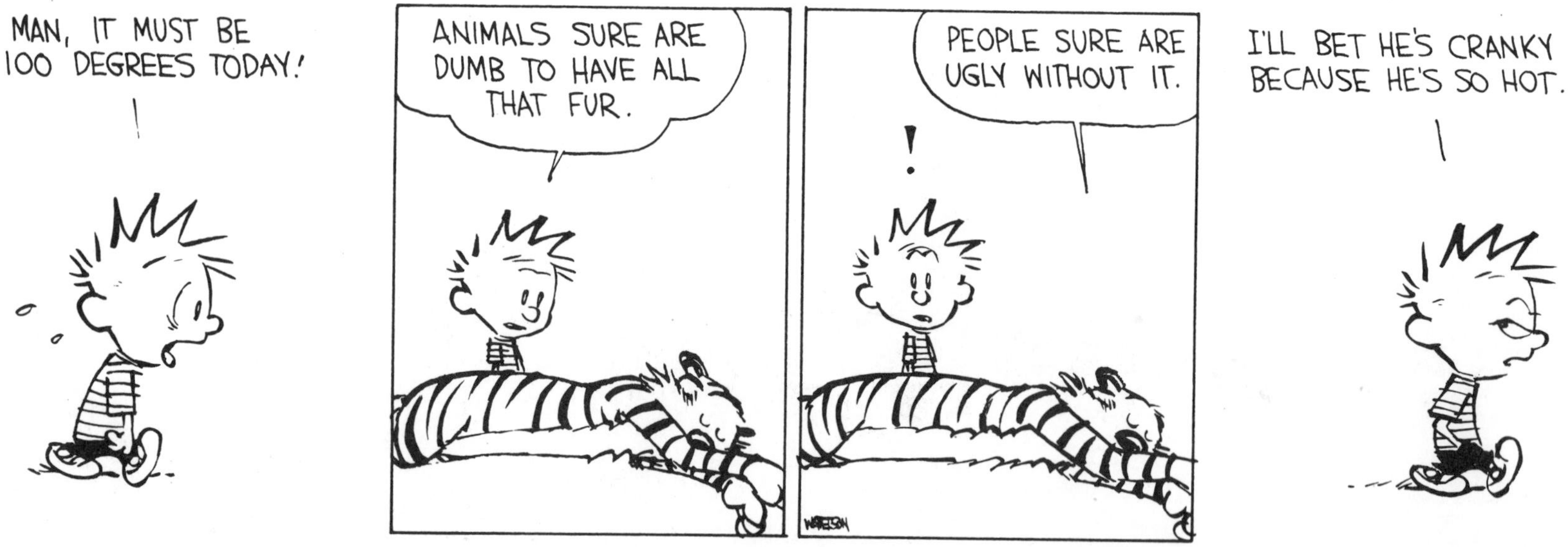
MAN, IT MUST BE 100 DEGREES TODAY!
ANIMALS SURE ARE DUMB TO HAVE ALL THAT FUR.
PEOPLE SURE ARE UGLY WITHOUT IT.
!
I'LL BET HE'S CRANKY BECAUSE HE'S SO HOT.

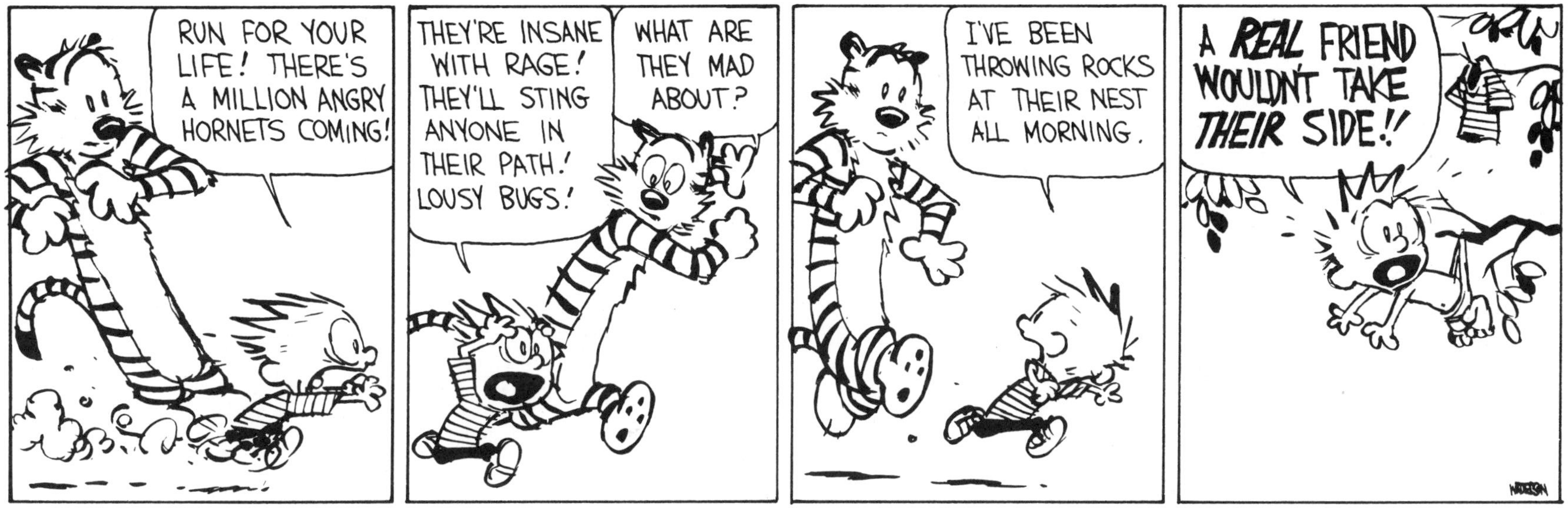
RUN FOR YOUR LIFE! THERE'S A MILLION ANGRY HORNETS COMING!
THEY'RE INSANE WITH RAGE! THEY'LL STING ANYONE IN THEIR PATH! LOUSY BUGS!
WHAT ARE THEY MAD ABOUT?
I'VE BEEN THROWING ROCKS AT THEIR NEST ALL MORNING.
A REAL FRIEND WOULDN'T TAKE THEIR SIDE!!

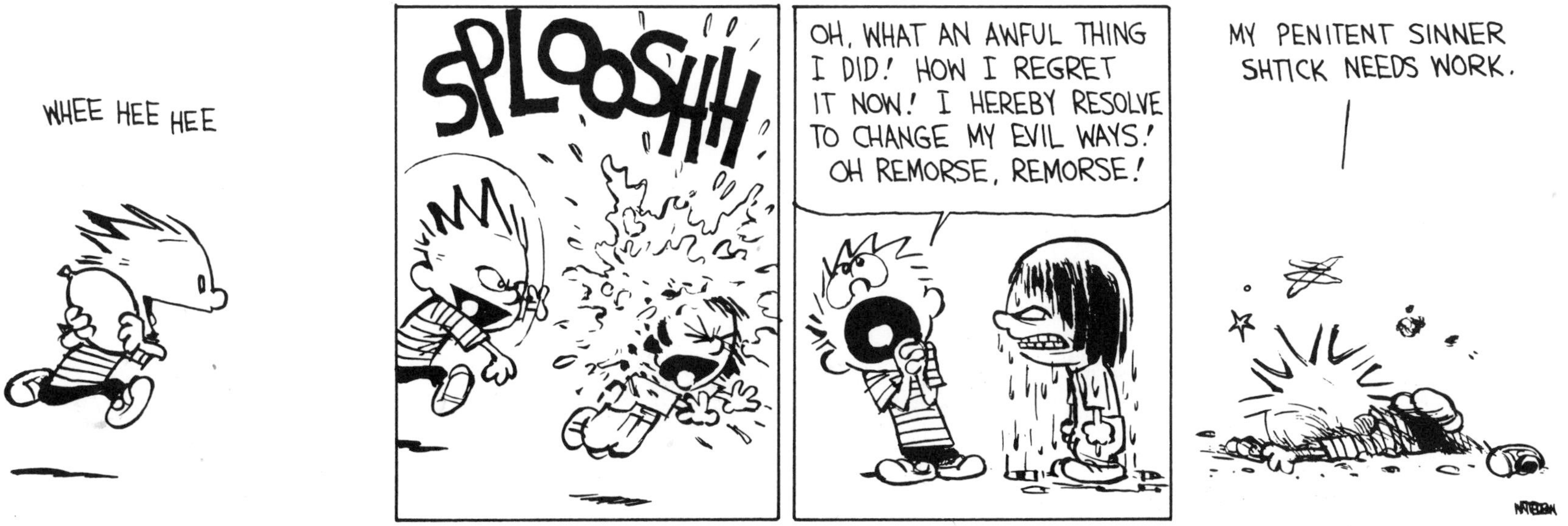
WHEE HEE HEE
SPLOOSHH
OH, WHAT AN AWFUL THING I DID! HOW I REGRET IT NOW! I HEREBY RESOLVE TO CHANGE MY EVIL WAYS! OH REMORSE, REMORSE!
MY PENITENT SINNER SHTICK NEEDS WORK.

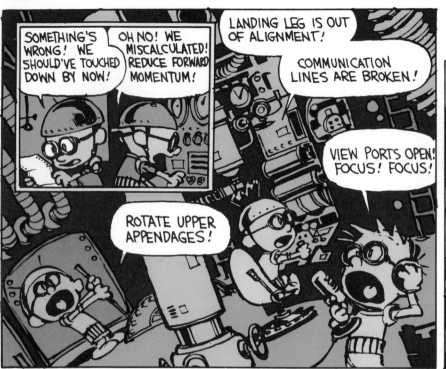

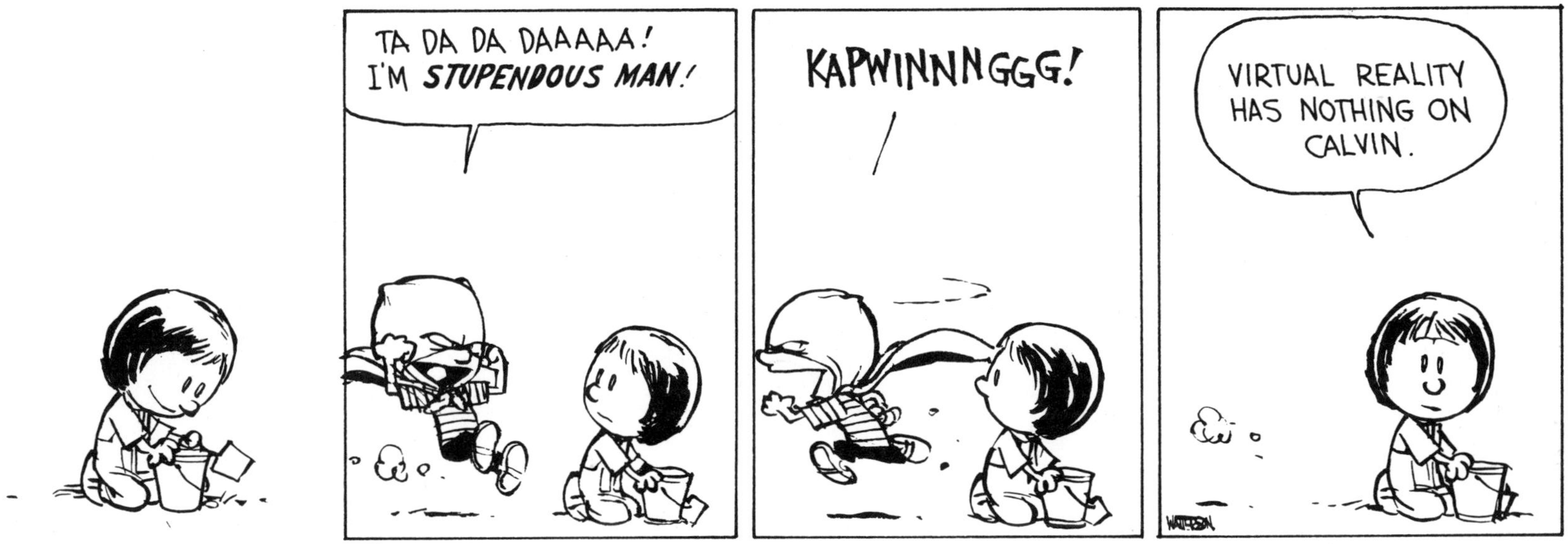
TA DA DA DAAAAA! I'M STUPENDOUS MAN!
KAPWINNNGGG!
VIRTUAL REALITY HAS NOTHING ON CALVIN.

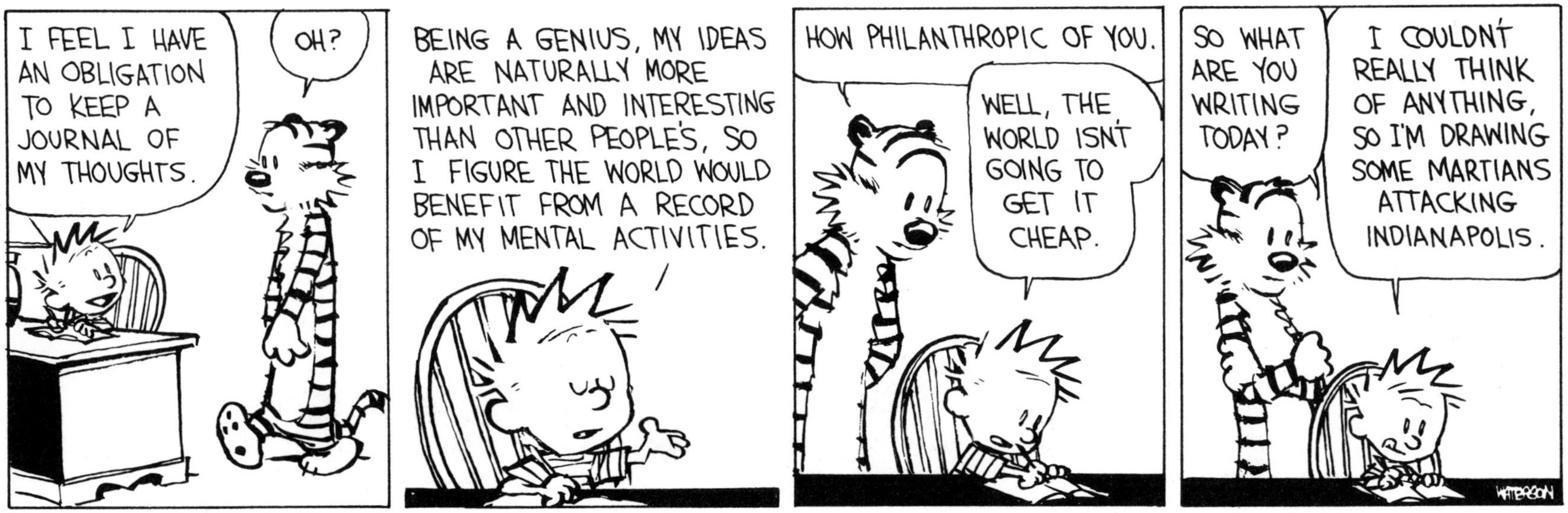
I FEEL I HAVE AN OBLIGATION TO KEEP A JOURNAL OF MY THOUGHTS.
OH?
BEING A GENIUS, MY IDEAS ARE NATURALLY MORE IMPORTANT AND INTERESTING THAN OTHER PEOPLE'S, SO I FIGURE THE WORLD WOULD BENEFIT FROM A RECORD OF MY MENTAL ACTIVITIES.
HOW PHILANTHROPIC OF YOU.
WELL, THE WORLD ISN'T GOING TO GET IT CHEAP.
SO WHAT ARE YOU WRITING TODAY?
I COULDN'T REALLY THINK OF ANYTHING, SO I'M DRAWING SOME MARTIANS ATTACKING INDIANAPOLIS.

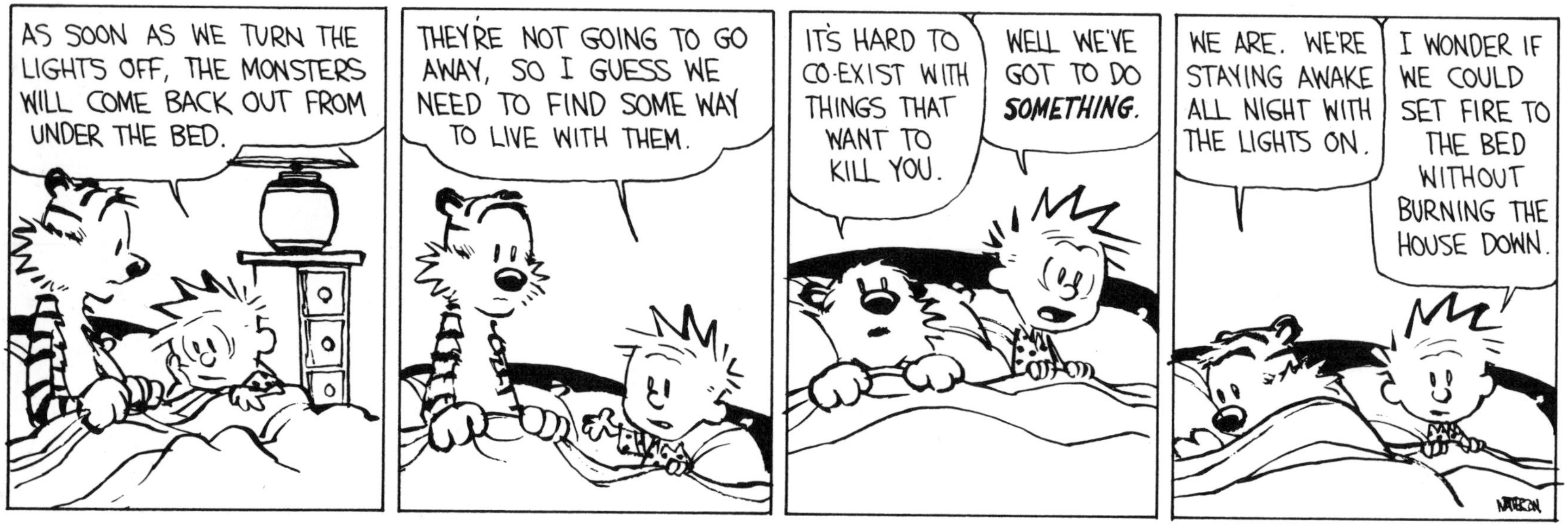
AS SOON AS WE TURN THE LIGHTS OFF, THE MONSTERS WILL COME BACK OUT FROM UNDER THE BED.
THEY'RE NOT GOING TO GO AWAY, SO I GUESS WE NEED TO FIND SOME WAY TO LIVE WITH THEM.
IT'S HARD TO CO-EXIST WITH THINGS THAT WANT TO KILL YOU.
WELL WE'VE GOT TO DO *SOMETHING*.
WE ARE. WE'RE STAYING AWAKE ALL NIGHT WITH THE LIGHTS ON.
I WONDER IF WE COULD SET FIRE TO THE BED WITHOUT BURNING THE HOUSE DOWN.

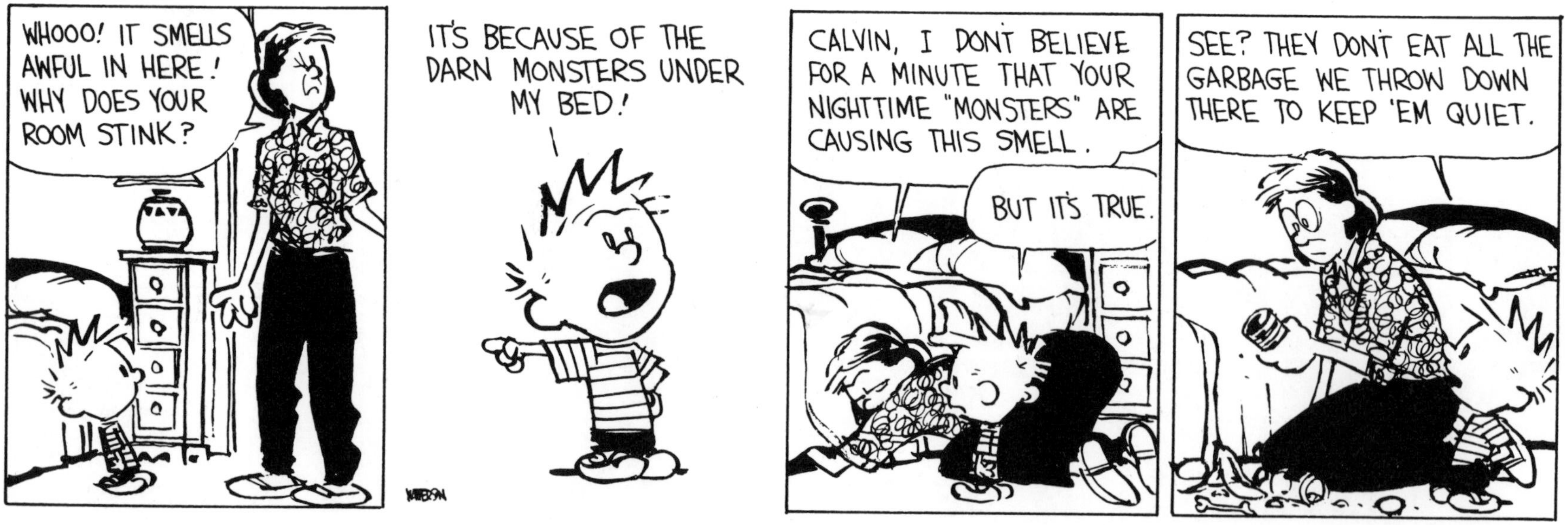
WHOOO! IT SMELLS AWFUL IN HERE! WHY DOES YOUR ROOM STINK?
IT'S BECAUSE OF THE DARN MONSTERS UNDER MY BED!
CALVIN, I DON'T BELIEVE FOR A MINUTE THAT YOUR NIGHTTIME "MONSTERS" ARE CAUSING THIS SMELL.
BUT IT'S TRUE.
SEE? THEY DON'T EAT ALL THE GARBAGE WE THROW DOWN THERE TO KEEP 'EM QUIET.

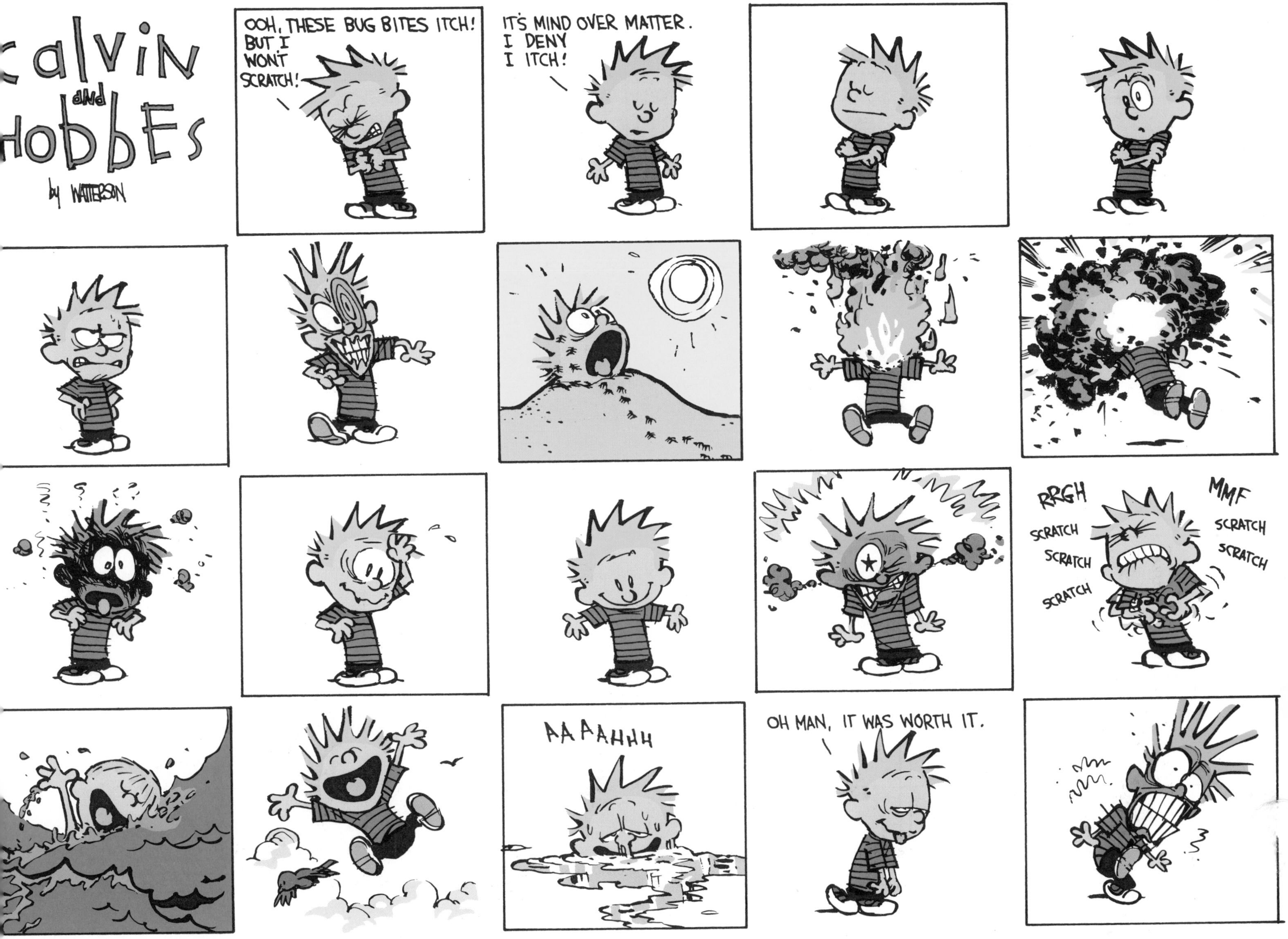
Calvin and Hobbes
by WATTERSON
OOH, THESE BUG BITES ITCH! BUT I WON'T SCRATCH!
IT'S MIND OVER MATTER. I DENY I ITCH!
RRGH
MMF
SCRATCH
SCRATCH
SCRATCH
SCRATCH
SCRATCH
AAAAHHH
OH MAN, IT WAS WORTH IT.

CALL ME CALVIN.

Actually, make that, "CALVIN, BOY GENIUS, HOPE OF MANKIND."

... OR "DOCTOR DESTINY" FOR SHORT.

(THAT'S "DOCTOR DESTINY, SIR" to YOU.)

MY JOURNAL IS OFF TO A GOOD START.

I WISH MY SHIRT HAD A LOGO OR A PRODUCT ON IT.

A GOOD SHIRT TURNS THE WEARER INTO A WALKING CORPORATE BILLBOARD!

IT SAYS TO THE WORLD, "MY IDENTITY IS SO WRAPPED UP IN WHAT I BUY THAT *I* PAID THE **COMPANY** TO ADVERTISE ITS PRODUCTS!"

YOU'D ADMIT THAT?

OH SURE. ENDORSING PRODUCTS IS THE AMERICAN WAY TO EXPRESS INDIVIDUALITY.

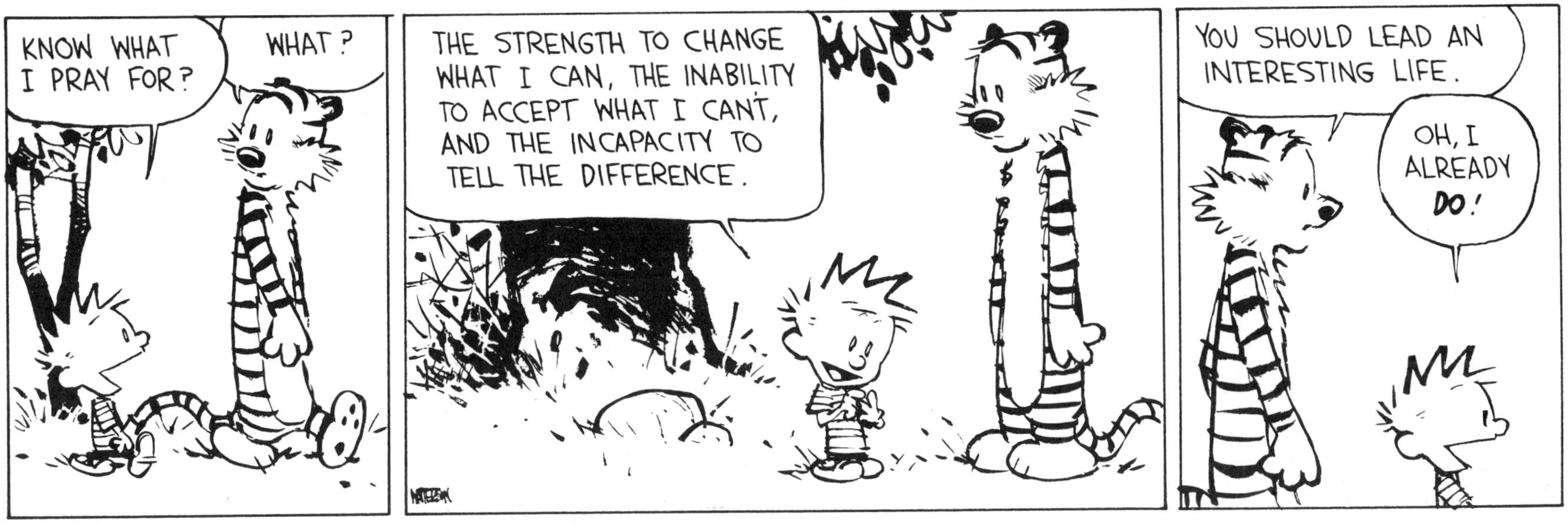
KNOW WHAT I PRAY FOR?
WHAT?
THE STRENGTH TO CHANGE WHAT I CAN, THE INABILITY TO ACCEPT WHAT I CAN'T, AND THE INCAPACITY TO TELL THE DIFFERENCE.
YOU SHOULD LEAD AN INTERESTING LIFE.
OH, I ALREADY **DO**!

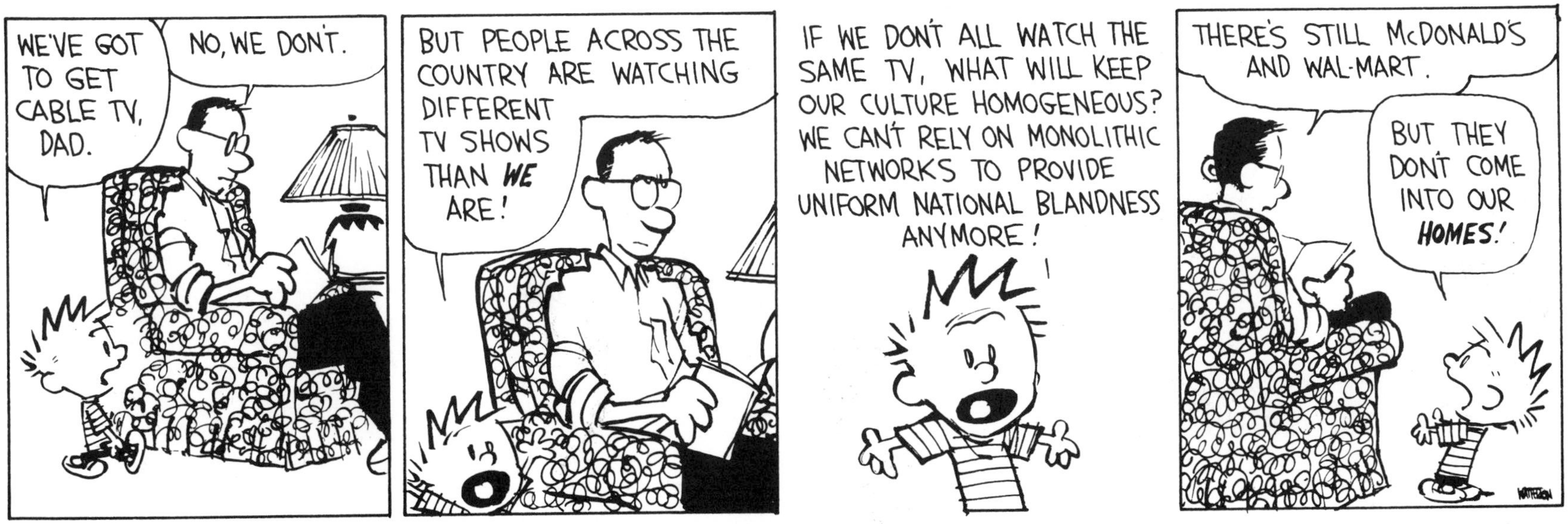
WE'VE GOT TO GET CABLE TV, DAD.
NO, WE DON'T.
BUT PEOPLE ACROSS THE COUNTRY ARE WATCHING DIFFERENT TV SHOWS THAN **WE** ARE!
IF WE DON'T ALL WATCH THE SAME TV, WHAT WILL KEEP OUR CULTURE HOMOGENEOUS? WE CAN'T RELY ON MONOLITHIC NETWORKS TO PROVIDE UNIFORM NATIONAL BLANDNESS ANYMORE!
THERE'S STILL McDONALD'S AND WAL-MART.
BUT THEY DON'T COME INTO OUR **HOMES**!

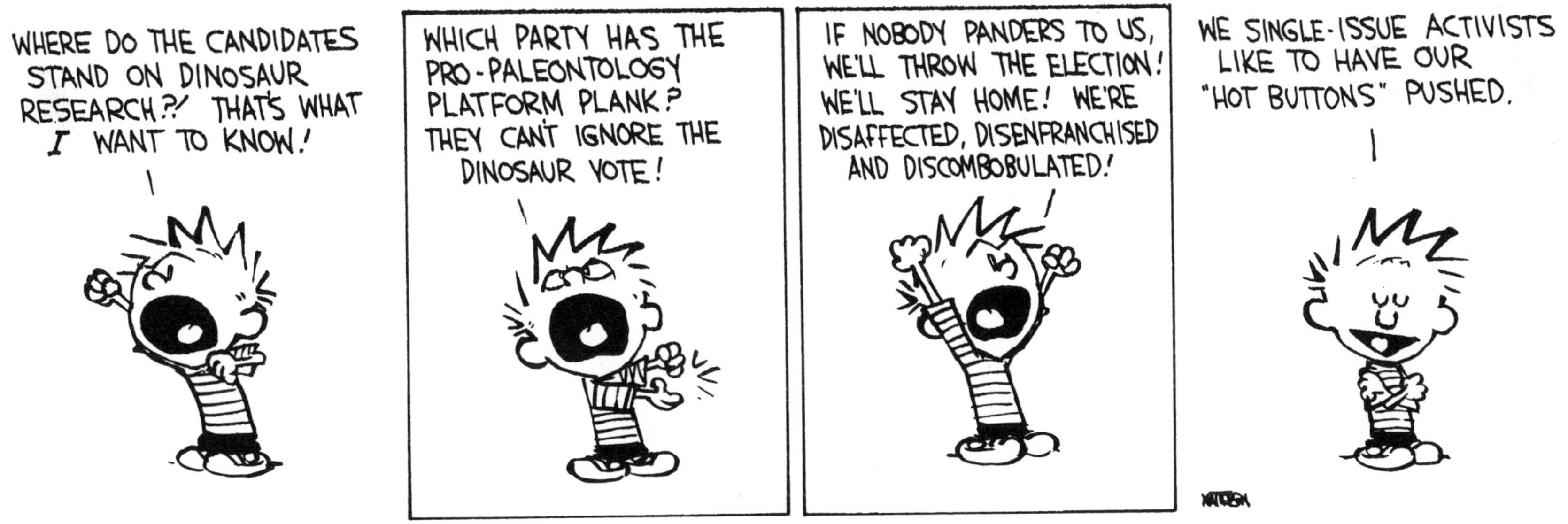
WHERE DO THE CANDIDATES STAND ON DINOSAUR RESEARCH?! THAT'S WHAT I WANT TO KNOW!
WHICH PARTY HAS THE PRO-PALEONTOLOGY PLATFORM PLANK? THEY CAN'T IGNORE THE DINOSAUR VOTE!
IF NOBODY PANDERS TO US, WE'LL THROW THE ELECTION! WE'LL STAY HOME! WE'RE DISAFFECTED, DISENFRANCHISED AND DISCOMBOBULATED!
WE SINGLE-ISSUE ACTIVISTS LIKE TO HAVE OUR "HOT BUTTONS" PUSHED.

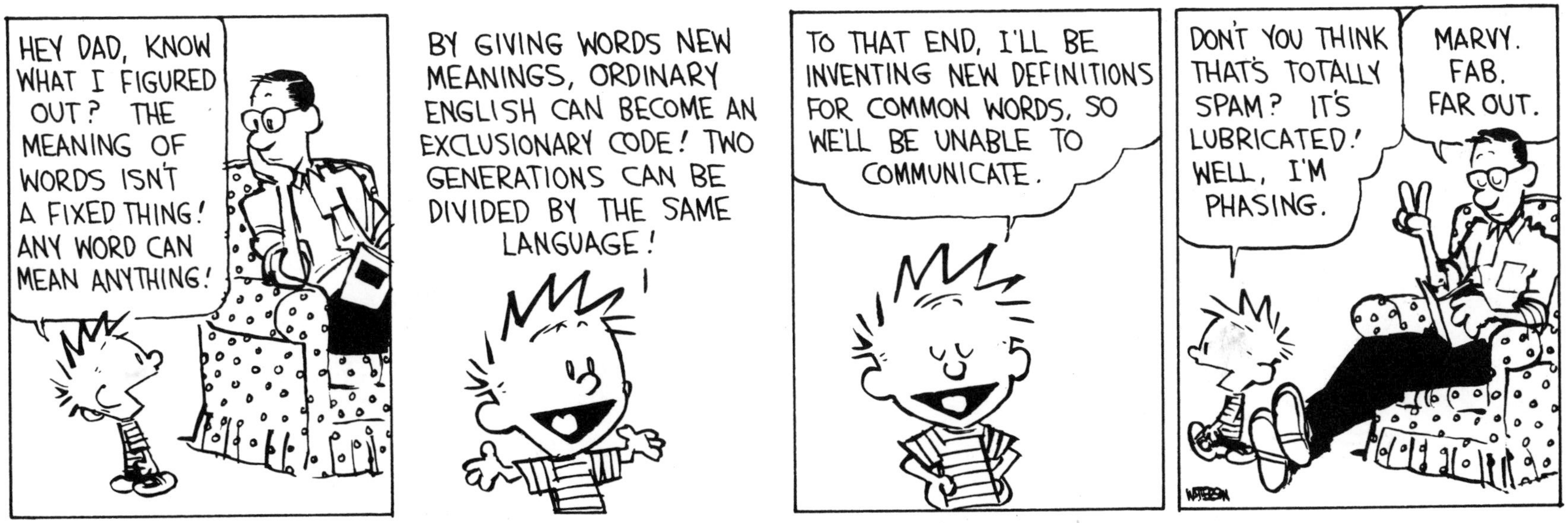
HEY DAD, KNOW WHAT I FIGURED OUT? THE MEANING OF WORDS ISN'T A FIXED THING! ANY WORD CAN MEAN ANYTHING!
BY GIVING WORDS NEW MEANINGS, ORDINARY ENGLISH CAN BECOME AN EXCLUSIONARY CODE! TWO GENERATIONS CAN BE DIVIDED BY THE SAME LANGUAGE!
TO THAT END, I'LL BE INVENTING NEW DEFINITIONS FOR COMMON WORDS, SO WE'LL BE UNABLE TO COMMUNICATE.
DON'T YOU THINK THAT'S TOTALLY SPAM? IT'S LUBRICATED! WELL, I'M PHASING.
MARVY. FAB. FAR OUT.

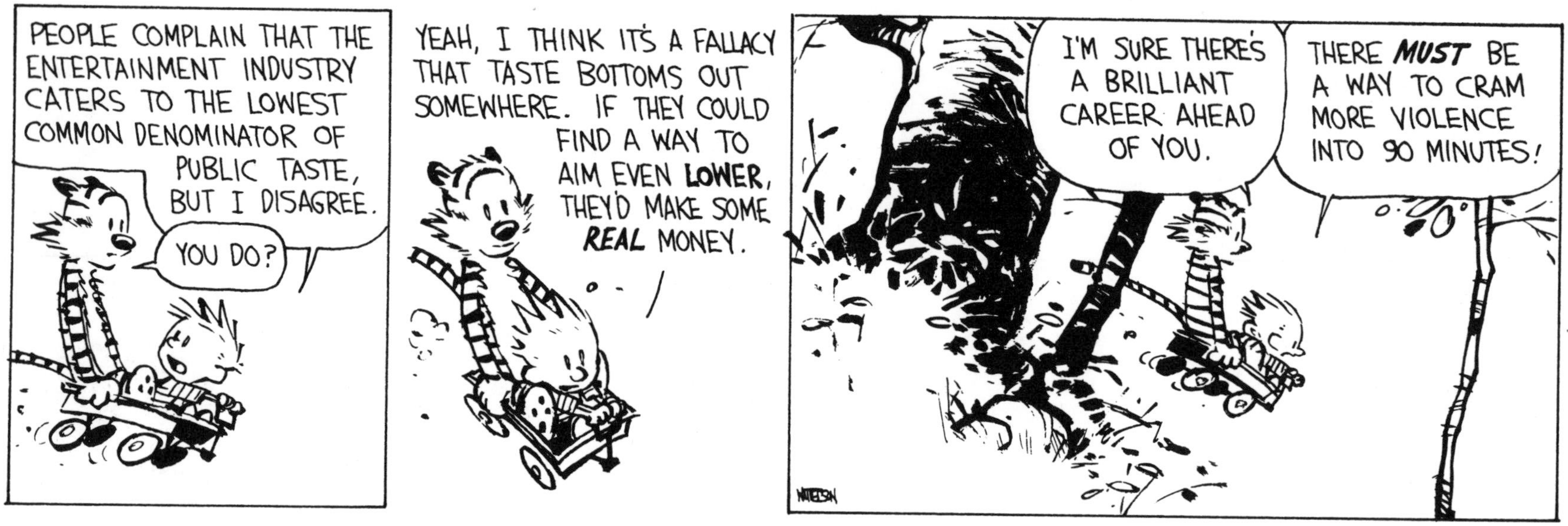
PEOPLE COMPLAIN THAT THE ENTERTAINMENT INDUSTRY CATERS TO THE LOWEST COMMON DENOMINATOR OF PUBLIC TASTE, BUT I DISAGREE.
YOU DO?
YEAH, I THINK IT'S A FALLACY THAT TASTE BOTTOMS OUT SOMEWHERE. IF THEY COULD FIND A WAY TO AIM EVEN **LOWER**, THEY'D MAKE SOME ***REAL*** MONEY.
I'M SURE THERE'S A BRILLIANT CAREER AHEAD OF YOU.
THERE ***MUST*** BE A WAY TO CRAM MORE VIOLENCE INTO 90 MINUTES!

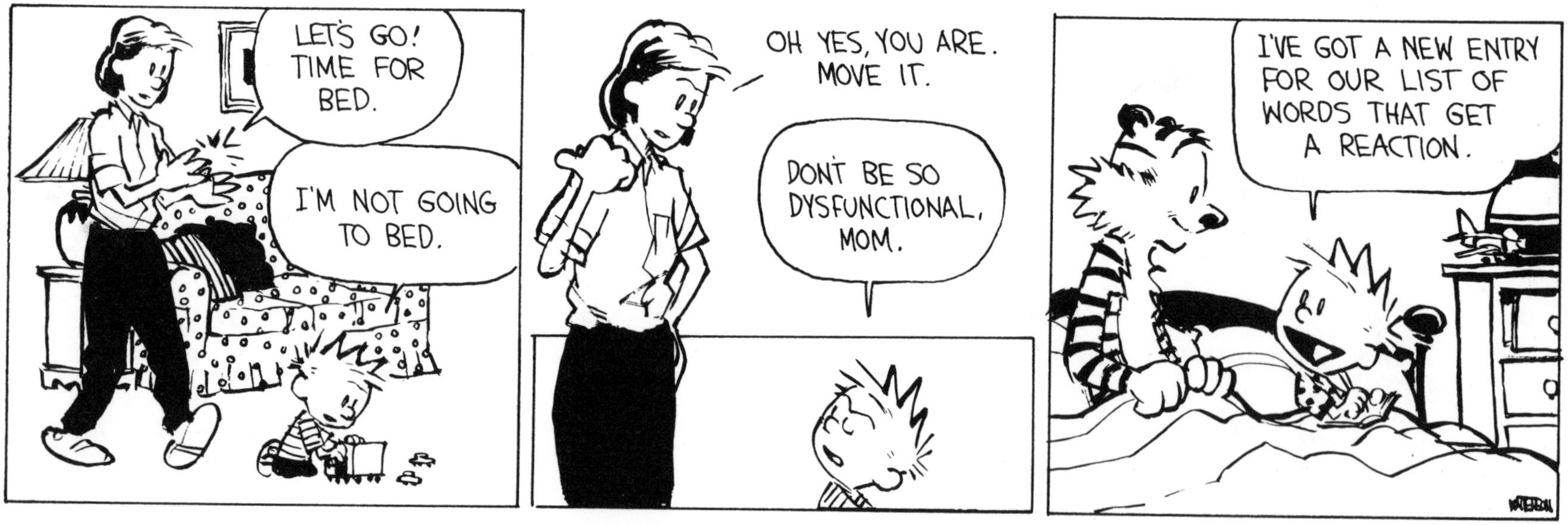
LET'S GO! TIME FOR BED.
I'M NOT GOING TO BED.
OH YES, YOU ARE. MOVE IT.
DON'T BE SO DYSFUNCTIONAL, MOM.
I'VE GOT A NEW ENTRY FOR OUR LIST OF WORDS THAT GET A REACTION.

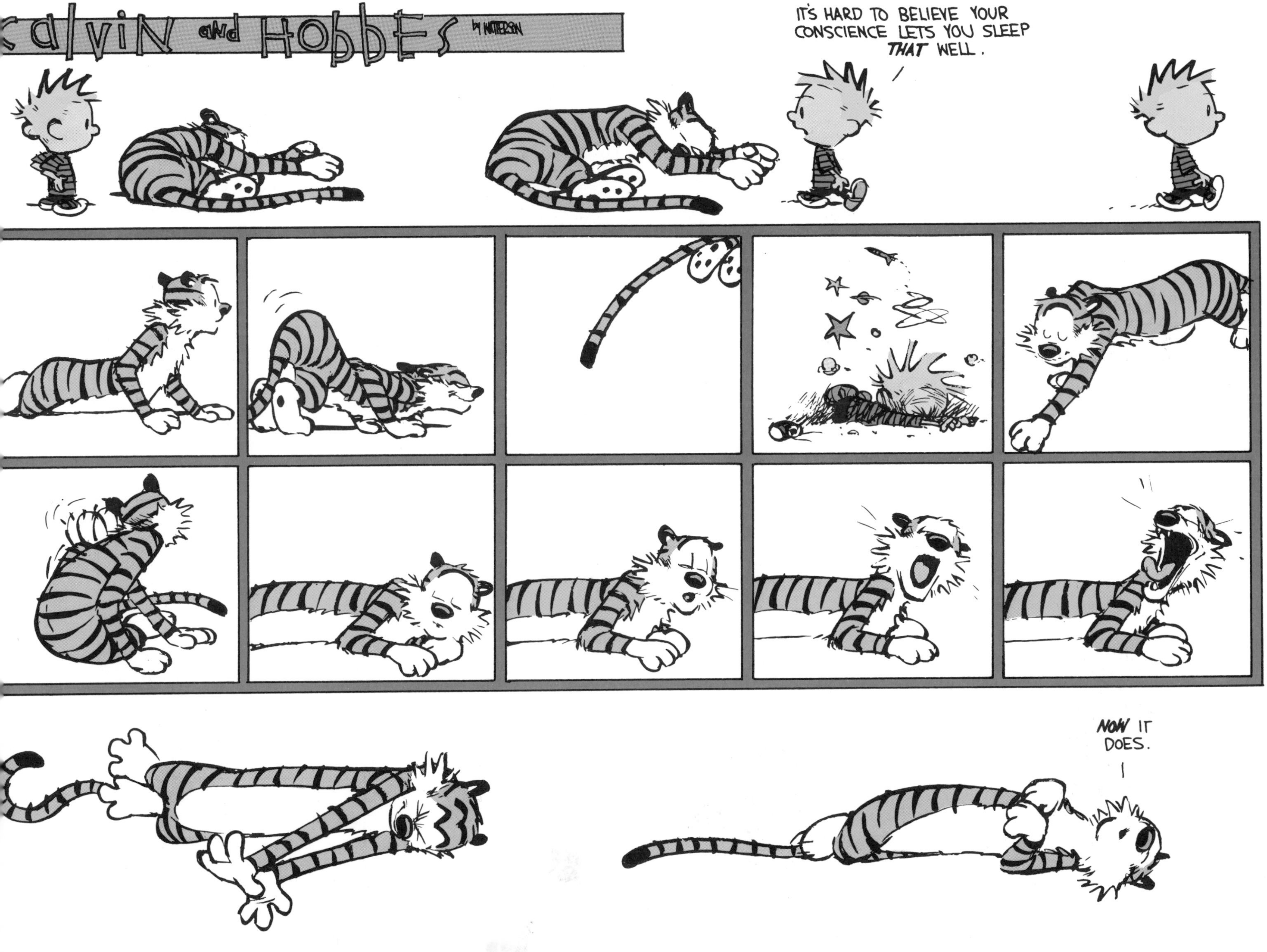
Calvin and HOBBES by WATTERSON
IT'S HARD TO BELIEVE YOUR CONSCIENCE LETS YOU SLEEP *THAT* WELL.
NOW IT DOES.

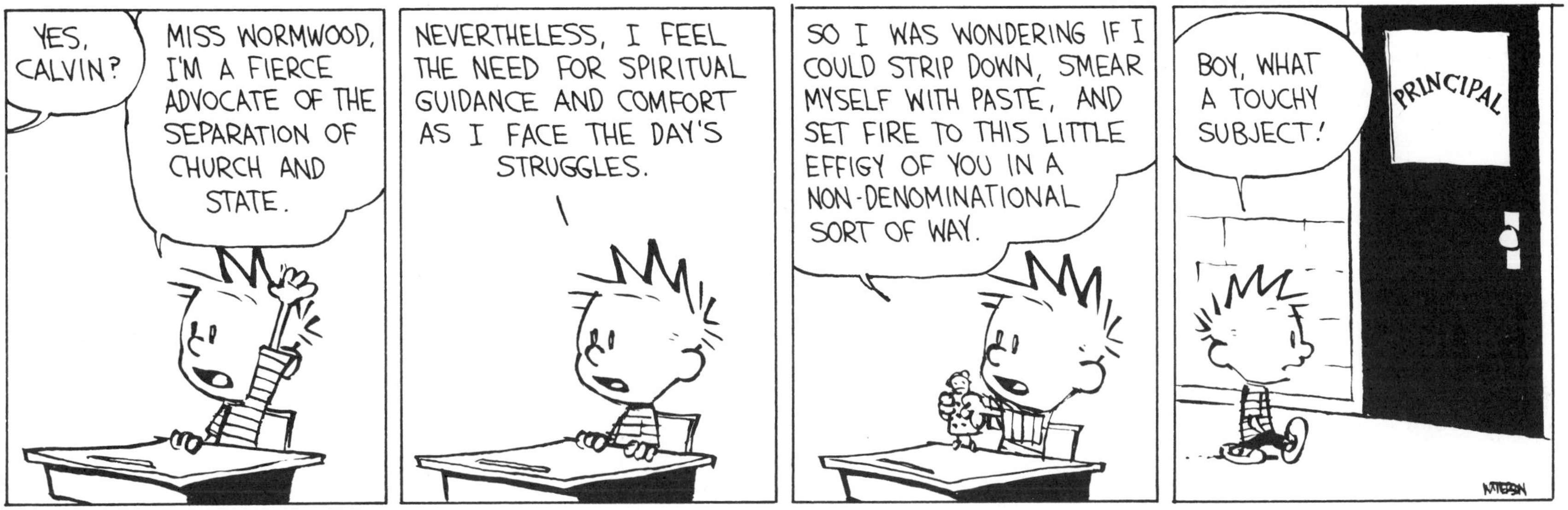

YES, CALVIN?
MISS WORMWOOD, I'M A FIERCE ADVOCATE OF THE SEPARATION OF CHURCH AND STATE.
NEVERTHELESS, I FEEL THE NEED FOR SPIRITUAL GUIDANCE AND COMFORT AS I FACE THE DAY'S STRUGGLES.
SO I WAS WONDERING IF I COULD STRIP DOWN, SMEAR MYSELF WITH PASTE, AND SET FIRE TO THIS LITTLE EFFIGY OF YOU IN A NON-DENOMINATIONAL SORT OF WAY.
BOY, WHAT A TOUCHY SUBJECT!
PRINCIPAL

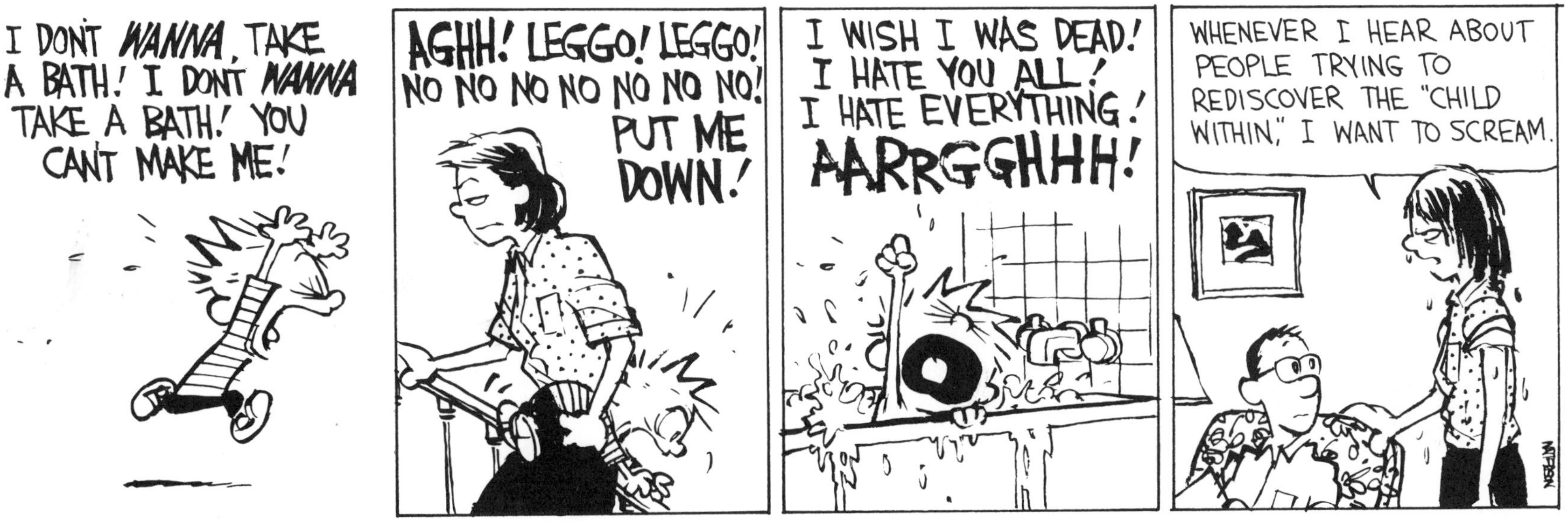

I DON'T WANNA TAKE A BATH! I DON'T WANNA TAKE A BATH! YOU CAN'T MAKE ME!
AGHH! LEGGO! LEGGO! NO NO NO NO NO NO NO! PUT ME DOWN!
I WISH I WAS DEAD! I HATE YOU ALL! I HATE EVERYTHING! AARRGGHHH!
WHENEVER I HEAR ABOUT PEOPLE TRYING TO REDISCOVER THE "CHILD WITHIN," I WANT TO SCREAM.

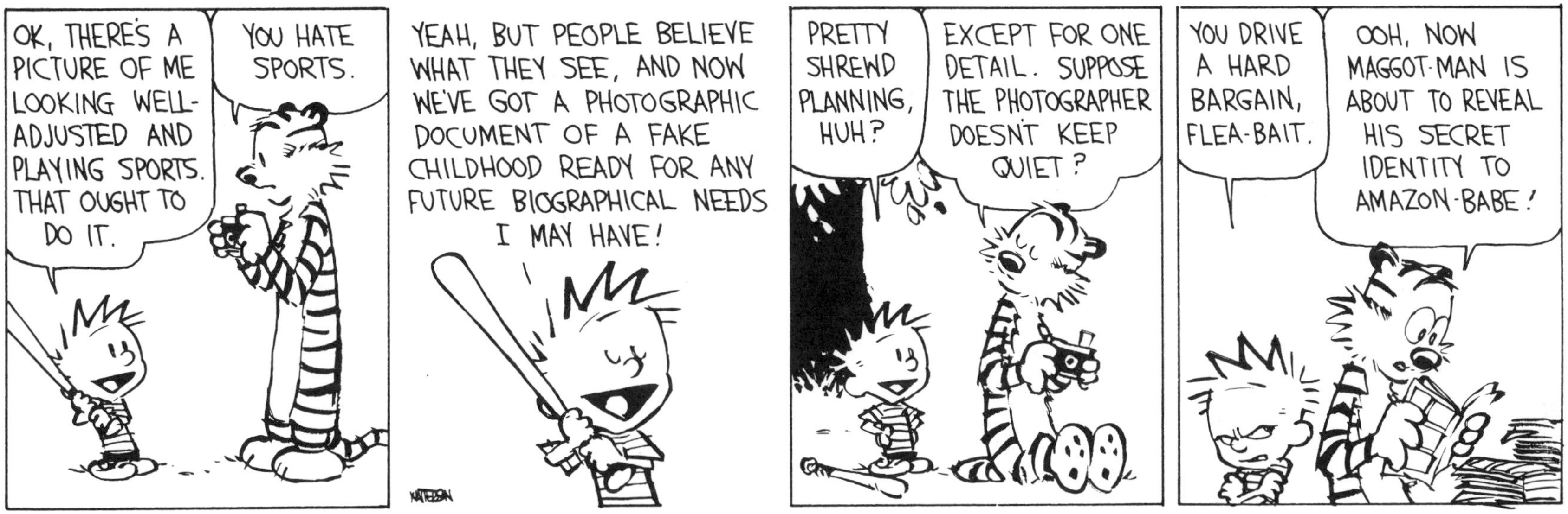
OK, THERE'S A PICTURE OF ME LOOKING WELL-ADJUSTED AND PLAYING SPORTS. THAT OUGHT TO DO IT.
YOU HATE SPORTS.
YEAH, BUT PEOPLE BELIEVE WHAT THEY SEE, AND NOW WE'VE GOT A PHOTOGRAPHIC DOCUMENT OF A FAKE CHILDHOOD READY FOR ANY FUTURE BIOGRAPHICAL NEEDS I MAY HAVE!
PRETTY SHREWD PLANNING, HUH?
EXCEPT FOR ONE DETAIL. SUPPOSE THE PHOTOGRAPHER DOESN'T KEEP QUIET?
YOU DRIVE A HARD BARGAIN, FLEA-BAIT.
OOH, NOW MAGGOT-MAN IS ABOUT TO REVEAL HIS SECRET IDENTITY TO AMAZON-BABE!

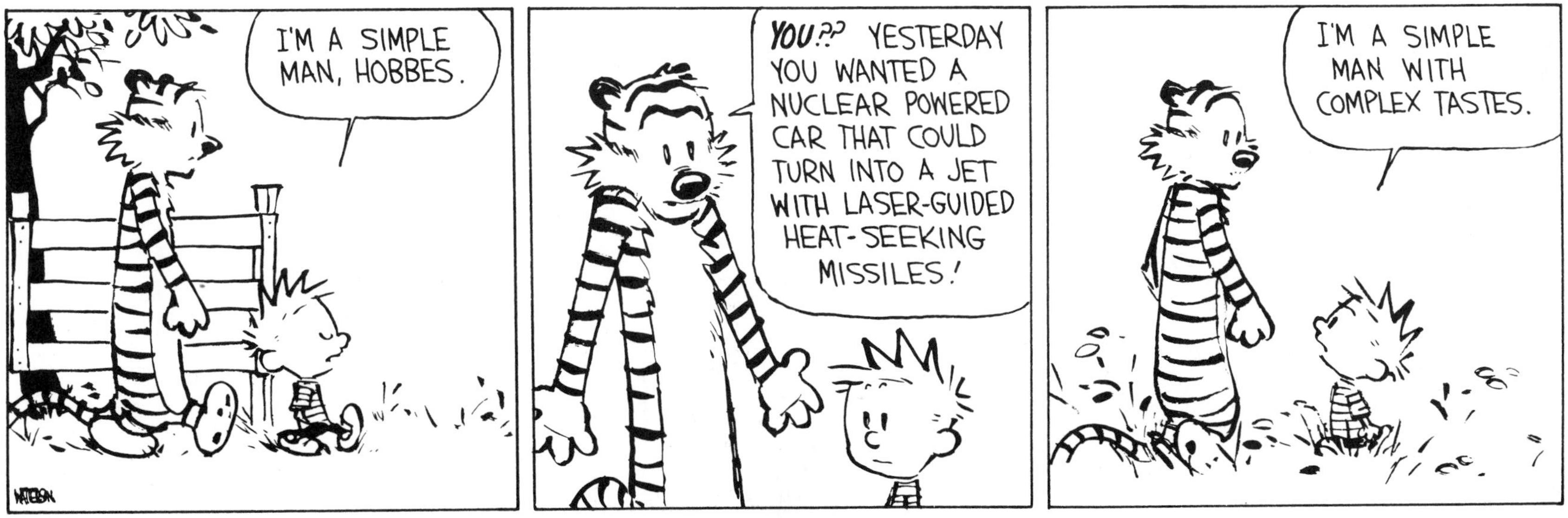
I'M A SIMPLE MAN, HOBBES.
YOU?? YESTERDAY YOU WANTED A NUCLEAR POWERED CAR THAT COULD TURN INTO A JET WITH LASER-GUIDED HEAT-SEEKING MISSILES!
I'M A SIMPLE MAN WITH COMPLEX TASTES.

CalViN aND HObbEs  by WATTERSON

I NEED TO MAKE FRIENDS WITH SOME LESS TERRITORIAL ANIMALS.

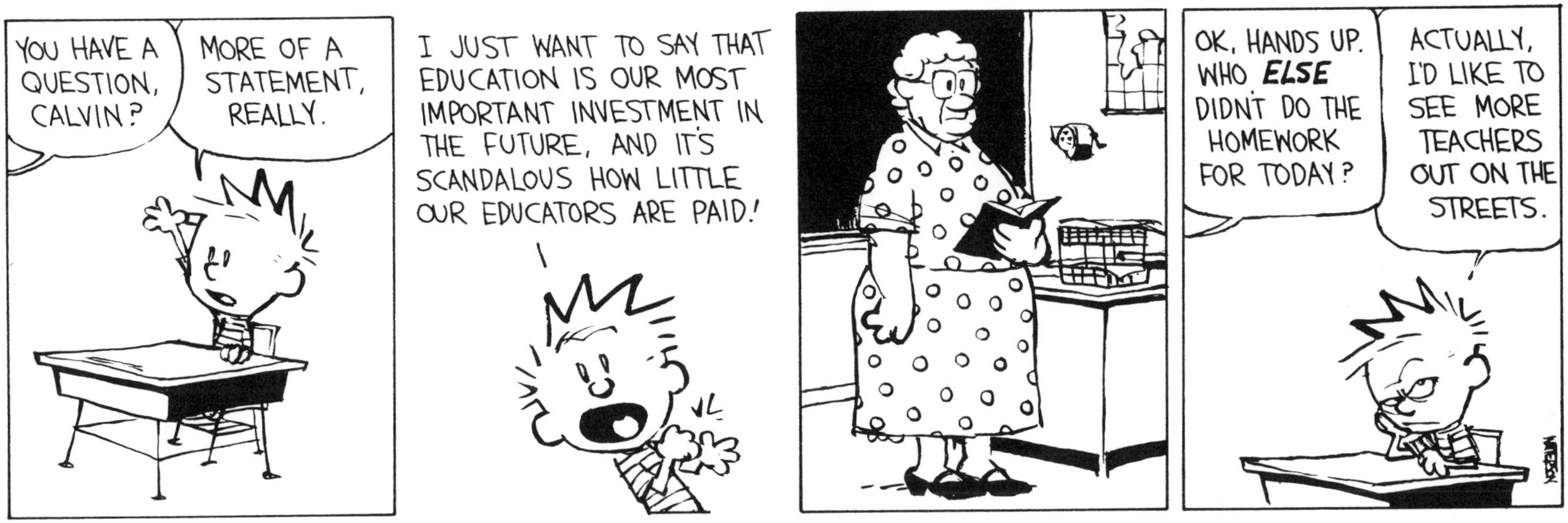
YOU HAVE A QUESTION, CALVIN?
MORE OF A STATEMENT, REALLY.
I JUST WANT TO SAY THAT EDUCATION IS OUR MOST IMPORTANT INVESTMENT IN THE FUTURE, AND IT'S SCANDALOUS HOW LITTLE OUR EDUCATORS ARE PAID!
OK, HANDS UP. WHO ELSE DIDN'T DO THE HOMEWORK FOR TODAY?
ACTUALLY, I'D LIKE TO SEE MORE TEACHERS OUT ON THE STREETS.

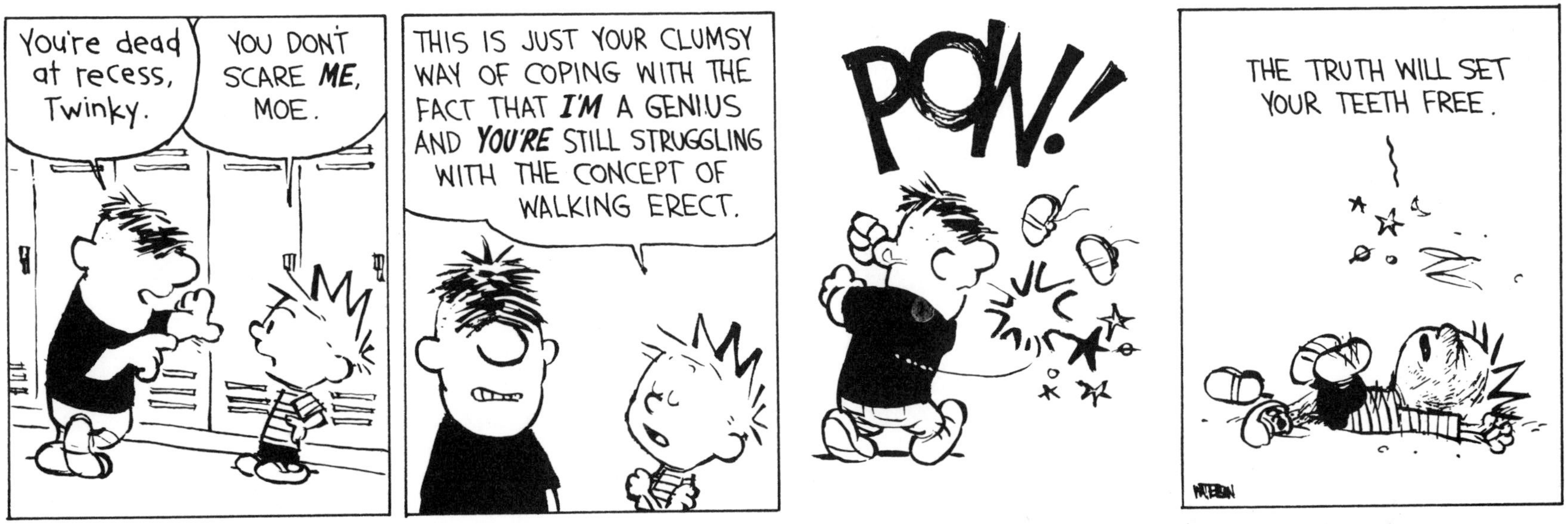
You're dead at recess, Twinky.
YOU DON'T SCARE ME, MOE.
THIS IS JUST YOUR CLUMSY WAY OF COPING WITH THE FACT THAT I'M A GENIUS AND YOU'RE STILL STRUGGLING WITH THE CONCEPT OF WALKING ERECT.
POW!
THE TRUTH WILL SET YOUR TEETH FREE.

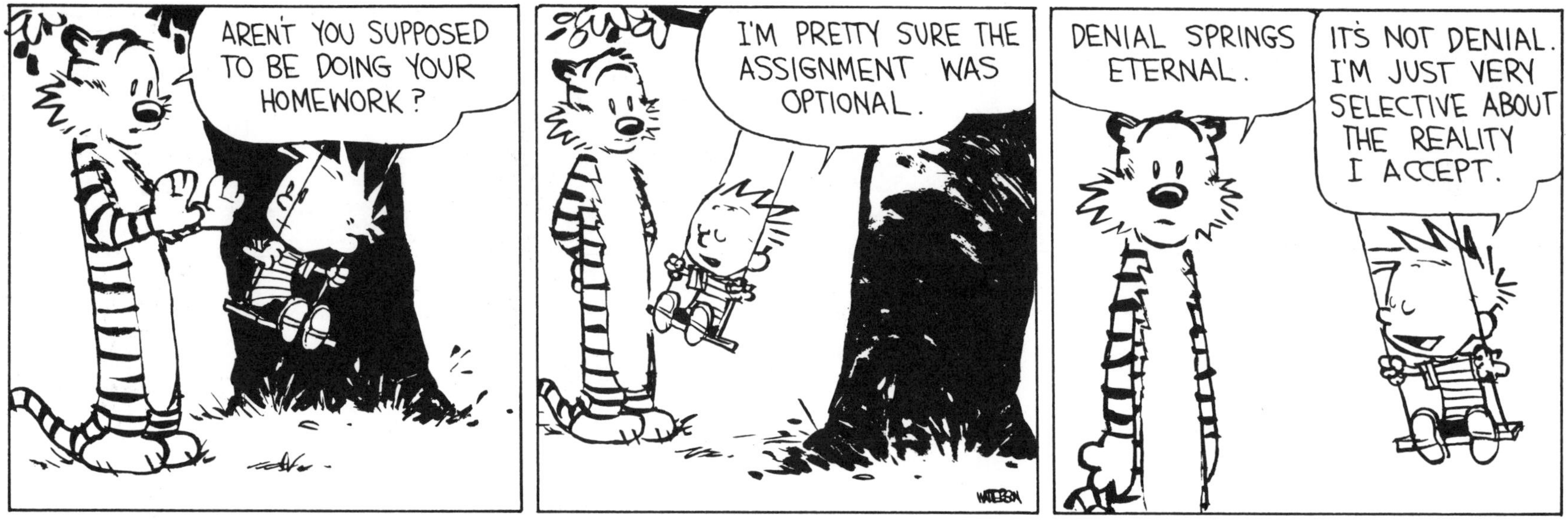
AREN'T YOU SUPPOSED TO BE DOING YOUR HOMEWORK?
I'M PRETTY SURE THE ASSIGNMENT WAS OPTIONAL.
DENIAL SPRINGS ETERNAL.
IT'S NOT DENIAL. I'M JUST VERY SELECTIVE ABOUT THE REALITY I ACCEPT.

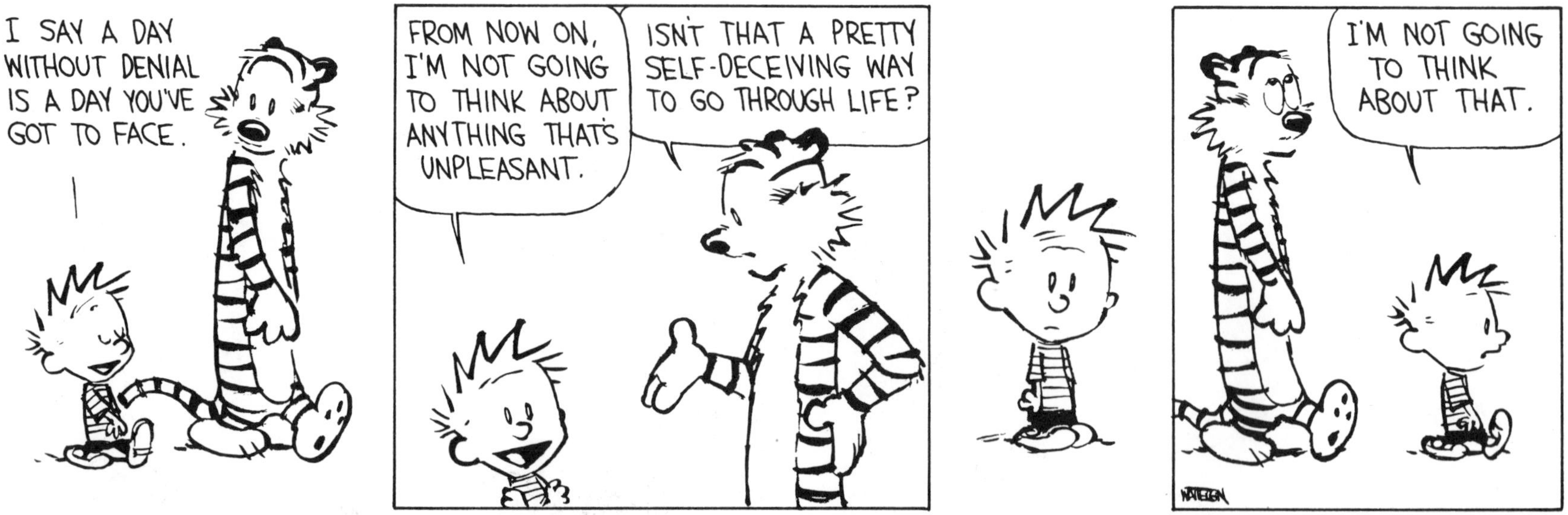
I SAY A DAY WITHOUT DENIAL IS A DAY YOU'VE GOT TO FACE.
FROM NOW ON, I'M NOT GOING TO THINK ABOUT ANYTHING THAT'S UNPLEASANT.
ISN'T THAT A PRETTY SELF-DECEIVING WAY TO GO THROUGH LIFE?
I'M NOT GOING TO THINK ABOUT THAT.

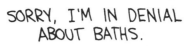

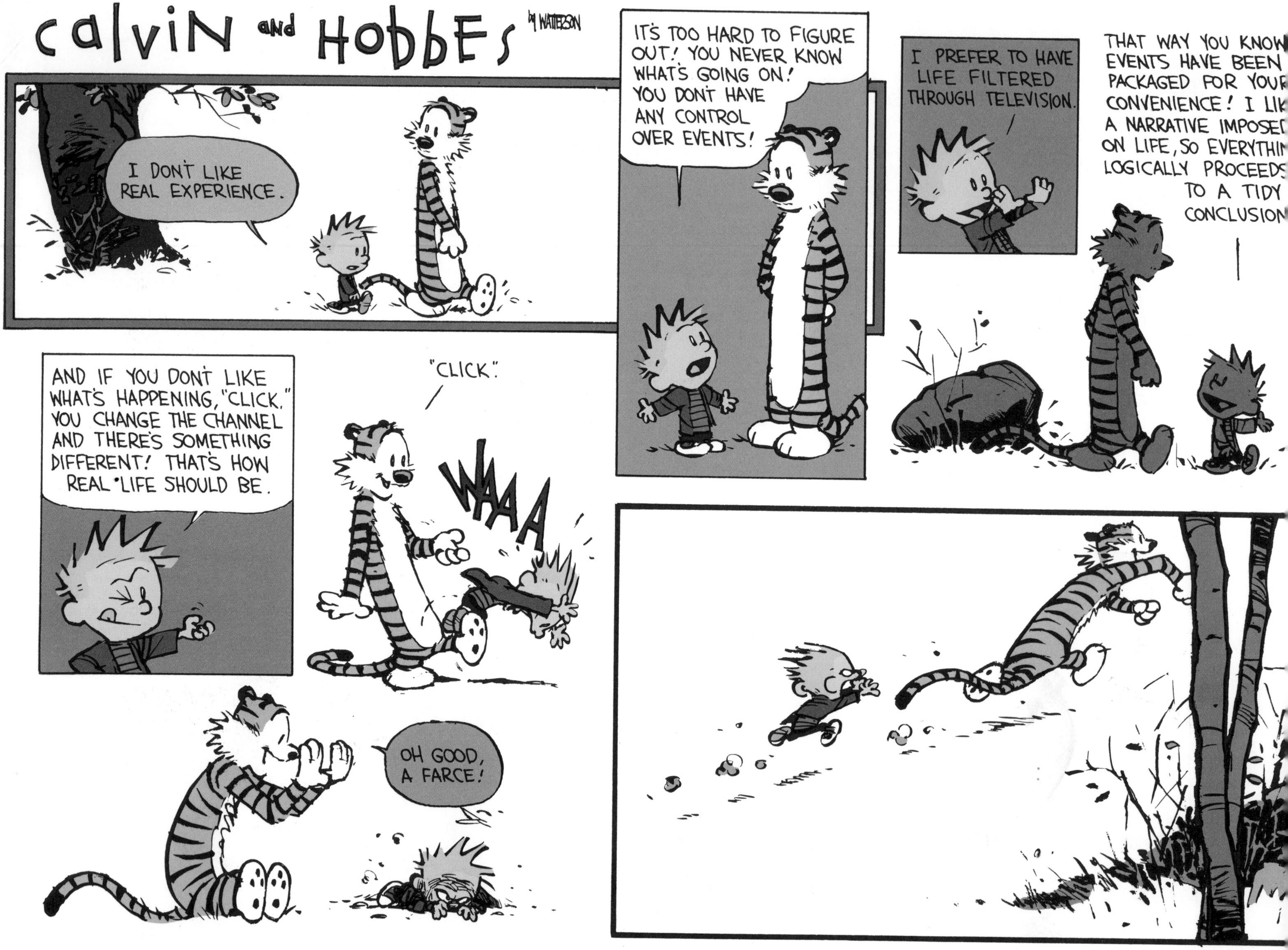

calvin and HOBBES by WATTERSON
I DON'T LIKE REAL EXPERIENCE.
IT'S TOO HARD TO FIGURE OUT! YOU NEVER KNOW WHAT'S GOING ON! YOU DON'T HAVE ANY CONTROL OVER EVENTS!
I PREFER TO HAVE LIFE FILTERED THROUGH TELEVISION.
THAT WAY YOU KNOW EVENTS HAVE BEEN PACKAGED FOR YOUR CONVENIENCE! I LIKE A NARRATIVE IMPOSED ON LIFE, SO EVERYTHING LOGICALLY PROCEEDS TO A TIDY CONCLUSION.
AND IF YOU DON'T LIKE WHAT'S HAPPENING, "CLICK," YOU CHANGE THE CHANNEL AND THERE'S SOMETHING DIFFERENT! THAT'S HOW REAL LIFE SHOULD BE.
"CLICK."
WAAA
OH GOOD, A FARCE!

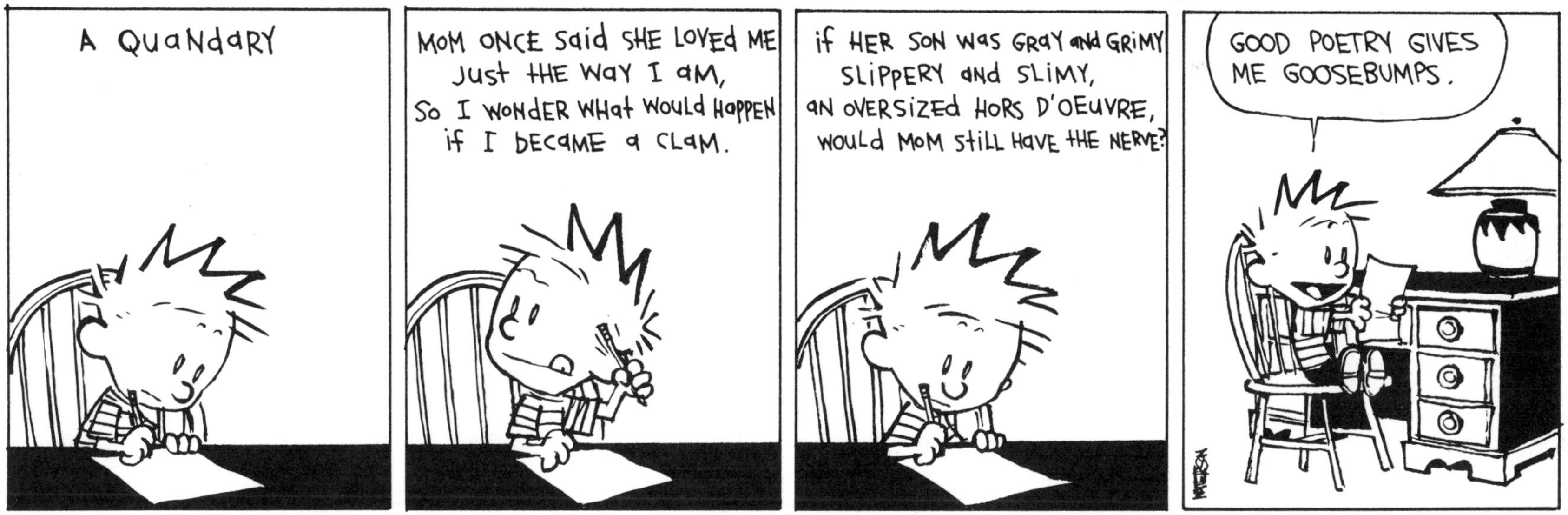
A QUANDARY
MOM ONCE SAID SHE LOVED ME JUST THE WAY I AM,
SO I WONDER WHAT WOULD HAPPEN IF I BECAME A CLAM.
IF HER SON WAS GRAY AND GRIMY, SLIPPERY AND SLIMY,
AN OVERSIZED HORS D'OEUVRE, WOULD MOM STILL HAVE THE NERVE?
GOOD POETRY GIVES ME GOOSEBUMPS.

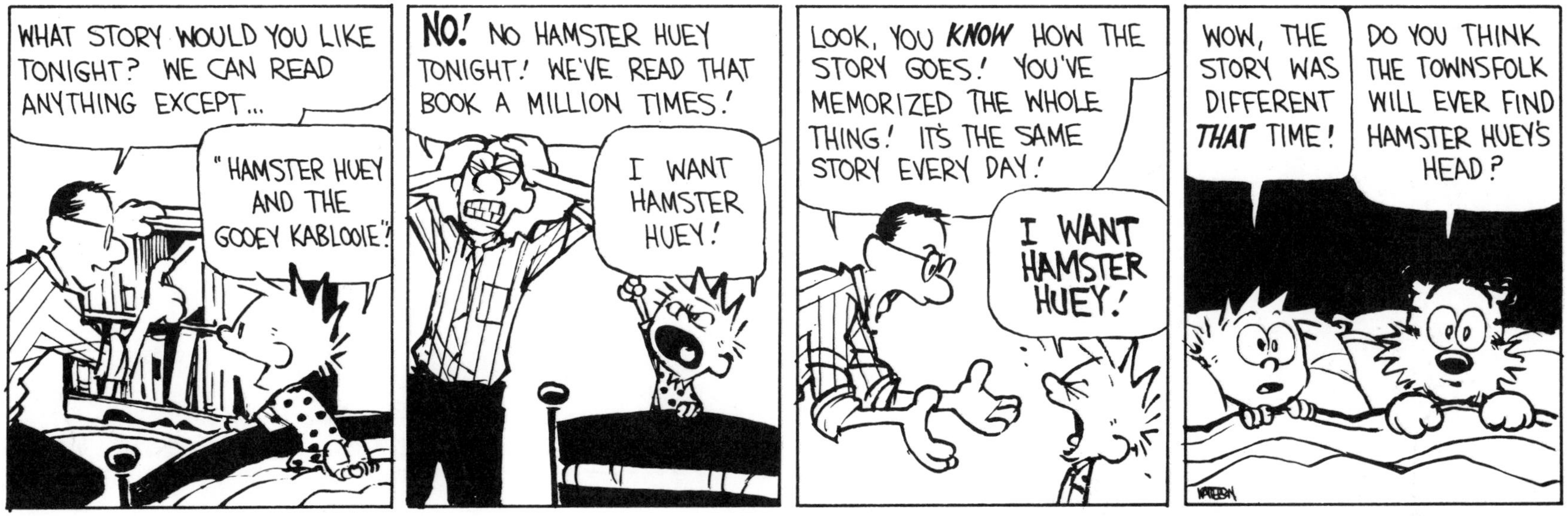
WHAT STORY WOULD YOU LIKE TONIGHT? WE CAN READ ANYTHING EXCEPT...
"HAMSTER HUEY AND THE GOOEY KABLOOIE"!
NO! NO HAMSTER HUEY TONIGHT! WE'VE READ THAT BOOK A MILLION TIMES!
I WANT HAMSTER HUEY!
LOOK, YOU KNOW HOW THE STORY GOES! YOU'VE MEMORIZED THE WHOLE THING! IT'S THE SAME STORY EVERY DAY!
I WANT HAMSTER HUEY!
WOW, THE STORY WAS DIFFERENT THAT TIME!
DO YOU THINK THE TOWNSFOLK WILL EVER FIND HAMSTER HUEY'S HEAD?

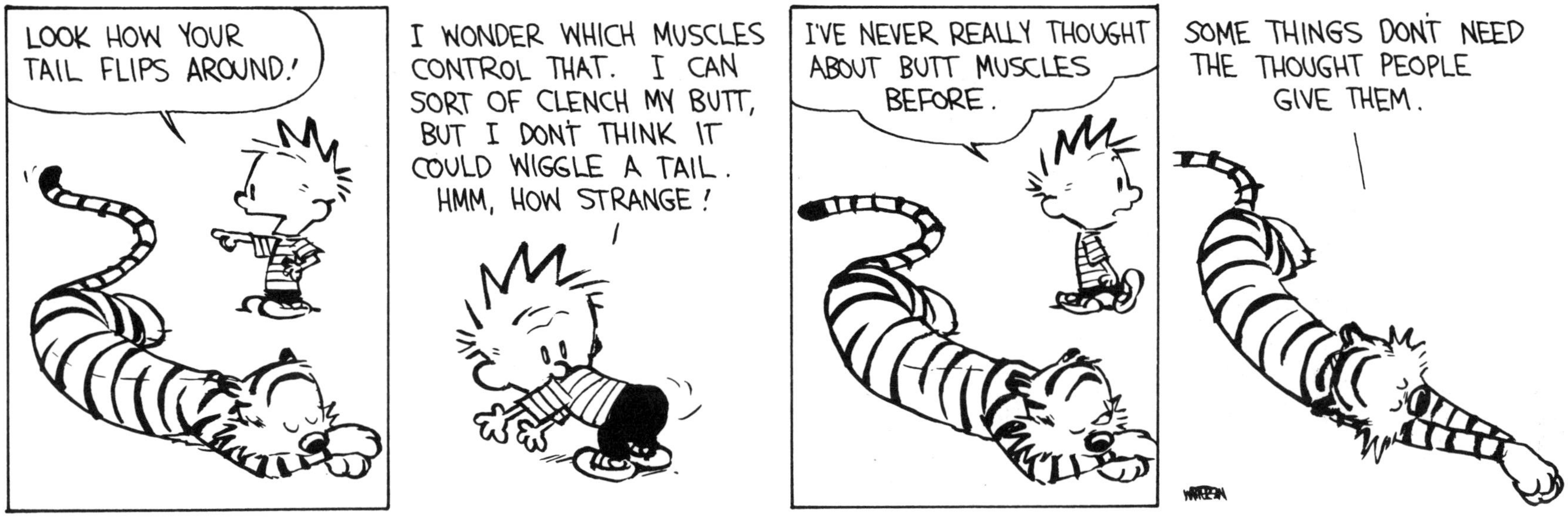
LOOK HOW YOUR TAIL FLIPS AROUND!
I WONDER WHICH MUSCLES CONTROL THAT. I CAN SORT OF CLENCH MY BUTT, BUT I DON'T THINK IT COULD WIGGLE A TAIL. HMM, HOW STRANGE!
I'VE NEVER REALLY THOUGHT ABOUT BUTT MUSCLES BEFORE.
SOME THINGS DON'T NEED THE THOUGHT PEOPLE GIVE THEM.

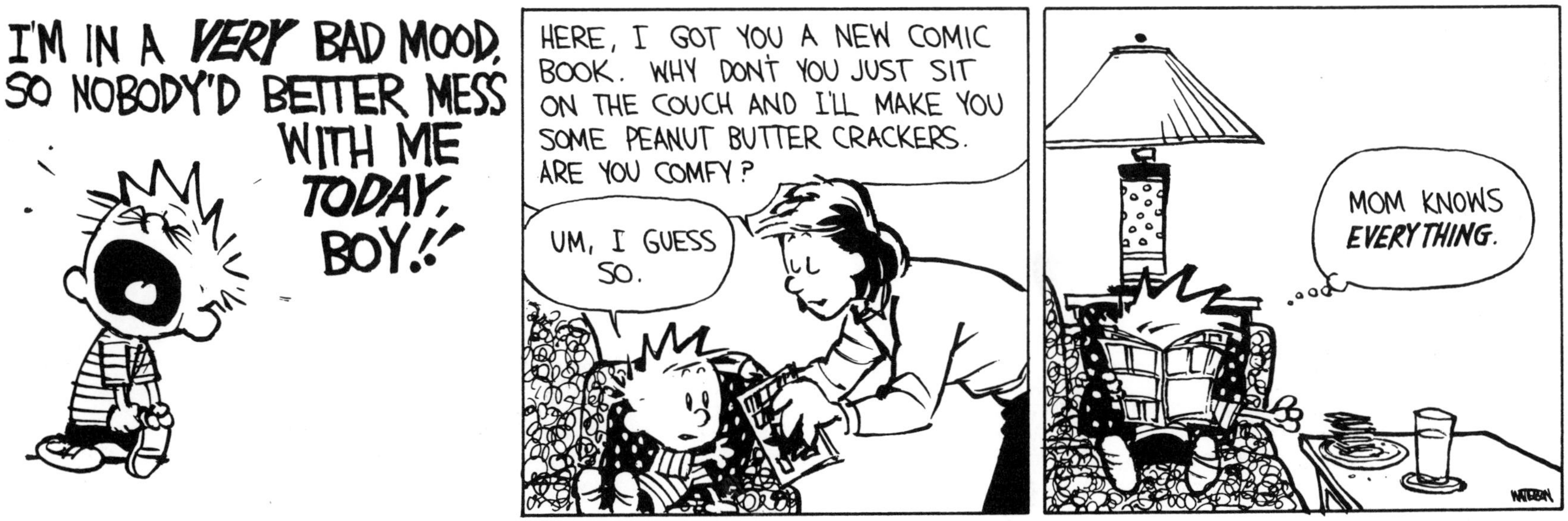
I'M IN A *VERY* BAD MOOD, SO NOBODY'D BETTER MESS WITH ME *TODAY*, BOY!!
HERE, I GOT YOU A NEW COMIC BOOK. WHY DON'T YOU JUST SIT ON THE COUCH AND I'LL MAKE YOU SOME PEANUT BUTTER CRACKERS. ARE YOU COMFY?
UM, I GUESS SO.
MOM KNOWS *EVERYTHING*.

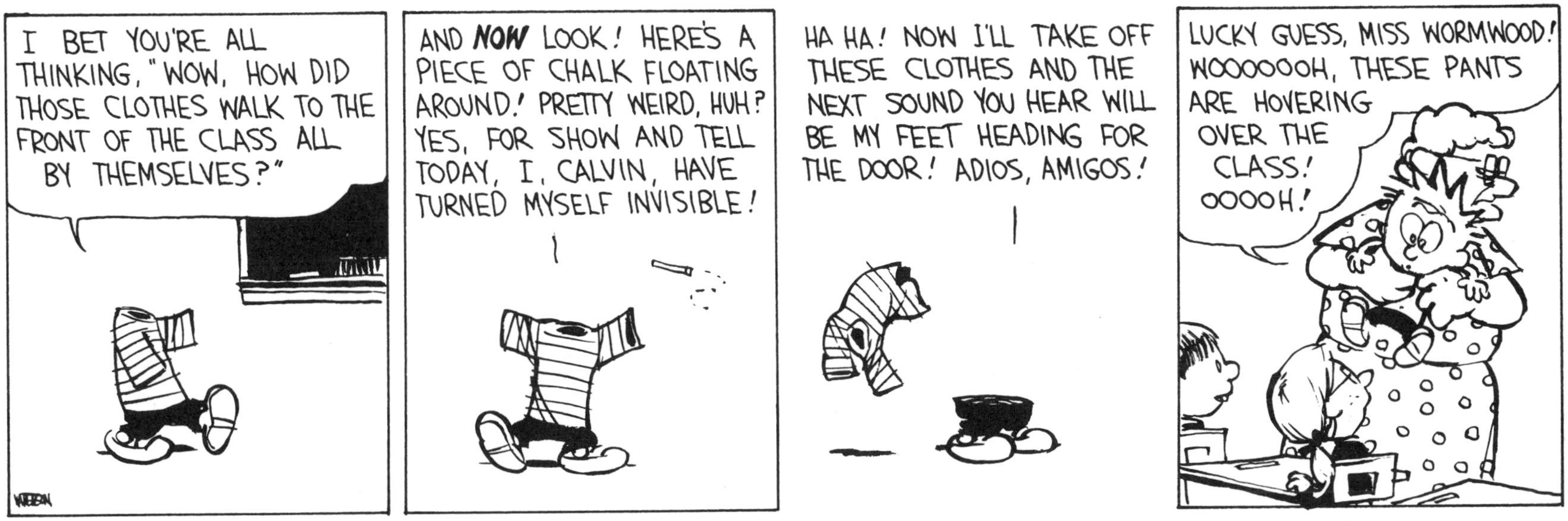
I BET YOU'RE ALL THINKING, "WOW, HOW DID THOSE CLOTHES WALK TO THE FRONT OF THE CLASS ALL BY THEMSELVES?"
AND NOW LOOK! HERE'S A PIECE OF CHALK FLOATING AROUND! PRETTY WEIRD, HUH? YES, FOR SHOW AND TELL TODAY, I, CALVIN, HAVE TURNED MYSELF INVISIBLE!
HA HA! NOW I'LL TAKE OFF THESE CLOTHES AND THE NEXT SOUND YOU HEAR WILL BE MY FEET HEADING FOR THE DOOR! ADIOS, AMIGOS!
LUCKY GUESS, MISS WORMWOOD! WOOOOOOH, THESE PANTS ARE HOVERING OVER THE CLASS! OOOOH!

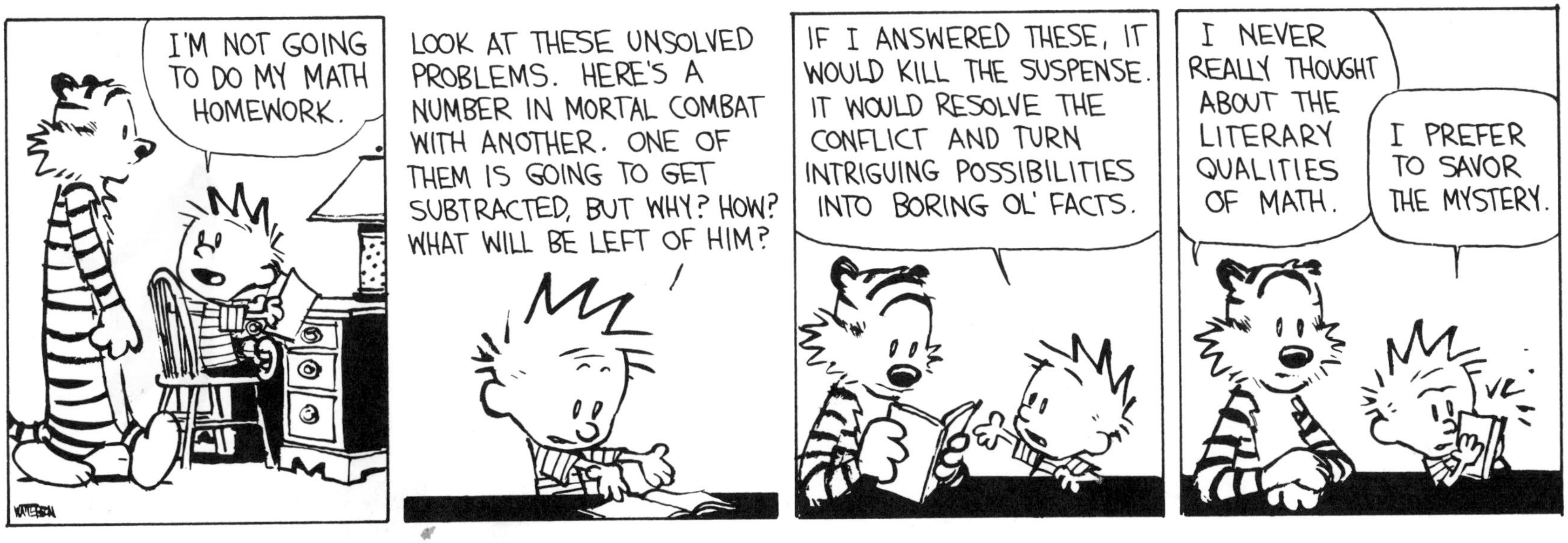
I'M NOT GOING TO DO MY MATH HOMEWORK.
LOOK AT THESE UNSOLVED PROBLEMS. HERE'S A NUMBER IN MORTAL COMBAT WITH ANOTHER. ONE OF THEM IS GOING TO GET SUBTRACTED, BUT WHY? HOW? WHAT WILL BE LEFT OF HIM?
IF I ANSWERED THESE, IT WOULD KILL THE SUSPENSE. IT WOULD RESOLVE THE CONFLICT AND TURN INTRIGUING POSSIBILITIES INTO BORING OL' FACTS.
I NEVER REALLY THOUGHT ABOUT THE LITERARY QUALITIES OF MATH.
I PREFER TO SAVOR THE MYSTERY.

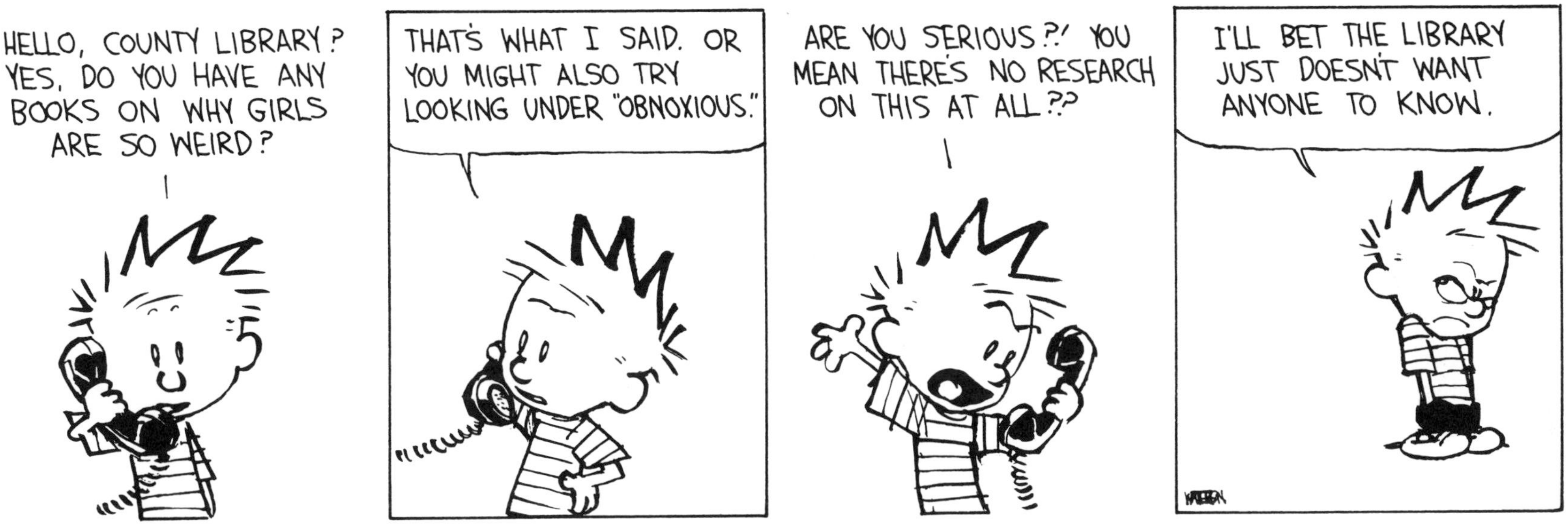
HELLO, COUNTY LIBRARY? YES, DO YOU HAVE ANY BOOKS ON WHY GIRLS ARE SO WEIRD?
THAT'S WHAT I SAID. OR YOU MIGHT ALSO TRY LOOKING UNDER "OBNOXIOUS."
ARE YOU SERIOUS?! YOU MEAN THERE'S NO RESEARCH ON THIS AT ALL??
I'LL BET THE LIBRARY JUST DOESN'T WANT ANYONE TO KNOW.

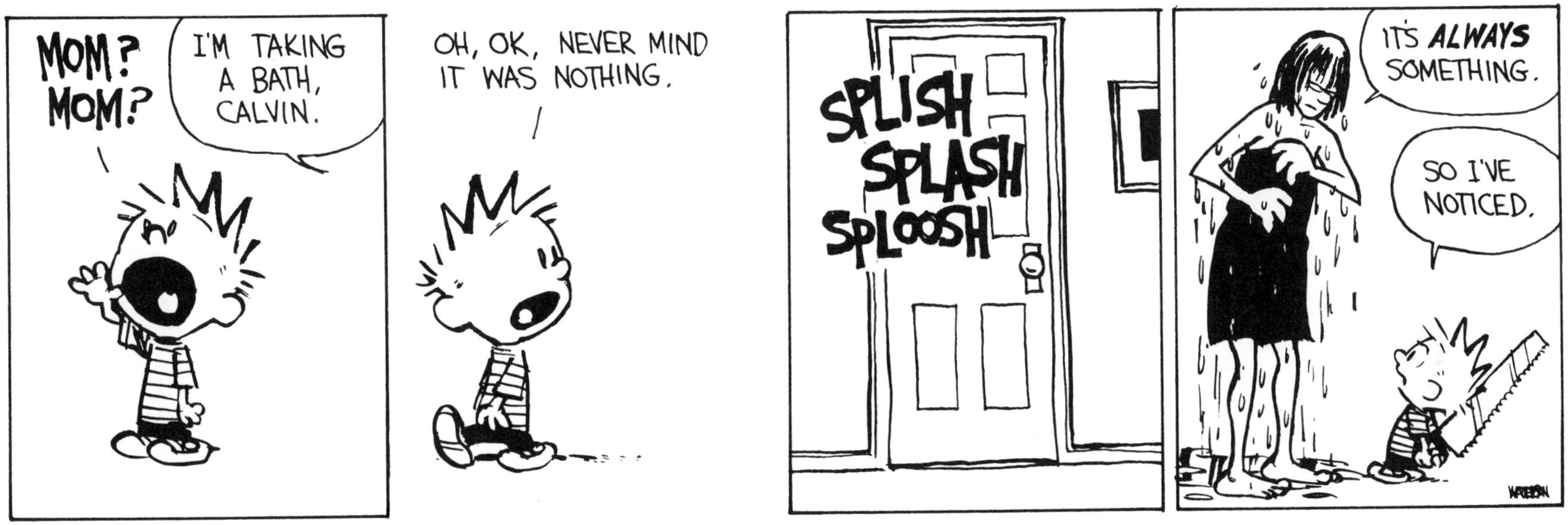
MOM? MOM?
I'M TAKING A BATH, CALVIN.
OH, OK, NEVER MIND IT WAS NOTHING.
SPLISH
SPLASH
SPLOOSH
IT'S ALWAYS SOMETHING.
SO I'VE NOTICED.

THERE REALLY OUGHT TO BE A FALL OLYMPICS.

BPBPBBPB

IT'S A HIGH PRICE TO PAY, BUT NUZZLING TIGER TUMMIES IS ONE OF THE GREAT PLEASURES OF LIFE.

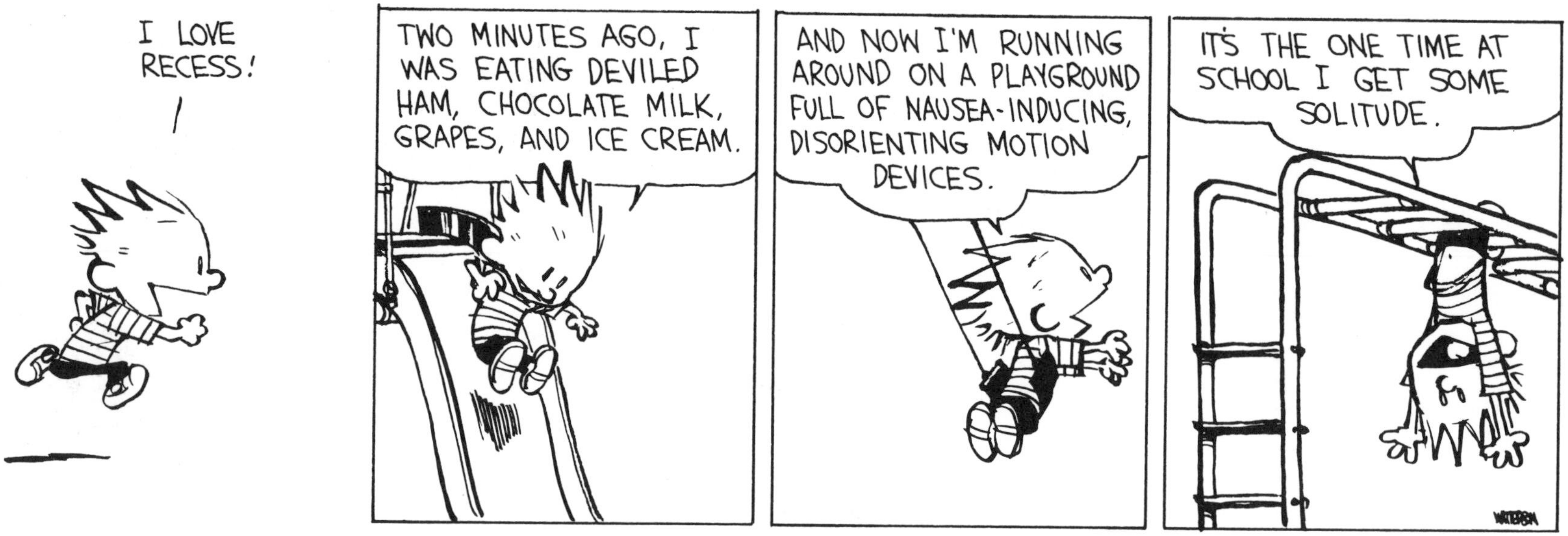
I LOVE RECESS!
TWO MINUTES AGO, I WAS EATING DEVILED HAM, CHOCOLATE MILK, GRAPES, AND ICE CREAM.
AND NOW I'M RUNNING AROUND ON A PLAYGROUND FULL OF NAUSEA-INDUCING, DISORIENTING MOTION DEVICES.
IT'S THE ONE TIME AT SCHOOL I GET SOME SOLITUDE.

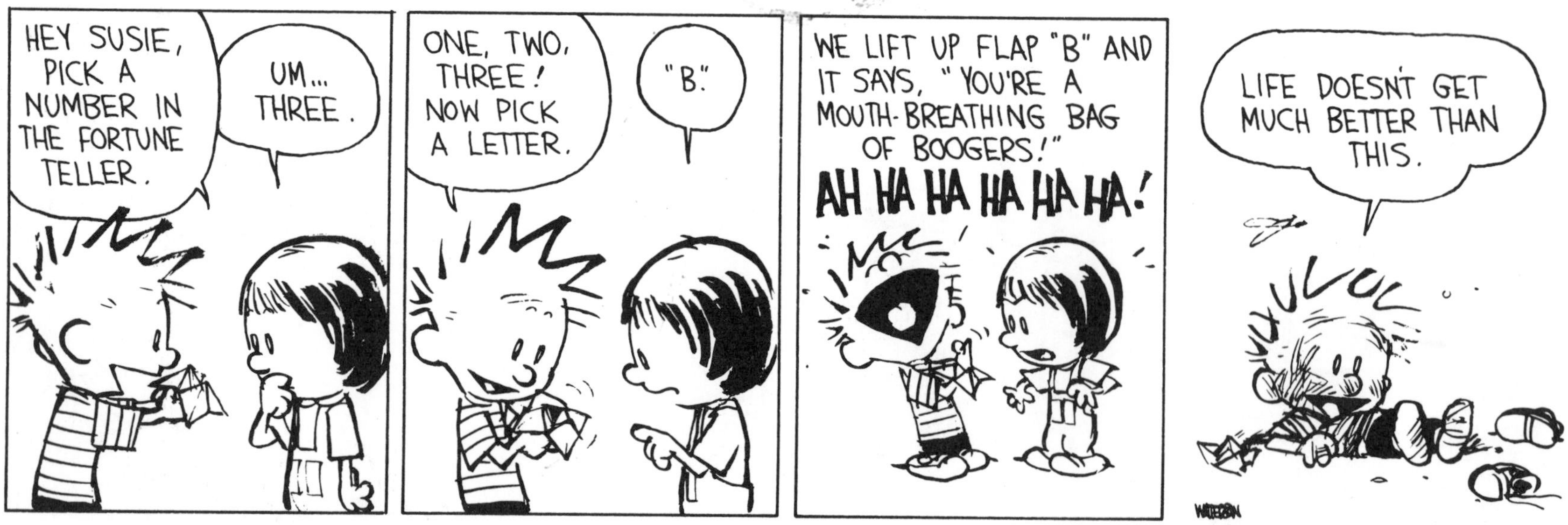
HEY SUSIE, PICK A NUMBER IN THE FORTUNE TELLER.
UM... THREE.
ONE, TWO, THREE! NOW PICK A LETTER.
"B."
WE LIFT UP FLAP "B" AND IT SAYS, "YOU'RE A MOUTH-BREATHING BAG OF BOOGERS!"
AH HA HA HA HA HA!
LIFE DOESN'T GET MUCH BETTER THAN THIS.

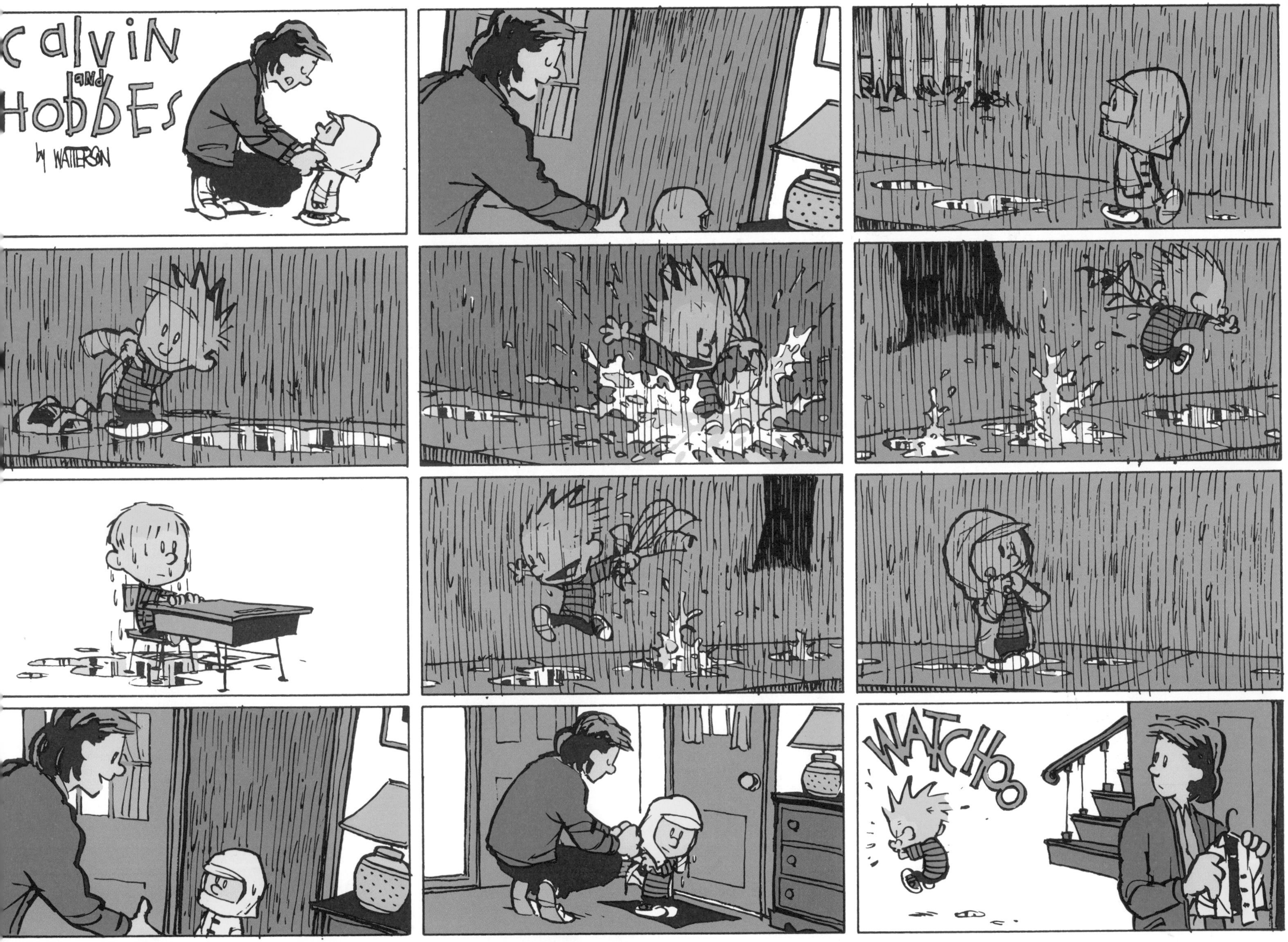
CALVIN and HOBBES
by WATTERSON
WATCHOO